In a wonderfully warm and inviting voic
fulness down to earth and into the heart.
abstract ideas into living words that draw the reader onward and inward. This is a wonderful complement to classics such as *Radical Acceptance*, and full of value for our too-hectic world.

—Rick Hanson, PhD, psychologist and author of *Hardwiring Happiness*

Her sensitive way of seeing and being has been honed through decades of mindfulness and compassion practice that spills out from her meditation into all the myriad facets of her life. You will get the chance to glimpse the world anew through her rich perspective and you will emerge all the richer for that.

—Vidyamala Burch, co-founder of 'Breathworks'; author of *Living Well with Pain and Illness*

If you want to take your mindfulness practice deeper, and widen it into new areas, then Ratnadevi is an experienced and engaging guide. In this well-crafted book she is generous with her own experience, along the way sharing the contents of her fridge and her heart, as well as her challenges and successes in living a mindful life. We are given practical tools for addressing a large range of issues, from the everyday to climate change, helping us become more alive to our inner world and more effective, helpful and fulfilled in our interaction with the outer world.

—Vessantara, author of *A Guide to the Buddhas*

Rich, multi-textured journey through mindfulness practice exploring how it relates to our inner world, how it is expressed through our bodies and how it impacts on our environment and the complex society we live in. An intimately personal and instructive book that draws on a wealth of personal experience and offers a wide array of methods and perspectives.

—Choden (Sean McGovern), co-founder of Mindfulness Association and co-author of *Mindful Compassion*

Our bodies tell us we need remedy for thirst, hunger, and fatigue. The signals are clear, and we ignore them at our peril. But what of our deep need for calm, for clarity, for a renewed brimming capacity for kindness—compassion for ourselves, and for others? The signals for these needs are harder to read, for they are found in our unrest, our anger or resentment—all the cloudy distractions from a life lived well. This book will help you read the signs and find the remedies for daily storms of confusion with stories to turn your mind, and rituals for restoration born of this writer's long and thoughtful practice. In a difficult world, on a busy day, peace is at hand: a few deft breaths guided by this book.

—Kim Stafford, author of *Singer Come from Afar*

Her guided meditation practices help me relax into a state of inner peace. She demonstrates how to relate to the parts that make life difficult, such as the inner critic, by listening for its positive intention. I am so grateful for Ratnadevi's practical guidance to trusting the wisdom of the body. What I enjoy most about the book are her quirky stories that bring mindfulness to life!

—Martha Lasley, co-author of *Coaching for Transformation*

This is not just another mindfulness manual, but a mindfulness book with heart and soul. It explores connections between mindfulness practice and art and creativity, food and everyday living, communication and relationships, nature and how we live on this planet Earth, as well as many other areas of life.

—Vajragupta, author of *Buddhism: Tools for Living Your Life*

BRINGING MINDFULNESS TO LIFE

RATNADEVI

LUISE HOLTBERND PhD

To Fran
for the pleasure of
mindful living
Ratnadevi x

Playspace Publications

Bringing Mindfulness to Life

Published in United Kingdom in January 2022 by
PlaySpace Publications

01, 12 Garrioch Drive, Glasgow G20 8RS, Scotland
www.playspacepublications.com
ISBN 978-0-9573340-8-3

Typeset & Design by Gerry Cambridge
gerry.cambridge@btinternet.com

Cover image by Ratnadevi

Printed and bound by
Imprint Digital, Exeter, UK,
using responsibly sourced paper.
https://digital.imprint.co.uk

To listen is to lean in softly with a willingness to be changed by what we hear.

—Mark Nepo

The door to the mind should only open from the heart.

—Joy Harjo

To my students and friends in the mindfulness community

Contents

PART II

PART III

~ Introduction ~

The brains of human beings seem built to process stories better than other forms of input. Thomas B. Newman[1]

When I teach on mindfulness courses and on retreats, I notice the atmosphere in the room changing when I tell a story or read a poem. It could be an ancient parable from the Buddha's times or the tale of that moment of mindlessness when I stumbled over an anchor chain on holiday and broke my ankle, a moment that led to discoveries about how to open to pain and still have a good time. It's as if doors and windows open to let in a fresh breeze, carrying the scent of adventure, tragedy, kindness or mystery. My listeners' eyes soften and their bodies lean forward a little: their whole being is involved, not just the thinking mind. Suddenly I am not the expert teacher so much as a fellow traveller traversing the landscape of shared human experience, pointing to certain marker stones that we all interpret in our own ways.

This book on mindful living is brimming with such stories, giving you a taste of how decades of mindfulness, compassion and insight practice shape my response to all kinds of experiences, whether pleasant, boring or exasperating. My hope is that reading it will make you, too, pause more often, take in the good things in life and remind yourself of your strength and wisdom when faced with challenges. You'll accompany me picking blackberries, cleaning the fridge, visiting the hairdresser or, more dramatically, backing the car into a gatepost, learning that the underfloor heating coils have been punctured by a builder, or living with a chronic illness.

What helps me to keep my cool, in a warm-hearted way, comes down to a few simple principles, such as:

Staying in touch with my body, in the moment, receptive to sensory experience.

Not letting my thinking mind, driven by its evolutionary inheritance to focus on danger, go frantic.

Deliberately cultivating appreciation, gratitude and generosity.

Making friends with all parts of myself – the solution to a problem is in the problem.

---

[1]Professor of Epidemiology and Biostatistics at UCFS

Being curious about the needs and values (such as ease, respect or safety) underlying any experience: it is the way to great resourcefulness, particularly in situations of painful communication.

Seeing the big picture, where I am in deep time and space and staying in touch with my calling.

Easier to read than to put into practice? Regular meditation and mindful movement practice, occasionally going on retreats and being part of a practice community definitely help. One of the topics I am interested in is how mindfulness can become ritually embedded in our societies: how to celebrate a mindful Christmas, for example, and how to support our daily meditation by creating a home practice space that is rich in symbolic meaning. Living in a century governed by materialistic values, we need all the help we can mobilise, in order to stay connected with what really matters to us and what leads to true and lasting happiness.

This book is also an invitation to journey together and have a fresh look at some of the pressing issues we face as human beings today: the Covid pandemic, climate change, pollution, political chaos and the adverse effects of digital media use. Are we just using our mindfulness practice as a refuge of peace and sanity for ourselves, or can it equip us with confidence and resilience to express our compassion in active engagement, in line with our values? I draw on the insightful and practical work of the Work That Reconnects (devised by Joanna Macy) that offers helpful narratives, encouraging us to face our feelings of powerlessness, despair, fear, numbness or anger and move towards deeper insights into interrelatedness.

This is not a systematic introduction to mindfulness – there are plenty of books out there which offer that. I imagine that you are someone who maybe has already had some brushes with mindfulness, or someone with a daily meditation practice or perhaps you are a mindfulness teacher. If you are new to it, I trust that you will learn from this offering the way a young child enjoys a story that may include words it doesn't yet fully understand. I trust your intuition to use this book in whatever ways serve you best. There is something here to entertain as well as provide further training and stimulation for your own practice. If you run courses yourself, it may give you some ideas for teaching mindfulness: how to make mindful movement a delectable adventure, or how to introduce some habit-defying improvisatory elements into walking meditation.

Mindfulness is a way of being present that integrates all parts of ourselves, and that is what this book encourages. My intention is to appeal to the inner scientist, child, parent, monk, teacher, smartphone user, to the reptilian brain that needs calming, the mammalian brain that needs connecting and the big frontal brain that wants to understand. It allows you to lean back and be told stories, then stirs you into activity and asks you to become a co-creator of a 'mindful living' project by trying some exercises, reflections and meditations in your own time.

In the process, you will get to know me: how, as a Catholic teenager, I learned to meditate with a Benedictine monk; what classical music training taught me about the principles of practice; the joys of marriage, playing with children and doing the housework; some of my inner critics and how I have learned to befriend them; how to deal with loss and separation.

A few words about the genesis of the book and how it is structured, which may also suggest some ideas about how to read it. I started writing it about eight years ago and some of the characters, like my 'Buddha daughter', feature at different ages, without following a chronological order. During that time-span my partner Larry and I got married; I decided to call him 'husband' throughout, for simplicity's sake. Many sections had their first airing as articles for the website 'Buddhist Door Global',[2] where I contribute a column also called 'Bringing Mindfulness to Life'. This gives completion and roundedness to every small chapter - you could dip into the book at random and it would (hopefully) make sense. Saying that, my editor and I have given the overall shape of the book a great deal of thought, so that reading it from cover to cover would also be a rewarding process, following an arc: with material of a of more introductory nature in Part 1; the nitty-gritty of living in a challenging world in Part 2; followed by reflections on a broad range of topics regarding mindful living in Part 3 and finishing with a Coda on how to be present in Part 4.

You will come across the same ideas and teachings again and again, brought to life in different contexts. I don't remember who said this, but I am sure it was a wise being: 'There are no new teachings, just deeper understanding.' May your own understanding deepen and lead to joy, peace and love!

Ratnadevi, December 2021

[2]https://www.buddhistdoor.net/column/bringing-mindfulness-to-life/

PART I

~ Getting Started ~

Dedication Ceremony

'I think we've gone too far.' Gingerly he reverses down the narrow village road, past the picturesque potted geraniums and rose-garlanded entrances, to – THUD! – collide with the wall at the corner of a driveway. A concerned neighbour appears and picks up the pieces of the shattered back light. Emerging from a shared, momentary freeze, we clamber out of the car and introduce ourselves as friends of Sue and Bob, the owners of the Welsh cottage. 'A moment ago my car was parked at this very spot,' she says with a worried expression. Clearly, we haven't made a very trustworthy first impression.

My husband Larry and I are here for a couple of weeks to write. And have a bit of a holiday. And a bit of a retreat. And do some artwork. And finish off a few bits and pieces of other work. But the main purpose is to write, definitely. Larry puts his laptop in Bob's study upstairs, overlooking fields and wooded hills. He wants to focus on getting his next collection of poetry ready for publication. I will work on this book in Sue's garden hut with a view onto her ornamental thistles, daisies and apple trees, all held in place by walls of grey Welsh granite, which also figures prominently in the adjacent Presbyterian church. We could join in with the service that happens there every second Sunday of the month, which is today. Hear some Welsh chanting, maybe. Or we could follow the boom of the loudspeakers, drawing a crowd of gregarious holidaymakers to the local carnival. We could graze through Sue and Bob's extensive collection of films, music, books and whiskies. But no, that's not what we are going to do – or are we? Given the wide range of our combined interests and the lure of local opportunities, some clarification and enshrining of purpose would probably serve us well.

For the time being, though, both of us stumble through the cottage, feeling somewhat discombobulated from the accident. Each time I step through a door or climb up the stairs, I draw in my head as if expecting to be hit by a beam. Maybe that would have been necessary fifty years ago, but the place has been modernised since, in line with contemporary needs for spaciousness and light. Where is the nearest garage to get the light replaced? The bumper received quite a scraping that will also need fixing. And it's actually not our car either... It belongs to a friend, who, because of ecological concerns, invited us to share it. I bet he didn't expect it to be bashed up quite so soon, though. We are ambling through the house, emptying our suitcases and bags of groceries, losing things or worrying about losing them: keys, diary, reputation. 'I think I just locked the garage key inside the garage,' Larry says. A false alarm, luckily.

Eventually we sit down on a wooden bench in the garden with a cup of tea. The ginger cat, Frank, who has come with us from our friend's house in Liverpool, briefly returns from his exploits in the (relative) wild. He acknowledges our temporary tribal belonging by curving his long-tailed body around our shins before heading off again into the sheep field at the back of the garden. The sheep keep their heads down, oblivious to any observers. My eyes come to rest on a mature oak leaning over the wall of another cottage garden. It feels solid. I remember Sue's story about the horrible boundary dispute they have had to endure for the past eighteen months with that neighbour. They've even been threatened with court action. So how are **we** doing, right now? What semiconscious hostile voices are spoiling our inner peace?

'My inner critic is pretty vociferous,' I start. 'Mine too – in fact there's a whole bunch of them,' Larry replies. Just naming this already makes us feel a little better, smiling in tacit sympathy, less 'in the grip of'. Then I go through a little 'parts work'[3] session with myself, out loud, like a radio play: 'How are you doing, mate?' First finding out how the critic is feeling (tense, stern, frowning), I enquire into his good intention for me. He (he does seem a little more male than female) wants to protect my good standing in the eyes of others and make me feel safe, respected and at ease. He seems to speak for both Larry and me. When I thank him for his vigilance, he tangibly relaxes.

Now some sadness arises, which I recognise as the presence of a little girl who is being admonished by her parents for having broken something – a precious porcelain cup that belonged to Mum's granny. They've been shouting at her, and she feels scared,

[3]This type of parts work is drawn from Internal Family Systems (IFS) by Richard Schwartz; see Chapter 'Befriending All the Parts'

disconnected and ashamed. I talk to her in a soothing voice, letting her know that I understand how she is feeling and how much she needs to feel safe and loved. Taking that in, she's more at peace again.

The inner critic who has been witnessing the conversation feels a lot lighter and even a little amused when imagining telling the story to our car-share friend and others. There is more of a sense of perspective: everyone knows how it feels to be afraid of being judged and most people are likely to be a lot more forgiving with others than with themselves.

Larry has been following the storyline with vivid interest, judging from his forward-leaning posture and focussed eyes. I have a sense that witnessing my process has had some calming effect on his own inner critic too. Now it's his turn and I give my attention to his different ways of restoring mental equilibrium.

Later that day, after some food and an exploratory walk around the village (still in the grip of the annual carnival), we set up a place to meditate, in front of the fireplace. There's a serene-looking little Buddha figure, and we have brought candles and incense. I pick some of Sue's daisies and purple-flowering marjoram and arrange them in two glasses either side of the seated statue. We close the window to dim the festive raucousness and perform an improvised dedication ceremony, loosely modelled on what is the custom at the beginning of the Buddhist retreats we go to.

First, we 'salute the shrine', chanting in Pali, then sit quietly for a few moments. The Buddha seems to smile kindly through the haze of pine-infused incense.

'I dedicate our time here, including our writing efforts, to the benefit of other beings,' Larry starts. As I let that sink in, something in me relaxes – this is not about being good or bad at anything, but about making a contribution to something bigger. This is about letting go of a fixed sense of self, into our essential interconnectedness. We take turns continuing.

'To anyone troubled by the difficult times we live in.'

'To our students, past, present and future.'

'To all the people in this valley, including the dance band.'

'To our generous friends, Bob and Sue.'

'To Pearse, our car-share friend.'

'I dedicate our time here to all our inner parts, the protectors and the exiled inner boys and girls.'

'And the inner boys and girls in everyone else.'

Mentioning the inner children has hit the spot for me – a sweet release of energy and deeper settling.

'To the free flow of creativity, beauty and insight.'

I have arrived – and I am ready to start.

Setting your Intention

Perhaps this story has struck a chord and brought to the fore some of your own inner critics? I wouldn't be surprised – most people's psyches are populated with such bothersome characters who cling to outdated and often counterproductive methods to (ultimately) serve you. It doesn't always feel like they are trying to help, though. If you want to learn more about the 'parts work' process I was describing and have a go yourself, you could jump to the chapter called 'Befriending All the Parts' now. Or stay and explore how to prepare yourself for any task or project.

What do we want to do, and why? If we don't clarify our intention, however loosely or formally, we are likely to be at the mercy of half-conscious inner parts pulling us in different directions. The book you wanted to read gets buried at the bottom of the pile. You sit down to meditate and find yourself composing an email to a friend. You go to the shops to buy groceries and end up browsing the nearby second-hand clothes shops. In themselves, all these activities meet valid needs, but we are likely to feel dissatisfied with ourselves if we 'fail' at our primary goal and end up judging ourselves for 'giving in to temptation'. Conversely, doing what we said we'd do feels good; it leads to self-respect and self-confidence.

Connecting with the 'why' also taps into our sources of motivational energy, so that whatever we do feels less like a chore and more like play, the kind of serious play children can get absorbed in for long periods of time. Flexibility is part of the skill set, of course; we don't have to slavishly stick to our resolve when other needs have become more important, but it's good to be aware of that.

If you want to empower your resolve with regard to a particular short- or long-term goal, try this out for yourself now, if you like.

Ask yourself these questions:

What do I want to do? Be clear and precise, i.e. 'spend thirty minutes in daily sitting meditation every morning', or 'get my tax return ready to send by tomorrow evening'.

What's important about that? Or: **What needs does it meet?**[4] For meditation, it could be inspiration, calm and centredness. For the tax return, completion and a sense of mastery. Your activity could also include an awareness of others' needs, in which case it meets a need for contribution and honouring our basic interconnectedness. (This is what we made conscious in our dedication ceremony in that Welsh cottage.) So what is important about the activity you want to do?

Allow yourself to fully experience that quality for a moment. This part of the process is extremely important – it's where our brains change in accordance with our values, so that it becomes more and more natural to apply ourselves to what we want to do. Rick Hanson has written a lot about this neuroplasticity, about 'letting in the good'.[5] Try this out for yourself right now, if you like. Say the word 'inspiration' (or any other quality that appeals to you) to yourself, and observe the subtle effect on your body and mind. Maybe there is a lightening of energy, a brightening behind the eyes?

What other parts of you are around and what needs are they trying to meet? This question is often neglected; however, the more knowledge you have of what could be called 'the shadow', the less likely you are to be tripped up by resistance later on. Maybe there is a part in you that doesn't want to meditate or work out your expenses, but wants to go on Facebook, for example, for relaxation and companionship. Give some space to exploring these other pulls, and be curious about the important needs behind them.

How could all these needs be met? Even just assuming that a win-win scenario may be possible calms down the inner warfare.

[4]Refer to the Appendix for a List of Needs
[5] Rick Hanson, *The Buddha's Brain*

So you want to meditate in order to experience inner peace, **and** you want to spend time on social media for a sense of belonging and connection? What could that look like? Meditate first, and then log on? Keep your friends in mind and enjoy the connection with them during a loving-kindness meditation? Look for a group to meditate with?

Having brought all our different agendas into consciousness, we are in a better position to wisely negotiate a range of different needs, without the confusion, distraction and excessive inner criticising that so easily eat the joy out of our lives. Wanting more peace and joy in life is often the reason people start to become interested in mindfulness practice. In the next chapter you will read the story of how that came about for me, as a torturously self-conscious German teenager, and what it is like for me now to practise and teach meditation as a Westerner, with a particular tangle of cultural roots.

~ Where we belong ~

Mindfulness meditation is thriving in modern societies, on ground that was prepared by the twentieth-century arrival of Eastern gurus and pioneering Westerners who immersed themselves in Far Eastern religions and practices. It is a fairly new cultural movement: the first English translation of the *Tibetan Book of the Dead* was published in 1927. Many people these days learn to meditate without much knowledge of the belief systems of which sitting practice is a part, while others' first taste of it may come as part of an introduction to Buddhism. The Dalai Lama advises Westerners not to give up the religion they are raised in; I gather he wants to reassure people that he is not trying to convert anyone to Buddhism and that 'isms' don't matter anyway to a follower of the Dharma.[6] It is easy to underestimate how tough it is on the psyche to make a break with one's religious and cultural heritage. For most of us, our parents and grandparents didn't meditate – how does that affect our confidence in our own mindfulness practice? And how is that practice enriched by what our ancestors did give to us, such as religious music, art and architecture? Entering this territory of questions, this section starts with the story of how I first learned to meditate.

Zen and the Benedictine monk

Dedicated to Pater Rupert Overlack

The first and most vital practice in everyday life is... to value those moments in which we are touched by something hitherto undreamt of.
Karlfried Graf Duerckheim*

Almost fifty years ago, I did a week of 'Exerzitien' (literally, spiritual exercises) at the Benedictine abbey in Gerleve, in Westphalia, Germany. My whole class went; it was part of our education at St Ursula, the high school run by nuns in my home town, Dorsten. We were around fifteen years old, deemed to be the right age for some serious soul-searching. The abbey was an hour's coach ride away. The tall, square church tower could be seen from miles

[6] Dharma is a Buddhist term which has multiple meanings, including 'the law' and 'the Buddha's teachings'.
* From: *The Way of Transformation: Daily Life as Spiritual Exercise*

away, dominating the flat, rural scenery. We had been told we would be sleeping in single rooms, in a modern seminar building, not in cells. 'Exerzitien' – the word had a medieval ring, suggesting spiritual self-examination, a rigorous routine of prayer and silence and some vaguely imagined mortifications of the flesh.

Our seminar leader was a monk called Pater Rupert. My parents knew of him – he came from Bottrop, the small industrial town where my father was born and brought up. It was about fifteen miles south of Dorsten, and my father took my sisters and me to weekly piano lessons there, with an older, matronly lady who apparently had also taught Pater Rupert.

'I bet some of you are wondering why you are here,' said Pater Rupert at the start of the introductory session. He appeared formidable and 'other', in his swathes of black cloth, made of densely woven cotton, shiny in places. It was a chilly late-autumn day, and his bare feet in leather sandals gave a glimpse of austerity. He had a slightly hoarse voice, as if he wasn't used to speaking much.

'Who thinks a Benedictine monastery is the last place you'd choose to come?'

Wearily, half the class raised their hands. He slowly nodded.

'OK – we'll work out how you can get something out of being here.'

He started to explain what the place was all about, speaking in short sentences, to the point, with a twist of dry humour, leaving long pauses to look at us with sparkling, intensely interested blue eyes, allowing us to look at him.

'The monks have periods of silence, throughout the night and at mealtimes.' Pause. 'I thought we could have a go at it, if you're up for the challenge.' Pause. 'We could try it overnight till after breakfast – see what you make of it.' Pause. 'You may be surprised. It heightens the senses – a bit like drugs maybe, only safer.' I was aware of some bird singing outside; I was sure he heard it too. The room seemed bright, a brightness not caused by the strong morning light but by a certain attentiveness in the group.

'I will teach you to meditate. This is a bit different from praying.' I had a sense he wasn't trying to be liked or accepted by us, he was just himself. What did he do that gave him this self-assurance, this quiet alertness? Pray? Meditate? Practise celibacy? I was drawn to the expression of ardour and asceticism in his slightly hollow cheeks under high, sharp cheekbones, his kind, wry smile. A long face, with a shock of greying curly hair.

'Do you not shave the crown of your head?' one of the boys interrupted. 'What do you call it – a tonsure?'

'Yes, a tonsure – we haven't been doing that for decades. You may be interested to know that originally it came from a medieval rite of initiation into monkhood: carrying a candle on one's head and letting it burn down to the skin.' He definitely had everyone interested now.

At the end of the session, chuffed to have the Bottrop piano teacher connection, I introduced myself to him. He beamed with pleasure at being reminded of his life before entering the order. He clearly remembered Mrs Lemming, the grand piano in her parlour and the way she played: very fast and a little sloppily. He said this with affection. He suggested we talk more later, which made me feel elated, special.

We had a go at sitting meditation that evening.

'Meditation gets you out of your head. It's about being, not doing. It'll give you the confidence to be who you truly are. You focus on an area just beneath your navel, the "hara".'

I was always undermining myself with self-doubting thoughts to do with my appearance and status in the class. I'd definitely give this a go – this 'getting out of the head'. We sat for forty minutes, kneeling on meditation stools on the carpet. As far as I remember, there were no further instructions. My back soon felt achy and weak. My mind was intensely active, trying hard to calm itself down, to suppress the constant stream of thoughts: 'I wonder how Lisa feels about me after what I said to her? Don't think! Focus on the "hara"… Where exactly is that supposed to be? I'm not feeling anything… I'm not very good at this, am I?'

The next morning after breakfast, I was hanging around with my two best friends in the inner courtyard of the seminar building, comparing our impressions of it all so far. (We had managed to keep to the overnight silence, which seemed to make our chattering more delicious.) We agreed we loved the space. Pater Rupert had contributed to the design. It was inspired by Zen: warm wood, raw brick and austere concrete, lots of light. There was a Zen garden: raked pebbles and big round rocks, placed just so. All over the interior walls were original paintings by pupils, properly framed, looking spiritual in an appealing, abstract way. Pater Rupert was cool. But we were sceptical about the 'self-discovery workshops' to come, involving free movement, painting and talking about our experience in small groups. We had been taught in the conventional, front-facing style. You sit on rows of benches, in pairs, facing forwards. You talk to the teacher, not to each other. You use your head, not your body. Apprehensively, we gathered in the seminar room.

'We will do a session of free dancing to the sounds of "The Moldau" by Smetana.' Pater Rupert was his calm, bright, confident self. 'You'll love it.' He winked to the groaning boys. 'The idea is to let the music express itself through your body, become you. Same thing as with meditation – don't let your head get in the way. It's a great piece of music.' He described the development of the symphonic poem, from the source to a stream to a river, a hunting party, a peasants' dance and the eventual merging with the big ocean, expressed through a final, triumphant shift from the minor to the major key.

'What do you think the big ocean might symbolise?' He obviously was trying to nudge us into some metaphorical thinking about God. I wasn't so sure thinking of God would help – it brought with it a whole array of metaphysical complications. In school we had just studied three different proofs of God, and I was feeling increasingly wary about a God that so desperately needed proving.

The playful introductory flute runs, with tentative pizzicato punctuations from the strings did indeed bring a spring to mind. I moved my fingers a little, experimentally. The passionately lyrical theme, when it finally emerged, played with gusto by the violins, moved me, literally. I felt a gush of hot sweetness in the centre of my chest, and extending my arms and leaning into the space around me made that response stronger. This was great – exhilarating, except when there were idling passages in the music with nothing much to carry me. I was also aware of intense resistance in the room. My life was centred around classical music; most of the class didn't share those tastes. It was the Beatles and the Rolling Stones for them, and in any case, most preferred not to move their awkward teenage body in front of anyone else at all. The boys in particular had a hard time; they stood like jammed logs in the semi-self-conscious swirl of movement around them. Pater Rupert was a solid presence at the edge of the room, holding it all. Ripples of movement wafted through his black habit like wind, and every so often he spread his arms in encouragement. 'Let go,' the gesture seemed to say. 'Flow! Fly!'

'Check out the Gregorian chanting.' Pater Rupert encouraged us to go to services in the imposing abbey church. I did that, once, and after that spent time in the church on my own. It was time to make up my mind about God, decide whether, in fact, I was a Christian. Liturgy didn't help; the repetition of the same phrases, hymns and movements had a hypnotic effect that made it hard to hear my own thoughts. And any thoughts that did make themselves heard were often the doubtful kind, at variance with the collective professions of faith that were a central part of the service. This painful tension wasn't very conducive to the kind of mystical, direct experience I was hoping for. I had an inkling that solitude was more conducive to my quest, as it had been for Teresa of Avila or Francis of Assisi. I played the organ in our local church, and what I enjoyed about it most was access to an empty church for practice.

So there I sat, on the hard, square bench in the dark abbey church, my long back uncomfortable, trying once more to be open and receptive, praying (how do you do it?) that God may make himself felt in me. Confusingly, I felt both a presence and an absence. The presence was in the building, filled with the yearning of human beings towards meaning, a long history of it. Otherwise, there was only emptiness and a sense of failure. But I trusted my impetus towards authentic meaning and direct experience, and had a strong inkling that meditation was the way to go.

*

I look up Gerleve Abbey on the internet. They still run courses for schoolchildren, still called 'Exerzitien'. By email, I enquire after Pater Rupert and get a short reply: sadly, he has dementia and doesn't remember much of the past. I would have liked to thank him for befriending me (we did have several chats after that initial one) and for framing one of my paintings for the seminar building. To let him know that the meditation stool I bought from him accompanied me for many years and that eventually I started meditating every day. That the week with him set me on the road to becoming a Buddhist order member, multidisciplinary artist, rhythmics teacher, retreat leader, yoga and mindfulness teacher and trainer, life coach and writer.

He belonged to the first generation of monastics who turned towards Zen Buddhism, in particular the teachings of Graf Duerckheim, for revitalisation of the Faith. I don't think he had quite recognised the weight of body-hostile baggage in the Christianised Western psyche; otherwise, he might have guided us more gradually and sensitively into an accepting body-based experience of ourselves. His workshops were more ideas-led than sense-oriented. He didn't teach us to have compassion when judging ourselves, or if he did, I didn't hear it. But he modelled a life of spiritual commitment and risk-taking, and the marriage of mindfulness and creative expression, for which I am deeply indebted.

Meditation: Some Tips on Practising a Self-led Body Scan

My first sitting meditation experiences would have been a lot more rewarding, I think, if they had been preceded by a body-based practice such as a lying-down body scan. This type of meditation, where you explore internal physical sensations throughout the body, is presented early on in mindfulness courses, giving an experiential taste of a kind of awareness that is different from our prevailing thinking-based mode of operating. Often people use recordings of guided body-scan meditations, but guiding yourself has a number of advantages, in particular allowing for more flexibility and a more organic approach. Here are a few general principles and tips to bear in mind.

Set up the best conditions: do some mindful movement beforehand. In any form of meditation, a balance needs to be found between alertness and relaxation, and in the supine position (which is usually recommended for the body scan) there is a natural bias towards relaxation, not to say sleepiness. Some people actually use the body scan to go to sleep, and if it helps with insomnia, why not? But I would argue that sleeping doesn't make use of the full potential of the practice to access and stabilise mindful attention, which is the prerequisite for mental and emotional health and resourcefulness in so many ways.

To counteract sluggishness, people commonly exert too much effort, but trying harder usually backfires and results in even more drowsiness. Sleepiness in any form of meditation is a rich topic and worth being curious about, rather than going for a quick fix: 'just keep your eyes open!' There is some advice, however, I find hard not to offer, just because it makes such a big difference. It is simply: do some mindful movement beforehand. Five or ten minutes of shaking, swinging, bouncing, generally livening up in a standing position or slowly rolling on the floor, feeling the contours of the bones against the earth, relishing the massaging pressure of gravity on tight muscles, will make it much more likely that you will feel the satisfaction of body awareness in stillness. Movement tones the body/mind[7] energy, enlivens you or calms you down depending on what you need. If you have moved your feet and toes, you are more likely to actually sense them in stillness, rather than just thinking about them and getting disheartened by 'not feeling anything'. During the scan itself, however, the recommendation is not to move. Having given ourselves the best possible conditions for relaxed awareness, we then work with what arises, with acceptance and curiosity. If we 'don't feel anything', then we explore that 'nothing' and our reaction to it.

Form a clear intention. What do you want to get out of this meditation and how do you want to engage with it? Do you want to use it to fall sleep? Or to fall awake? Inhabiting the body with lucidity enables a profound shift of awareness, from a narrow, problem-oriented mentality to one that is tangibly connected with a vital flow of energy through the body. It can bring about a sense of peace, vitality and connectedness with a larger reality. It sets you up for more choice-full living. Setting an intention for any type of mindfulness practice, or indeed any undertaking, involves getting a sense of some of those qualities that you are longing to experience more of. Just thinking about states such as calm, presence or kindness already gets you in the mood. Try it right now! Simply

[7] I use the expression body/mind to refer to the integrated, holistic nature of our being.

ask yourself: what do I need right now?[8] Calm? Ease? Confidence? Clarity? A sense of belonging? Allow some time for it to emerge and then breathe with it. Feel the quality in your whole body. See, you are already meditating! This is a way of naturally generating the energy and resolve to give the practice your best shot. It is much more effective than summoning pure willpower.

Accept what is and let go of expectations and striving. This may sound somewhat contradictory to intention-setting, and it is! Shifts in awareness often occur when we embrace seeming opposites: setting a goal while abandoning any goal orientation. This will assist us in connecting with the truth of our present-moment experience, which tends to be messier than we like but is the only gateway to those wonderful states of mind we desire. The reason we are separate from them is our resistance to feeling what is already here: a niggling pain in the shoulder, a vague sense of boredom, confusion. We don't want these feelings, and this 'not wanting' keeps us locked in discomfort. We want results for our efforts, and soon. So part of the intention can be an encouragement to do our best to be present with what is, knowing full well that sometimes that isn't easy. Be open to any outcome, and trust that 'being with what is' will bring unforeseeable shifts in energy.

Follow your natural interest and stimulate your curiosity. When guiding yourself, it doesn't always have to be systematic, for instance starting with the toes and ending at the crown of the head. Any part of the body will do for a starting point, and it may be most organic to begin with a place where there is some natural interest, perhaps because of some discomfort or a ripple of pleasurable release as a result of lying down. Breathe into that area, and then use awareness of the breath as a guide and anchor throughout. What is the effect of the breath on this tight spot you are investigating? Does it respond differently to inhalation and exhalation? Curiosity is a quality of mindfulness that comes into its own during the body scan, helping to maintain the necessary freshness and lucidity. What is really going on in that part of the body I call my calf? The richness and complexity of the felt sense can't really be adequately put into words, but perhaps there's some pressure, tingling, a sense of

[8] You may want to refer to the list of universal needs in the Appendix.

volume. Be inquisitive: ask questions that feel fresh. Where does my body end and the floor begin? You could ask yourself this right now... Which is the lowest part of my body that I feel the breath in? Allow yourself to get absorbed in the exploration. Soon you will feel some changes in energy that give you access to a more intuitive way of guiding yourself. Something in you just knows where to go next or which line of enquiry to take in this fathoming of the inner body-world. Give yourself over to the experience, and let the journey unfold from there, till eventually you are aware of the whole, breathing body. The sense of this 'me' may also appear in a new, liberating light.

Secular or Spiritual? Reflections on Roots and Values

As a German ex-Catholic, a trained musician and an ordained Buddhist who now lives in Scotland and teaches 'secular mindfulness' to groups and individuals, where do I feel spiritually and culturally at home? In a cathedral, a tenement flat converted into a Buddhist centre or a hired community hall; when singing German folk songs, British carols, chanting Tibetan mantras or staying silent; when being faithful to traditional Buddhist teachings and the communities preserving them or in the company of freethinkers who forge their own individual paths? It appears that all of these threads are coming together to create a new, distinctive fabric, a warp and weft of tradition and innovation. This has happened for immigrants through the ages: a relative rootlessness is experienced as a loss, a yearning and an awareness of significant values. A voyage of cultural integration eventually brings forth new, creative forms of expression. Within that process, there is an inevitable, necessary voice that warns: 'Make sure you don't lose anything precious, anything essential.'

Such voices are also part of an ongoing discussion in the emerging modern mindfulness world, as ancient Eastern spirituality comes face to face with Western psychology, and each is influenced by the other. Hundreds of thousands of people from all walks of life are now 'doing mindfulness', as courses are held in places as diverse as hospitals, schools, parliament, businesses, prisons, the army, yoga studios and private therapeutic treatment rooms. Mindfulness teacher training has become an attractive addition to the career portfolios of many. What exactly are they all doing? What assumptions, originating in their cultural, religious or areligious upbringing, do they bring to their mindfulness practice? What are they really looking for: methods to reduce stress within otherwise unquestioned materialistic ways of life? Or something a bit more radical and transformational: guidelines for better living that examine the roots of both personal conditioning and systemic structures? What are the new or emergent support structures for lifelong practice? Where do people go for continued support when their eight-week mindfulness course has finished: a mobile phone app, a Buddhist centre, drop-in sessions at their place of work or community centre, or self-organised groups of friends? What are the new rituals emerging within such new communities – how do you celebrate a mindful Christmas, for example? And what role do such 'Sanghas'[9] play in addressing the most pressing and urgent concerns of our times, the fragile political and environmental state of the world?

At the heart of this enquiry are needs and values: how they often unconsciously govern our behaviour; how they are exploited by clever manipulators of market interests; how we choose and cultivate them and how they affect our well-being and that of other living beings. Historically, this has been a religious matter. Organised religion was and is there to orchestrate ritual reminders of what matters, of what moves the heart. It uses music, drama, colour and scent to powerfully affect people's emotions, to stimulate faith and give moral direction. The church also did and does a whole lot of other things connected with vested power interests which make many modern Westerners wary of religion. They don't appreciate the notion of hell as punishment for any misdeeds. These days, many people interested in spiritual development (although they may not call it that) instead turn to mindfulness, because it is 'secular'. Definitions of 'secular' put it in negative terms: it is not connected with spiritual or religious matters. Apart from the sound of a meditation bell, whether analogue or ringing from a mobile phone, there are no religious implements. There are no clerical hierarchies; the teacher doesn't

[9] 'Sangha' is a Sanskrit word meaning 'community'.

wear any special garments and doesn't expect any deferential treatment. You simply pay them for a service.

In practice, it is less clear-cut. When Jon Kabat-Zinn[10] entered the big lecture hall of Glasgow University during a mindfulness conference, the auditorium (I almost said the congregation) rose to their feet, and the reverent hush brought to mind elements of guru worship. Not that he did anything to engender that; if anything, he seemed a little uncomfortable with it. His answer to the question of whether he sees himself as a Buddhist was a little ambiguous. He did write this:

> The early years of MBSR [Mindfulness-Based Stress Reduction] and the development of other mindfulness-based clinical interventions were the province of a small group of people who gave themselves over to practicing and teaching mindfulness basically out of love, out of passion for the practice, knowingly and happily putting their careers and economic well-being at risk because of that love, usually stemming from deep first-person encounters with the dharma and its meditative practices, often through the mediation of Buddhist teachers and acknowledged masters within a number of well-defined traditions and lineages.[11]

I have seen passionate altruism demonstrated by many 'secular' mindfulness teachers and practitioners, but it is perhaps not the first thing we associate with the term, even if we would like our teachers to 'walk their talk', to embody calm and compassion. Secularity has connotations of individual autonomy and rationality, where nobody will be asked to believe anything that science can't prove; there is no Immaculate Conception in mindfulness. It is a scientific discipline, evidenced by thousands of research papers. Unlike religion, it doesn't concern itself with the provision of ethical guidance.

But maybe, in being so careful to distance itself from religion, secular mindfulness misses an opportunity. There is a difference between preaching the law and sensitively stimulating ethical awareness. My experience of introducing the topic of values into

[11] Jon Kabat-Zinn in McCown, Reibel and Micozzi (2010), p. xii.

[10] Kabat-Zinn was the first person to introduce mindfulness courses into the American health system and is seen by many as the father of the mindfulness movement.

mindfulness teaching has been encouraging; people welcome the conversation. They enjoy homework exercises such as gratitude practice and 'random acts of kindness', and they listen eagerly to research accounts that explain how generosity leads to enhanced well-being. 'Finding a sense of meaning' or an 'anchor' is frequently listed among the reasons for being on a mindfulness course. It seems that in the face of the many severe problems assailing the world, there is a pressing need for a more consciously and widely cultivated values-based orientation. It is disturbing that 18 per cent of young children in the UK don't feel their life is worth living.[12] Where does a sense of meaning come from in this fast-moving, materialistic, digital media-suffused, extinction-threatened age? I don't agree with the Dalai Lama when he says, 'I think the best people to stimulate awareness about what's happening and what needs to be done are not the politicians or leaders but the scientists. They are the real gurus in these matters.'[13] My impression is that scientists get more excited about what can be done (creating new organisms from stem cells, or artificial intelligence, for example) than whether, how and why it should be done. I think it may have to be us, anyone starting to wake up and consider more mindful ways of living, who are asked to clarify their ethical stance and take responsibility.

The topic of climate change is an obvious platform for a contemporary exploration of ethics in mindfulness. I think many of us sense how caught up we all are in cycles of systems-driven craving and consuming. We know what it is like to be addicted to comfort and habits that don't give us what we really want, but just a sense of dissatisfaction and existential hunger. Commercial advertising is very good at tapping into our free-floating needs, untethered to religion or any clear moral ground. A mindfulness course or retreat is a context where our deeper emotions and values can first be recognised and named and then galvanised to play a part in 'The Great Turning'[14] towards truly sustainable living. We can both rest in the moment, letting ourselves be deeply nourished by the beauty of landscapes in rain and sunshine, and take responsibility for protecting the fragile ecosphere. Part of that is

[12] YouGov survey quoted in *The Guardian*, 10.2.2019.

[13] During a think tank meeting on climate change in Dharamsala, quoted in *Tricycle*, Spring 2019.

[14] A term used by Joanna Macy to describe the worldwide movement from exploitative industrial societies to sustainable growth societies.

recognising that 'mindfulness' doesn't exist in a cultural vacuum; it has roots in the rich soils of both the East and the West. The earth has been cared for by countless generations and has passed into our care now. From that recognition arise confidence and a sense of agency; we are not alone, but part of past and present communities.

The gifts we have received from our ancestors are most likely a bit of a mixed bag. I was at a workshop with Makere Stewart-Harawira, Professor of Indigenous, Environmental and Global Studies at Alberta University, who was visiting Scotland to see the coalmines run by her great-great-grandfather. Her work focuses on the environmental degradation caused by coal mining, which led her to descend into the womb of the earth and connect with her family history. She found herself down in the narrow, dark mines, weeping and struggling to make sense of it all. It is confusing: we may be simultaneously proud of the technological achievements of past generations and appalled by their exploitation of the poor and their lack of consideration for future generations. We like our electric light and central heating and don't quite know how to square that with knowledge of the darker environmental ramifications of such 'necessities'.

In the midst of these complexities, we can feel spiritually adrift, perhaps more so than at any other time in human history. By cultivating appreciation of our teachers and guides in the many arenas of our lives, we nevertheless gain a degree of inner confidence and belonging.

Meditation: 'Where we belong' – Earth Breathing and Gratitude to Our Teachers and Ancestors

This is a meditation designed to help you find your confidence by connecting with your somatic and cultural roots. It's not so much about analysing the perhaps mixed blessings received from your parents or caregivers, but choosing to tune into a more generic, felt sense of lineage and belonging. It can be done lying down or in a sitting position.

Settle into your physical posture, particularly sensing the contact areas of your body with the earth. Tuning[15] into a felt sense that you are part of the earth, like a tree or a mountain, rooting down. Sensing the earth like a welcoming presence, inviting you to let go, absorbing any habitual tension you may be able to release easily.
Breathing out and letting your awareness descend into the earth. Allow the awareness of your body to merge with the body of the earth; vast, warm and still. Allowing a sense of belonging to suffuse your body, resting in it.

Aware of the in-breath, let your body be filled with life-giving energy from the earth. Whatever the qualities of the earth you sense – warmth, spaciousness, stillness – let yourself be nourished by them.

Rest in the moment with your breath, extending your body awareness down into the earth with the exhalation and receiving energy from below with the inhalation. Give yourself over to this 'earth breathing', allowing the thinking mind to naturally calm.
Your roots also extend into time, into the past, to your previous meditations and insights. You are not starting from scratch, but building on your past efforts. Let the freshness of presence in this moment be combined with confidence arising from your past realisations.

Now opening to a sense of your biological ancestors, your parents and their parents, and the long chain of generations before them, right back to the dawn of human consciousness. Connecting with their practical survival skills and spiritual beliefs and practices that sustained and inspired them; their reciprocal relationship with plants and animals, their knowledge of healing. Connecting with the best of that creativity and resourcefulness, in its many manifestations, throughout the millennia.

Bringing to mind some of your ancestors' cultural and spiritual achievements that now enrich your life: music, literature,

[15] In guided meditations, the 'ing' form of verbs suggests a sense of presence, flow, equality and non-duality, the sense that the teacher is not telling anyone what to do, but is suggesting they are all in this exploration together. It is worth making use of, even it can sound a bit odd, grammatically.

architecture, scientific knowledge. Allowing yourself to be uplifted and nourished by this current of creativity and beauty. This is part of your heritage.

Now bringing to mind a meditation teacher whose presence and teaching open you to the sources of deep peace, compassion and understanding in your own heart. Treasuring that vital link to experiences that may be quite subtle and hard to put into words.

Reflecting that they in turn have been inspired by their teachers and have nurtured that connection. People have been meditating and navigating the depths of the human mind for many thousands of years and all that is present in you now. You can relax and let yourself be supported by that stream of love and wisdom.

Allow your heart to be filled with gratitude and continue to sit in a more formless way.

Why Meditate? Deepening Connection with Ourselves and the World

We are all prone to experiencing considerable levels of stress on a daily basis as we try to cope with prevailing threats, such as the rise of right-wing populism and climate change, together with more personal challenges and pressures amplified by social media. Mindfulness meditation is generally regarded as a helpful strategy for maintaining desirable levels of calm and well-being. But not everyone agrees.

Ron Purser, professor of management at San Francisco State University, has created a bit of a stir with his book *McMindfulness* (2019). He states that 'Instead of changing the world, mindfulness has become a banal form of capitalist spirituality that mindlessly avoids social and political transformation, reinforcing the neoliberal status quo.' I agree with him that focussing on personal well-being without considering systemic conditions could be a questionable strategy for resolving the problem of suffering. A metaphor comes in handy here: pulling drowning bodies out of a river may seem like a noble and compassionate act, but would it not be as useful, indeed more so, to ask 'How come so many people are drowning?'

There are different levels on which this crucial question can be considered, and the sociopolitical perspective is one of them. It would be wonderful if more people could lead their lives in more self-determined ways, with better working conditions, more free time, access to better education and more meaningful leisure activities, and so on. But in my opinion, at the root of the question 'How come so many people are drowning?' lies a deeper, existential enquiry related to our values and how aware we are of them. We can't just blame capitalism when we don't know what we really want and are easily drawn into addictive and mind-numbing ways of spending our time that don't bring greater happiness and might actually increase our suffering.

Together with a growing number of other 'secular' mindfulness teachers, I incorporate working with values as an integral part of my courses and retreats (without presenting them as articles of religious belief). In my experience, this reduces the likelihood of falling into the pitfall of quietism or, indeed, into the pitfall of black-and-white thinking. An 'either/or' way of thinking doesn't serve us in these critical times; it is not about either blissing out on the meditation cushion or saving the world – it has to be both. One of the meanings of mindfulness, next to 'being present in the moment', is to 'remember our purpose', to recall what we set out to do or which qualities to embody.

Why do we meditate? For me, and for many others I have heard answer this question, it is not just about personal peace and happiness but also about contributing to the welfare of others. We gain so much ourselves from being in the presence of contented people who thrive in their places of work and in their relationships, who are fulfilled enough in themselves to be able to really listen to what others need. So doesn't it make sense to do our best to add to others' happiness and create the conditions for it? Bringing to mind, at the beginning of a period of meditation practice, our interconnectedness with life means our 'highest intentions are present in the same way that breath is present'.[16] As for

[16] Jack Petranker, in an email exchange in the Mindfulness and Social Change Network. He is the Director of both the Center for Creative Inquiry and the Mangalam Center, both in Berkeley, California.

Jack Petranker, each time I sit down and reflect on my motivation for meditating, 'the momentum that fuels social change will be there too'. It is present now, as I write this passage, and it is present when I prepare for a workshop for Extinction Rebellion activists to help them avoid burnout. Without my regular morning meditation, I believe this work would be far less effective – I would be more prone to feelings of overwhelm and despair, and less able to maintain compassionate awareness in the face of suffering.

There is another pertinent question when it comes to looking at mindfulness in relation to social change: **what kind of meditation** helps us make the bridge from 'self' to the world seemingly 'out there'? When we breathe mindfully, we can reflect on sharing the breath with other living organisms. But unless the insight of interconnectedness pervades our experience most of the time already, we probably have to remind ourselves to bring that perspective to the our breath-focused meditation, whereas the very essence of loving-kindness practices is to open our hearts to all life, including ourselves.

I would like to introduce you to a simple and easily accessible **loving-kindness meditation that starts with gratitude.** Thinking of something positive that happened to us opens the gates of energy flowing from and towards us, bringing us into connection with the world. Gratitude is an easily available way of noticeably shifting mental states towards more positivity, thus creating confidence in the possibility of change. It is hard to think of contraindications, except perhaps a reaction to an overly moralistic stance ('you should be grateful!') that would deny or minimise an actual painful experience. As with any other meditation, acceptance of what we feel is a necessary foundation.

The orientation towards positive states (and acceptance is one of them) is the essence of loving-kindness practice. It can be useful to think of it as having less of a 'doing' than a 'being' tone. Trying too hard to wish ourselves or others well can often be experienced as counterproductive, leading to tension, a feeling of inauthenticity and self-blame if it 'doesn't work'. Rather, we can cultivate the subtle art of recognising the states of calm, contentment and joy that are already there (perhaps as a result of recalling something we feel grateful for) and letting the experience linger in body/mind awareness. The prolonged somatic experience of a positive feeling, for at least twenty to thirty seconds, is what changes brain chemistry and creates new neural pathways.[17] Becoming more familiar with the expansive way of being that follows our attunement with important values makes it more likely that we can access these states when we really need to, in the heat of challenging situations and when important decisions have to be made.

Meditation: When Needs are Met – from Gratitude to Loving Kindness

In the following meditation we combine a general kindly inclination of the heart with recognition of the specific needs and values in a given situation. (Needs refer to more immediate experience, whereas values have a more long-term relevance.) This lends authenticity and imaginative, empathic acuity to the practice. I invite you to have a go at this now.

Connect with your present experience with openness and acceptance. What is going on in body and mind?

Remember things/people/events that inspire gratitude. For example, you might recall that your brother phoned you when you were ill.

Taking time to identify the needs and values that are met by these experiences. In this example, these may be to matter, to feel loved, cared for and supported.

Experiencing the beauty of these needs in the moment and wishing yourself the fullness of these qualities. You may repeat these words in a warm and gentle tone of voice: to matter, to feel loved, to be supported. And listen to the impact of these words, perhaps

[17] Rick Hanson, https://www.rickhanson.net/take-in-the-good/

as a felt sense of warmth, glow or tenderness in your body. Letting it suffuse your body/mind experience, breathing with it.

Bring to mind other people and wish/imagine their needs being met. Traditionally this could be a friend, followed by a neutral person, then someone you have difficulties with and then broadening it out. Or you could do it more organically, homing in on whomever appears in your mind. Reflect on what's important to them; if you know them personally, this could relate to their current life experience. For example, if they are stressed about the process of buying a house, you may initially wish them a speedy completion of the process, and then ask yourself what that would give them: states of mind such as ease, calm, safety and so on. You could picture them looking relaxed and at ease.

So you focus on universal needs and values rather than the strategies to meet those needs. With people you don't know, universal needs such as safety, happiness, a sense of meaning and fulfilment are certain to hit the spot. Gently repeat those words and feel them resonate in your heart.

~ Establishing a Regular Meditation Practice ~

Overcoming Obstacles to Practice

In writing, habit seems to be a much stronger force than either willpower or inspiration. John Steinbeck

When you feel diligent and enthusiastic you meditate, and when you feel lazy you meditate. Ajahn Chah

It's week two of an eight-week mindfulness course. I've just led a lying-down body-scan meditation, and the atmosphere is calm and mellow as we gather back in a circle. A couple of people report feeling transported into a 'numinous' kind of state, seeing colours and feeling the sound of the bell in their body. Soon after, however, the mood seems to change markedly when I suggest that they split into groups of three to discuss the previous week's home practice assignment. Shoulders stiffen and there are apologetic murmurings, nobody meeting my eye. I am guessing that quite a few inner critics have joined us here in this hired kung fu studio in the south of Glasgow, together with somewhat ashamed, criticised inner children.

Shame thrives in secrecy, and talking honestly helps to dispel it. People become quite animated as we put up on the flip chart a list of common obstacles to daily home practice:

- No time.
- Too hard to get out of 'doing' mode – there is so much else that needs to be done.
- Cultural conditioning: don't be selfish.
- It's too intense to stop and experience all that underlying tension.
- Feeling awkward and self-conscious.
- It's hard to change habits.
- Resistance to doing 'homework'.

The standard advice about learning a new skill is to give it the benefit of the doubt and persist through the teething troubles, which are only to be expected. Trust that the difficulties will work themselves out as practice becomes more established. What is required initially, it seems, is a leap of faith.

We are training ourselves in being more and more frequently aware of our experience as it happens, both in formal ways, when doing a body scan, mindful movement or sitting meditation, and in more informal ways, during conversations for example. This makes our experience more vivid, both the pleasurable and the painful aspects. We enjoy the sunshine more and feel our sadness more directly. With regular practice, what soon becomes apparent is that sometimes mindfulness practice comes easily and feels natural, and sometimes it just doesn't and we struggle in some way.

Often this is related to wanting a different experience from the one we are having. This is true even of experienced meditators. Repeated practice helps us gain perspective, stay relaxed and non-judgemental and not expect too much of ourselves at any given time. It takes time for the brain to rewire itself so that awareness becomes a more constant companion in our lives. Then, gradually, we experience more freedom of choice in our responses and are less prone to reacting based on habitual, old-brain survival impulses. Seeing these changes and sensing that we experience more of what motivated us in the first place is encouraging, and naturally makes us want to practise more. It is heartening to feel even small improvements in inner calm, a more reliable sense of perspective on repetitive thinking or more enjoyment of the small things.

Steinbeck's comment that it's not willpower or inspiration, but habit that is the key to success also merits some consideration. Recent research finds that on average it takes sixty-six days to form a new habit – about the length of an eight-week course! And regularity in the first few days seems to be a key factor. Showing up for practice instils confidence in ourselves as someone committed to this particular path of self-development.

But yes, at the beginning we can feel awkward, slightly hypervigilant. The other day when walking with a friend whose hearing is bad in one ear, I wheeled my bike on my left, rather than the familiar right side. It felt strange and precarious, but interesting. I sensed muscles in my upper back and neck that I didn't know I had, particularly when trying to turn my head towards my friend without running the bike into him. If I did this daily for a couple of months, it would probably feel normal; it would have become one of the thousands of actions I perform daily on autopilot. Which would be a shame, in a way...

Newness of experience is refreshing, which is why most people like going on holiday. It's a trade-off, giving up the comfort of the familiar for the thrill of aliveness. Regular mindfulness practice is unique in that it becomes a soothing routine, like the first cup of tea in the morning, *and* we do it to wake up, to be present in this unrepeatable, precious moment.

One of the reservations voiced by a woman in my mindfulness group was the intensity of experience: she was afraid of being overwhelmed by emotions. Dr Willoughby Britton[18] has done some important research into the possible adverse effects of mindfulness, and stresses that people have different 'windows of tolerance'. The message 'no pain, no gain' can be unhelpful. People with a history of trauma often find that focussing on the breath is *not* helpful – on the contrary, it can make them more anxious. So it is important to have a sense of choice. Maybe the feet or hands are better anchors for grounding experience in the present. And there should be no shame attached to taking care of oneself, choosing to sometimes distract ourselves from emotional pain and discomfort.

The obstacle of being seen as selfish is an interesting one. As a young woman I lived for several years at Taraloka, a Buddhist retreat centre for women in Shropshire, England. A new group of retreatants would arrive on a Friday evening and sometimes question us team members about our lifestyle. 'Seems like you live here in a bit of a bubble,' the more outspoken ones would say. 'No worries about money, everything provided for you, plenty of time to sit around and do nothing – seems like a cushy option to me. What about the state of the world? Are you not simply escaping your responsibilities?'

After a week of meditation their views would often change dramatically, and they would express admiration and gratitude for what we were doing. Honestly facing our experience is one of the most courageous and quietly revolutionary things we can do. Our capitalist economic system counts on us trying to escape

[18]https://www.fitmind.co/podcast-collection/dr-willoughby-britton-meditation-harmful

our existential discomfort through food, drink, ceaseless entertainment, restless digital communication and a stream of new acquisitions. At Taraloka we were not depriving ourselves of pleasure, but leading simple lives aimed at contentment, with few distractions. In Buddhism this is called the Middle Way between hedonism and asceticism. It is made possible through practising mindfulness and kindness.

Even so, there is perhaps a danger that the inner contentment encouraged by mindfulness practice could lead to complacency and passivity with regard to the state of the world, which, according to countless specialist reports, is in severe danger of systemic collapse in many fields. For me, the answer does not lie in *not* meditating or *not* going on retreat, but in going deeper. With more penetrating insight, the felt sense of our interconnectedness with all life naturally leads to compassionate activity that is courageous and joyful even as it embraces suffering.

Transferable Skills: Getting into new Habits

Something has passed from potential to actual; you've started something new, brought something into the world. It's magical and relatively rare. Beginnings are terrible times, and so are ends. Vincent Deary

Our battles with our habits speak of dreams yet to become real.
Mary Oliver

At the beginning many people are easily inspired by meditation and get glimpses of its potential to make life a lot more satisfying. They also realise that daily practice is of the essence and want to make space for that in their busy lives. And very often the enthusiasm and resolve crumble within a short period of time. The question is: what does it take to continue the new practice when the thrill of the new has flattened out?

On a mindfulness teacher-training event, we role play how to get across to our students the idea of daily meditation practice. We practise in groups of four: one teacher, three pretend students. 'You have one minute each: go!'

'You just have to do it; use your willpower!' A semi-retired GP starts her pitch, with a determined set of her jaws. 'The research shows the benefits of formal practice,' a clinical psychologist puts forward phlegmatically. 'Think how much more you enjoy life when you meditate,' a yoga teacher says enthusiastically. 'Well, let's face it: it's not that easy,' I begin my spiel, with what I hope is an encouraging smile.

Changing our routines and habits, and making space for a new regular activity such as meditation, is one of the hardest things to do. We start off with the best of intentions, our goal placed firmly in front of us, only to find that, embarrassingly, it doesn't take much in the way of inner or outer distractions to lure us off course. For the first couple of days after the mindfulness class, we heroically stick to our new regime; then on day three, at the appointed hour, a friend calls unexpectedly. Following from that there are emails to be checked, the washing machine needs emptying and by then everyone feels hungry. Or we come home and feel vaguely uncomfortable, a little out of sorts. The day hasn't been easy. We feel like doing something relaxing, soothing and ordinary, like watching a movie, checking Facebook – anything that gives us some respite from... well, ourselves. Perhaps we tell ourselves that we are still practising mindfulness, just more informally, as part of everyday life. Or that we are being kind to ourselves. That may all be true, but on some level we also know that we have let ourselves down. We may feel a little disappointed, a little guilty, which can then make us want to distract ourselves even more thoroughly – have a drink, binge on chocolate, buy something online. And of course, this is all very 'normal' behaviour, encouraged and sanctioned by our consumer society. All in all, it's very easy to underestimate the temptations and obstacles to implementing our good intentions. Unlike Odysseus, we don't ask the crew to tie us to the mast of the ship to be able to withstand the awful attraction of the sirens' song. And so once again we go under; we get swallowed up in the comfort of the familiar.

I am trying to remember what made me practise the piano, on a daily basis, for around twenty years of my life. What gave me the patience and persistence, aged eight, to learn to play a scale with both hands in parallel, starting with the little finger of the left hand and the thumb of the right hand, each on a C, an octave apart? The action was a lot harder than placing both thumbs on middle C and running the fingers outwards, in an easy symmetry of movement that produced, however, rather dissonant musical results. I remember the awkwardness of those first attempts to advance from C to D, trying to push down the ring finger of the left and the index finger of the right hand at the same time. Staring alternately at those fingers, I could almost sense something switching around right inside my brain. Performing this difficult action for the first time was a kind of birthing, holding the breath and somehow making the belly muscles squeeze the keys down, expelling air from the back of the throat at the same time. In front of me was a sheet of music, and I had to link the sound and the action to little black, oval shapes situated at specific places on or in between five horizontal lines, and to make the matter more complicated, coded differently for the right and left hands and with variations that indicated the length of each note, as well as symbols that indicated levels of loudness.

The whole process seems almost too complicated to disentangle into words and sentences. I put down my pen, press my ring and index fingers onto the arms of my chair and instantly access it again: the perfect, effortless, elegant coordination of the arms and shoulders into that precise and powerful contact of the pads of the fingers with the surface. I use about 30 per cent more strength on the left, non-dominant side, reinforcing the weaker finger, to make the two notes sound equally loud or the left even louder. Emphasising the lower note but not letting it come sooner than the higher. I can almost hear it: the warmth and mellowness of the sound, the bass note enveloping the overtones beyond the octave. These subtleties that bring the music to life give a personal touch that cannot be achieved on an electronic keyboard. It took uncountable hours of practice to programme my body to be able to do this, putting up with the discord of innumerable wrong notes and faulty timing and the emotional strain of experiencing repeated failure when measured against standards of perfection.

Was I trying to please my teacher, my parents and my favourite uncle, the organist; competing with my best friend and my siblings who were all learning to play; imagining a scintillating future as a concert pianist; harbouring some romantic notions of sublime transcendence through music; welcoming the challenge and the sense of mastery; or simply enjoying the sound of the music while playing it? It was probably a mixture of all of those, enough motivation anyway to help bear the frustrations of those first efforts and get admitted to a prestigious conservatoire, make a living teaching the piano for a few years and perform in a couple of concerts. Now I don't play the piano much; my practice has shifted to other areas, to other art forms and to yoga and meditation. Living in a flat, I am aware of the neighbours.

On this Sunday morning, however, I sit down at my trusted old upright Bechstein and open the pages of a book of music: Bach's French Suites. First, I limber up by playing some scales in D minor, the key the first suite is written in. Playing one octave very slowly, precisely, then doubling the tempo over two octaves and then progressing into even faster triplets over three octaves. Then starting again. 'Repetition is the mother of all learning', as the Romans said. To any casual passer-by, what I am doing would sound like the archetype of 'practice'. You can imagine the movie that would go with it: the Victorian setting, the tale of forbidden passion. During the first run I feel fairly present, aware of the rise and twist of the wrists as I take the thumb under the middle fingers and stretch for the black keys, aiming for smoothness and economy, controlling the volume and evenness of attack. More and more, the scale plays itself, with very little intervention by 'me'; it's largely automatic. The psychologist Vincent Deary, whom I quoted at the beginning of this chapter, writes that word with a capital A.

The decisions we commonly think 'we' make, he writes, have 'already been made by the agents and routines that make up the Automatic, and then consciousness gives it the nod, mistaking its accent for agency'. 'We' are just hosts to decision-making processes, consisting of our past learning, encounters, places, wishes and dreams that come together as a team to work it all out among themselves. Do you think it is 'you' who decides to get up and answer the phone? Your body will already be half off the chair before some notion of not wanting to be disturbed arises and you leave it ringing. Some stronger factors have won the game, but are they any more 'you'? This big Automatic and the questionable agency of a 'me' are what we are up against when for some reason the idea of doing something new is introduced into our lives.

When some dream wants to 'become real', as Mary Oliver says. For me, the current challenge consists in instituting writing as a regular part of my life. I want to get this book finished. Meditating daily has now been part of the Automatic for many years, although I still feel the lure of easier options at times. I do it before breakfast, after some stretches, on my accustomed cushions, in front of a little shrine. I light candles and incense. It is built firmly into the fabric of other routines and rituals. But trying to get myself to stick to my resolve regarding writing requires all the resources of inner strength and ingenuity I can muster, plus tolerance for some seemingly necessary slacking off. I let myself do this little distracting task on the computer, say, checking the weather forecast first, before opening my Word document. And then, before diving in, I first have to work out how to switch off the ringer on my new phone. Easy little confidence-boosting achievements.

We try to render as much behaviour as possible automatic, as quickly as possible. It frees up energy and capacities to deal with emergencies or anything that may threaten the equilibrium. Most species content themselves with applying their available mental and physical powers to handling current dangers, whereas our human brains have evolved to also apprehend future calamities and to rehearse over and over those we have survived. In the process we have grown addicted to thinking, sometimes about dangers and sometimes pleasures, but generally with a bias towards the negative. Given a little lull in the daily run of things, we will start daydreaming, pondering, brooding, reminiscing and fantasising. Not only that, but we attach great importance to the content of this ongoing plotting; it is a large part of our identity and shapes our character, for better or worse. 'I have had a lot of worries in my life,' Mark Twain famously wrote, 'most of which never happened.'

At the piano I am turning over ideas for this chapter while my fingers go through their limbering-up routines with relative ease and confidence, all by themselves. I am making little adjustments and refinements as I go, or more correctly, those adjustments are being made by some complex interplay of memory, sound, sight and tactile perceptions, musical convention and some degree of conscious intentionality. In the meantime, my mind wanders; now it's contemplating walking meditation.

One form of walking meditation involves pacing up and down a pathway of ten yards or so. (Not dissimilar to playing scales, come to think of it.) You are aware of your feet on the ground and other sense impressions, such as your arms brushing against your clothing or your face against the air. After a while you may choose to investigate what happens at the turning points. When and where in the body do you feel the first stirrings of the impulse to slow the momentum of your walk, and how does the body navigate that U-turn? Unless someone prompts you, you will probably not notice that you tend to turn the same way each time. It's a revelation to find how strange it feels to swivel round the other way. Strange and a little thrilling. By modifying an unconscious habit, the light of awareness has the chance to break though the dark, smothering cloud cover of the Automatic. It is a little unsettling, refreshing and brings a sense of freedom: you could go anywhere! Or choose to keep walking up and down the path, practising being mindful within those particular confines. This means noticing when and to what extent the Automatic rules the game, both in terms of physical movement and thought patterns, making forays into mindful presence and gradually learning to dwell in this state more and more fully and easefully. And does mindfulness practice then become the new Automatic? And does that not defeat the purpose? An interesting conundrum!

So is learning to meditate like learning to play the piano? Can we draw on transferable skills? We all have some previous experience of acquiring new abilities and establishing new patterns in our lives – if not playing an instrument, then eating with a knife and fork, reading and writing, riding a bike, playing football, maybe learning a new language or how to throw pots. We know it can be done; we can draw some encouragement from that. We know we can overcome the inertia of the familiar, override the need for comfort and security in following old habits, and expose ourselves to the discomfort, repeated failures and initial gracelessness of acquiring new skills. These formerly awkward actions are now relatively easy to do – they have left their marks, sculpted us. They are now inscribed on our muscles, bones and nerves. They have also become part of the fabric of our outer life; we are surrounded by the implements of our hobbies and interests. Our social networks are intertwined with what we like doing. There are maps and timetables in our minds and bodies that take us to the right places at the right time without us having to think about it. The Automatic takes care of it now, and we love the ease and comfort of that.

I am now playing a Bach piece that I have never played before, an allemande, slowly and evenly, as I was taught to do, diligently repeating the bars that didn't go right, thus letting the correct notes and most suitable fingering stamp themselves into my brain. It's all about repetition, isn't it? Establishing and reinforcing certain pathways in the brain. In order to maximise the effect, I don't just repeat the same phrase over and over the way I want it to sound in the end, but I vary the rhythm, speed and loudness. It becomes a little improvisation of sorts. Confidence in being able to eventually play those difficult passages as smoothly and calmly as the easy parts grows by making detours into the surrounding territories of even faster, even louder. Like learning to handle knife and fork unselfconsciously under most circumstances by managing bouncy peas, slushy mashed potatoes and cutting stringy meat with a blunt knife. Children know how to make learning into play, which makes it more messy and time-consuming, of course.

There is a certain peacefulness in this, the music and the practising, but I am also aware that I tense up my mouth, I frown and clench my jaws a little, as I have probably always done, starting from those early attempts at playing a scale. It seems that a certain attitude has been incorporated into me, together with the music, a subtle reaction to potentially getting it wrong, to being found lacking in some way. Not that I was subject to any of the draconian educational measures one of my piano teachers told me about. He was forced to put wine-bottle corks between his fingers to increase his hand span, and his teacher had a wooden ruler ready to flick over his fingers when he hit any wrong notes. In fact, I have been given a lot of encouragement in my musical development, but still, shaming is part and parcel of our educational culture. Could this be part of the resistance we face as adults when learning a new skill: the fear of making ourselves vulnerable to potential ridicule? And if this is so, how can we work with it? How can we make sure we practise the things we do want in our lives and don't involuntarily reinforce other unwanted habits of wilfulness?

The 'failures' are of course a necessary part of perfecting any skill. In 1984, the Turing Institute in Glasgow was involved in helping NASA fly the space shuttle. The early computers they used collected data on vast numbers of failures and simulated shuttle crashes. The data were fed into a learning algorithm which eventually led to better control of the object. I am pretty sure the scientists involved didn't feel bad about those 'failures' - in fact, they may even have been excited about them. When we reframe failure as opportunity, as a necessary part of any learning, much unnecessary tension can dissolve.

One or Two Marshmallows?

I spend a lot of my time on pursuits that can be called 'practice', be it meditation, yoga or playing the piano. They could be seen as states of postponed satisfaction, since the very notion of practice implies greater skills or a sense of accomplishment at a later stage. What really excites me, however, is finding that inner switch to enjoying the present moment at any stage of the process. When I remember the possibility of presence while practising that fast right-hand run in Beethoven's 'Spring' Sonata for violin and piano, at different speeds and in a variety of rhythms, it can yield as much satisfaction there and then as eventually playing it with Dan, my violinist friend. In meditation, there is also an element of skill development: training the mind in sustained attention on the breath, for example. We can easily belittle this part of the experience, longing for the imagined end result of sustained, effortless peace and bliss.

In the famous Stanford marshmallow experiment in behavioural psychology, a group of toddlers had to choose between short-term gratification and long-term reward. They were left alone in a room and told that they could either eat a marshmallow now or wait for fifteen minutes to receive two of them. The little ones who were able to postpone gratification went on to do better in many areas of life as adults.

During my childhood in Germany, we didn't have marshmallows, but we did have something known at the time as

'Negerkuss' (literally a 'negro kiss'), a treat similar to the Tunnock's Teacakes sold here in Scotland. Heavenly sweet egg-white fluffiness heaped on a waffle bed and contained within a perfect dome of dark chocolate; the architecture of it was as thrilling as the name (which has since been abandoned in favour of the less offensive 'Schokokuss' or 'chocolate kiss') and its sensuous potential. You would shape your tongue into a lance to pierce through the first bittersweet leaf-thin layer, withdraw to consider the break pattern, flick off some of the chocolate splinters with the tip of your tongue and then scoop up the airy body to melt into gooey satisfaction against the roof of your mouth. The licked-clean round waffle, with its criss-cross texture was then savoured with as many little crunchy bites as possible.

If I had been one of the children in the Stanford marshmallow experiment, presented with the choice of immediate pleasure or more of it in the future, what would I have done, I wonder? If my current life choices provide a clue, I think I would have relished the marshmallow there and then. I wouldn't necessarily have bought into the assumption that two marshmallows are an improvement on one. The accumulation of wealth for future material security and status has never been a compelling vision for me. I'd rather be rich in time now than work a nine-to-five job that compromises my core values in order to chase a substantial pension in a future that may not actually arrive. However, if the choice offered had been between the marshmallow now and satisfaction of a different order later, say, quality time with an adored adult, I may well have resisted the temptation.

The key to making choices we can embrace wholeheartedly and stay faithful to, lies in connecting with the needs and values they meet for us.

Meditate or Do Something Else? The Two Hands Exercise

We can easily feel bad about ourselves for not following through with our intention to meditate or doing mindful movement. This exercise introduces a creative and effective way to motivate ourselves to practise, without judging or shaming. It gives us the felt sense that all our inclinations, whether we feel drawn to meditate or to watch a movie, meet important needs and that we can find ways to meet them all: it's not either/or.

Get clarity about the two alternative activities you want to consider: Meditating versus? Spending time with the kids; Facebook; going for a walk; doing some work prep; watching a movie?

Hold your hands in front of you, cupped like open bowls. One of them represents meditation, the other the alternative activity. Decide which wants to be explored first.

Say it is 'watching the telly with the family' first. Ask yourself what needs are met by that: Relaxation? Belonging? Ease? Stimulation? Learning? Let yourself feel the goodness of the qualities that arise and imagine them as a coloured liquid or light in the bowl of your hand.

Then do the same with the other activity. If it is meditation, the needs may be for calm, centredness, nourishment, meaning? Whatever you find, enjoy the sense of it in the body/mind and imagine it as coloured liquid or light in the other hand.

Slowly bring the two hands together, till the hands form one bowl shape. Observe how the contents of the hands mingle. Let yourself feel all the needs simultaneously – what is it like when they all meet? Stay with that for a while.

Now join the palms of the hands together, letting the essence of the qualities become like a jewel cupped in the centre. Bring your hands to your heart and imagine the jewel being absorbed into it. Hold your hands over your heart and enjoy that connection.

Be open to any ideas, images or strategies arising from this experience.

One consequence of doing this exercise may be that you approach your meditation practice less like a chore, but more as a leisure activity, that brings you a sense of ease, pleasure and connection.

~ Ways of Moving ~

Yoga: Part of the Mindfulness Revolution?

Mindful yoga is a lifetime engagement – not to get somewhere else, but to be where and as we are, in this very moment, with this very breath, whether the experience is pleasant, unpleasant or neutral.
Jon Kabat-Zinn

On my way to Hillhead Library on Byres Road, the lights turn red. Like many other pedestrians in this country, I often ignore the lights when it's safe to do so. It's just easier, smoother, to keep going. Interrupting the forward momentum of purposeful walking, putting the brakes on, as it were, creates friction and feels a tad uncomfortable. But recently I have started to experiment with always stopping and taking the opportunity for a mindful pause, a 'three-step breathing space' as it is called in mindfulness programmes. So I let my awareness descend to the sensations of my feet standing on the concrete pavement, feel the weight of the books pulling on my shoulders, my slightly raised heartbeat and my breath, deepened by walking. From the corners of my eyes I take in other pedestrians gathering around the busy Botanic Gardens crossing, mostly young people: students, probably, as it's the start of term. I admire a girl's dress sense: a knee-length, vintage wool skirt over naked legs, ankle boots, fitted jacket, the colour of her socks matching her long, curly red hair. She is absorbed in looking at something on her mobile phone. There are four young men, facing me on the opposite side of Great Western Road, although I can't actually see any of their faces because they are also bent over their mobile phones, bodies turned slightly away from each other as if seeking some privacy.

The thought occurs to me that the typical human silhouette, the shape the brain recognises as a fellow citizen, must be changing: more hunched. It seems as if these days every spare moment must be spent in some device-related activity; otherwise one may uncomfortably stand out. People feel the pressure to keep up with their friends on Facebook, spending – I read in a psychology magazine recently – on average two hours a day.

One of my mindfulness course participants, a social work student, mentioned a game she and her mates sometimes play: they all put their phones face down on the table and the person who cracks first has to buy the drinks. Okay, I'd been rather carried away by my thoughts during this mindfulness break. I turn my attention to the breath in my belly some more, then the lights change.

Something else is making a growing appearance in the cityscape: yoga mats. They peek out of shopping bags and bike baskets or are slung over the shoulder in a designer yoga-mat bag, the materials, colours and patterns as varied as those of any other successful market product. According to the World Health Organisation, we busy, wealthy people are more stressed and depressed than ever, and increasingly, people from all walks of life are looking for ways to restore some sanity. Yoga has now been on the Western map for over a century, and some research has demonstrated its stress-reducing and other health benefits. More recently, mindfulness courses have mushroomed, with hundreds of studies proving its effectiveness in areas such as depression and anxiety, chronic pain, immune dysfunction, chronic fatigue, cancer, addiction to drugs and alcohol, and more. It's offered on prescription by the NHS and widely used in third-sector healthcare, schools, universities, businesses, government and even in the army.

Mindful movement, often in the form of yoga, forms an integral part of these courses. Together with sitting meditation, lying-down body-scan meditation, walking meditation and other mindfulness exercises, mindful movement awakens sensory awareness of what is happening in the present moment and encourages a non-judgemental, curious and kind-hearted stance towards it. One learns to rest in an open and spacious way of being, from where thoughts are seen for what they are: just thoughts, not reality. In this way the human tendency to get caught up in anxious and ruminative thinking, which can easily spiral down into depression, is kept in check. Whereas typically in a yoga class students are not encouraged to share their experience, a mindfulness teacher is trained to facilitate a process called 'enquiry'. The students are asked how the practice went, and, in dialogue, certain themes are brought into focus, such as non-striving or acceptance of experience, whether pleasant, unpleasant or neutral. With the help of audio recordings, people are expected to do homework of up to an hour daily, and during class there is the opportunity to look, often in small groups, at obstacles to regular practice. So clearly, a considerable degree of personal commitment is required from the participant compared to going to a weekly yoga class with a teacher who will do all the talking and won't ask whether you have done any practice at home.

Although mindful movement is on the syllabus of any mindfulness teacher training, many facilitators, who are often healthcare professionals, lack confidence in teaching this part of the programme. They are not in the habit of practising yoga, unlike Jon Kabat-Zinn, the doctor who started the big secular mindfulness movement when he founded the Stress Reduction Clinic at the University of Massachusetts Medical School in 1979. They have concerns about health and safety, so may quietly omit it from the programme altogether or offer only a very limited, safe choice of poses, which students easily get bored with. This is hardly surprising; teaching yoga well takes years to learn and requires commitment to personal practice. The same is true for teaching meditation, of course. It is said that 'mindfulness is caught, not taught'; the teacher's embodiment of qualities such as calm, openness, curiosity and kindness has a lot to do with the success of a course. As more and more people start teaching, sometimes after a very short training course and little personal experience, some leading teachers have raised concerns about mindfulness being presented in a way that does not do it justice.

Rooted as it is in ancient spiritual practice, yoga can potentially provide many of the benefits of a mindfulness class. These days it comes in all kinds of forms: with or without music, incense, chanting or meditation; sweat-producing, acrobatic or gentle; aligned with a particular tradition or more eclectic. My guess is that some forms of yoga and some teachers unwittingly perpetuate the same driven, competitive attitudes people long to have respite from. I got involved in yoga in my early twenties, when I was still living in Germany. My first instructor, Dharmapriya (Mike Sherk), was a passionate follower of the Iyengar method, and he was also my first Buddhist teacher. His disciplined and vigorous approach appealed to the idealistic part of my youthful self. On a retreat we'd get up at 6 am, do a 'double meditation' of forty-five minutes each with a leg-stretch in between, followed by ninety minutes of intense yoga asanas, savasana and, at last, brunch around 11 am. He was kind and generous, offering me free one-to-one yoga sessions, which laid a foundation for life. I owe him a lot. But in an Iyengar class with him or other teachers in the years to follow, I often felt emotionally tense, on my guard and with a running background commentary of judgement and comparison. I was probably feeling like that at other times and in other circumstances too, I was just learning to be more aware of it. I stuck with yoga and meditation because I intuited, based on some experience, its potential to be a tool for healing, personal transformation and true happiness. But along the way I often suffered the painful tension between that potential and the barriers to its realisation created by wilful, goal-driven styles and approaches. Some thirty years later I understand the territory so much better.

Brain science has provided some helpful narratives. Our brains have an inbuilt negativity bias, scanning the world for potential threats. The harsh, commandeering tone of voice from a teacher could be perceived as such a threat. The older parts of the brain switch on the survival system: certain hormones get released, the heart rate and blood pressure speed up, digestive juices stop flowing as we prepare to fight, flee or freeze. Whereas animals recover quickly from even traumatic experiences, get up, have a shake and keep going, for us, things are more complicated. Negative experiences tend to linger, because we start thinking about them; we almost can't help ourselves doing this. This easily takes the form of judgement: 'I'm just not up to this; I'm not good enough.' Or we harbour judgement of others, often detectable in 'should-thinking': 'He shouldn't have said that.' By going over and over the same loop of thoughts, we cement contracted, anxious, tense states into our body/mind and easily slide into chronic anxiety and depression. It seems unfortunate that our brains have evolved to work that way – but it looks like we are wired for survival, rather than happiness.

Looking at things from this biological angle protects me from some unnecessary suffering. I'm less caught out by self-judgement when I get anxious from time to time, knowing it's just a natural part of being human. I feel connected to those early humans, my ancestors. They kept in their minds the dangers of, say, a drought in a particular part of the savannah at a certain time of year and made some adjustments in terms of travel routes or food storage. They are the ones more likely to have survived and passed their genes on to me than the happy-go-lucky ones: 'Why worry – look, the grass is green now.' But nowadays, these deeply engrained brain habits can work to our disadvantage. In our densely populated, information-overloaded, fast and competitive times, people struggle to ever switch off their anxious thoughts and enjoy states of deep relaxation. Adrenalin and other stress hormones ceaselessly flood our body systems, and our health and well-being decline. In addition, for many of us traumatic childhood experiences have left their traces in our nervous systems. It's not easy to be a human being! But we also have the capacity to be aware of these patterns and make changes; the brain is malleable and capable of all kinds of development. Sage individuals in many cultures have discovered and utilised the power of meditation to find deep peace; now Western science has cottoned onto this amazingly effective, non-invasive, pill-free way to improve our mental and physical well-being, and we are witnessing something of a mindfulness revolution.

But learning to meditate is not easy: it requires a willingness to face ourselves, with all those half-conscious inner experiences we have avoided all day long by keeping ourselves busy. If you are seen to be idle, you risk being thought of as unsuccessful. For some, the physical discipline of yoga can be an easier way into reconnecting with our inner lives and finding some relaxation. Yoga is particularly good at activating the parasympathetic nervous system, the 'soothing' system, that normally swings into action when danger abates. Neurochemicals are released that relax the muscles, lower blood pressure and heart rate, get the digestive juices flowing again and make us feel content and peaceful. We need a healthy balance between these two states, being aroused for action or relaxed. Yoga can be an excellent way to help us achieve this balance; it can be invigorating when we feel sluggish and calming when we feel hectic. As we are likely to be generally overstimulated, speedy, tense, 'in our heads', approaches to teaching yoga that activate the soothing system are particularly valuable. Our organism recognises certain triggers that signal safety: a warm, soothing tone of voice, reassuring touch, slow breathing, yawning. In a yoga class I benefit from frequent encouragement to stay engaged with my physical experience, to take time between poses to feel the effects, to appreciate and savour feelings of well-being, to recognise and then let go of striving, judgement and competition. Straining to reach that perfect yoga pose demonstrated by the teacher has the effect of confirming that well-entrenched, nagging inner critique: you are not good enough. These kinds of thoughts serve as the nucleus for clouds of negative mood. Overriding body feedback in order to attain impressive poses can of course also easily lead to injury. Donna Farhi is one of the many gifted yoga practitioners who suffered debilitating back injuries through unwise practice. She now says, 'The practice should serve you; you are not a slave to the practice,' and asks whether we can 'develop an accepting relationship to a less than ideal outcome'.[19] Like her, I include the Feldenkrais method in my yoga, as it places more value on process and attitude than on achieving results.

There is a difference between mindfulness and relaxation. Mindfulness entails openness to our responses to experience, whether tight or relaxed, fearful or calm. One of the most helpful aspects of mindfulness training is learning to move towards what is difficult, the shadowland of our psyche, with curiosity and acceptance. Often poetry is used to convey this counter-intuitive attitude; an often-quoted poem is 'The Guest House' by Rumi. As the master of the guest house we are encouraged to let in all visitors, 'even if they're a crowd of sorrows / who violently sweep your house / empty of its furniture'. In a perhaps less-known poem by Wendell Berry, 'To Know the Dark', we are asked to go into the dark 'without sight / and find that the dark, too, blooms and sings / and is traveled by dark feet and dark wings'. Yoga is an excellent way to overcome our instinctive bracing against uncomfortable experience, as we are encouraged to 'play the edge' of a stretch, to surrender to the body's wisdom.

At its best yoga as a form of mindful movement combines many benefits: deep immersion in body-based experience; stretches and sequences that work all parts and systems of the body; subtle, energetic aliveness; a spirit of curiosity, acceptance, open enquiry and creative flow. It allows us to bring wise and kindly attention to the patterns of the mind, with the aim of letting the benefits of the practice take hold in everyday life.

[19] In 'Bringing Yoga to Life'

North-Easterly Winds and Balanced Effort

The forecast for the three-day retreat on Holy Isle (off another island, the Isle of Arran, which is off the Scottish mainland) seemed fine: sunny spells and moderate wind speeds. So the size of the swell at the Lamlash pier comes as a bit of a surprise. The Holy Isle ferry is still anchored out at sea, bobbing perilously on the whitecaps, looking rather slight. Grant, the kindly Buddhist ferryman, explains that it is not so much the strength but the north-easterly direction of the wind that is the problem: we may not make it across today. He will make a decision in two hours, when wind and waves may have calmed down. He doesn't sound too hopeful, though. There are seventeen of us, keen to 'come to our senses through yoga and meditation', the title of the retreat, and another ten on their way on the second mainland ferry. Most people go to the corner café for tea and scones and to get out of the chilly breeze, while I sit down in the rickety ticket cabin with Grant to have a chat and discuss our options.

I have been running retreats here for many years and feel myself slotting back into island time, that sense of surrendering control and respecting the larger forces of the natural elements. There are pauses in the conversation when we just watch the gulls and the clouds, flowing fast over the Holy Isle hills, just a fifteen-minute boat ride away. I am used to some people arriving late or leaving early, but this is the first time the whole group may only get over to the retreat centre a day late. Grant has some ideas: there is the Arran Lodge nearby, and we make phone calls. It looks like we can all find accommodation there in single and double rooms with a group discount and will be able to use a function room for an evening session. He takes me over in his car so I can have a look. Everyone is so helpful – it warms my heart.

Zipped up in windproof jackets and woolly hats, the group reassembles with their wheelie bags and yoga mats, some looking cautiously hopeful, others a little apprehensive. Maybe half of them have been on retreat with me before. I wave them closer, momentarily feeling rather more like a tour guide than a retreat leader, and explain the situation. In the back of my mind is a sense of the potential of this moment, to see it as an opportunity rather than an annoying obstruction, and which way it goes to some extent depends on the stance I take. Part of my awareness has descended through my back and my legs into the ground, drawing on the support of the huge, steady body of the earth. I do my best to speak calmly and slowly, making myself clearly heard above the racket of the breakers against the pier. People look alert and present, paying full attention to the details of what I'm saying. The luggage will be driven to our accommodation, and we'll walk along the shore. Everyone has to organise their own dinner, as the lodge is self-catering. The village shop is open until late. In all likelihood we will be able to get across to the retreat centre early tomorrow morning, in four ferry runs, and there will be porridge waiting for us. 'The retreat starts now,' I say with an encouraging smile, 'enjoy every moment'. People are nodding, and there is a noticeable absence of complaints or fretting, and a readiness to adjust to changed circumstances.

But as a species we are very good at worrying, and it takes conscious effort and training to spot and resist the compulsion to assume the worst. After the evening session at the lodge, several people approach me. 'Will there be a gluten-free breakfast option when we arrive?' 'Are there spare blankets in our rooms?' The questions themselves are fair enough, simply an expression of basic, universal needs for safety and comfort, although... how should I know about blankets, having just arrived myself? I pick up the underlying anxiety, nervous systems spilling over with adrenalin. I catch myself repeatedly wondering about a couple of people who haven't arrived yet; there is no reply to my messages. A famous quotation from Shantideva, written around 700 AD comes to mind: 'If you can do something about a situation, why worry? And if you can't do something about a situation, why worry?'[20] (It turns out later that I had made a mistake and listed them on the wrong registration sheet – they were not due to come on this retreat at all!)

Does mindfulness practice help us to be less stressed in unforeseen circumstances like this? One would hope so, but I think it depends on how you practise. When you focus on the object of meditation (for example, the breath) in a slightly wilful way, an attitude that is common in our task- and result-driven world, you will probably experience inner thoughts, difficult emotions, unpleasant body sensations or outer sounds as unwelcome intrusions, as

[20] *Bodhicaryavatara*, (ch. 6, v.10).

obstacles to try to overcome. Meditating can then feel like a bit of a struggle. You have the best of intentions, yet however hard you try, you never quite get back to that lovely peaceful state of mind that once bowled you over.

Another style of practising is more open and relaxed, allowing everything that arises to be part of the meditation, pushing nothing away. Someone noisily blows their nose? Thank you for the wake-up call. You can't stop thinking about your work? It shows how much it matters to you, and maybe the energy of the needs behind the thoughts can be creatively integrated into the meditation. In my experience, this is a more successful way of preparing for life's ups and downs, more flexible, kind and encompassing, and with less of a self to bolster up with some success story. It is surprisingly elusive, however. In the name of relaxation it is only too easy to fall into the opposite extreme to wilfulness and go a bit dreamy, flat and unengaged, or even to fall asleep.

Halfway through our Holy Isle retreat, I introduce the participants to an exercise called 'Following Hands'. It is a variation on a tai chi partner exercise and involves one person lightly placing a hand on the back of someone else's hand and being led by them through space. The idea is to get some somatic insight into the art of following the breath in sitting practice. You go wherever your partner takes you: up and down, in circles, at different speeds, sometimes pausing. You feel your body stretching up, bending down, twisting and turning, all in response to the guidance of your partner's hand, first with eyes open and then closed. After a while I instruct the followers to try a little harder, to exert some control in order not to lose the contact under any circumstances. The character of the movement now changes – people clasp their supposed leaders' hands, and it looks more like a jerky fight than a dance. There is also a fair bit of laughter. Then I encourage people to go to the other extreme: 'couldn't care less'. The hands disengage? Never mind. It's okay to 'be away with the fairies', planning your next meal or your holiday. The tone of the movement now is a little listless, sluggish and uninspired. After a while I encourage the group to find a balanced kind of engagement, neither trying too much nor too little. 'How do you know you got it right?' I ask.

When we debrief after the exercise, people talk about a dance-like quality, a sense of pleasure and flow, of ease and pliability, of losing oneself in the activity. When we sit down to meditate on the breath, we go through the same stages of trying too much and too little before settling into an enjoyable, sustainable state of balance that is constantly renewing itself. 'Being on the ball' is an apt synonym for mindfulness, suggesting the image of someone continuously adjusting their balance to stay on a revolving body.

I've recently added a further, rather fun stage to this exercise: this time you only touch with the tip of your index finger, and when it's your turn to follow, you do your best to maintain the connection, but you also allow the rest of your body more freedom of movement. Your free arm may swing into an expressive arc in space, your back may curl and wind away from your partner or your legs might engage in a sprightly wee jig. Perhaps the participants are getting a little more than they have signed up for, but, warmed up by the previous exercise, they are enthusiastic to try and seemingly relish it. I don't think many of them would have come, though, had I mentioned the word 'improvisation' in the course description. The fact is that improvisatory skills are a great bonus for meeting life's unpredictable twists and turns with grace and equanimity. A balanced and creative approach to meditation prepares us to stay tethered to our awareness under all kinds of circumstances, whether the wind blows gently from the south-west or fiercely from the north-east.

Walking in Nature

A study at Glasgow University[21] compared natural and non-natural environments for physical activity, including walking, running and cycling, and found that being around trees and grass lowered stress levels. It showed that the positive effect on people's mental health of being in nature was 50 per cent higher than can be expected from going to the gym. Two thousand physically active people took part in the research – a sizeable experiment. When I cycle home through Kelvingrove Park after teaching my early-evening yoga classes in town, I have noticed a new phenomenon: adults of all shapes and sizes jogging, jumping, pumping and stretching, usually gathered in small groups around a trainer with

[21] https://www.sciencedirect.com/science/article/pii/S0169204611003665

great shouting power, all dressed in the expected brands of sports outfits. Every week there seem to be more outdoor fitness enthusiasts, and it can be a challenge to wind my way through all this commotion. 'Bike!' someone in the group will shout, and bodies disperse with general goodwill and humour. It's heartening to see people getting out and taking care of themselves in this way, and no doubt for many, doing exercise with others is motivational. I know I wouldn't respond well to the militaristic style of vocal encouragement myself. I prefer cycling, walking and doing yoga and tai chi under the big ash tree in the arboretum near where we live, by myself or with another more reflective soul.

When choosing some form of movement as an arena for mindfulness practice, students often ask me whether running, jogging, hillwalking or swimming would be appropriate. I usually endorse any kind of cardiovascular training people enjoy, as it has an important part to play in dealing with anxiety and depression. Among other health benefits, vigorous exercise enhances the action of endorphins, chemicals that improve natural immunity and mood, and make us better able to deal with pain.

Walking is famous for its relationship with mental well-being. Robert Macfarlane mentions in his book *The Old Ways* that many long-distance walker-writers were depressive, trying to outstride their sadness or 'the Horrors', as the nineteenth-century author George Borrow described his affliction. They did this not just by putting in the miles and reaping the benefits of increased circulation and hormones on the brain. People like Borrow or the poet Thomas Edward were 'walking as a way to make sense of themselves.... The mind is a landscape of a sort and walking might be a way of crossing it.'[22] The mind/body is altered by the landscape it traverses, as we all know when we yearn to get out of the city or for any change of scenery. After walking the Broomway, a path across vast coastal sand and mud flats to the island of Foulness, Macfarlane described himself as 'sandflat and serene'. I believe the emotional healing of the self through walking comes from a kind of self-forgetting, replacing self-confirming, often negative, inner dialogue with attentiveness to the detail of the shifting landscape, maybe particularly when alertness to what is underfoot is essential for safety and survival. Macfarlane knew that humans can't outrun the tide when it comes in, and he was aware of many

[22] Macfarlane in his 2012 IQ2 lecture on 'Landscape and the Human Heart'

people who had died in the flats. This knowledge heightened his perception when walking that borderland.

The inclination of thought is altered by physical experiences of transition as simple as stepping out of the door. A new life, with new opportunities for relating to self and environment, opens. The American poet and farmer Wendell Berry describes the transition from walking on land to being afloat in a canoe on a rising river: 'There would... be several uneasy minutes of transition. The river is another world, which means that one's senses and reflexes must begin to live another life.' We can easily, of course, simply adapt our patterns of worry to the new environment. The element of danger, while slapping us into awareness, can stimulate the inner defence system with its anxious, adrenalin-fuelled thought patterns.

Although it is possible to walk fast and be acutely aware of the environment, one's heartbeat, body heat and so on, mindful walking as part of a toolkit to work with depression and anxiety is not necessarily always so vigorous or strident. It is perhaps more akin to the 'sauntering' Thoreau mentions, walking 'with the abandonment of all specific ends'. Yes, even the abandonment of the aim to cure oneself of painful mental states. This is a relatively new concept to the Western mind.

Many poets and philosophers have used walking as a way of thinking creatively. For example, Nietzsche: 'Only those thoughts that come from walking have any value.' Or Jean-Jacques Rousseau: 'When I stop I cease to think; my mind only works with my legs.' But maybe this is an overly romantic and one-sided view. Macfarlane writes in *The Old Ways*, 'Sometimes walking is the mind's subtle accomplice; at others its brutal antagonist. As you will know if you've ever walked long distances for day after day, fatigue on the path can annihilate all but the most basic brain functions.' I resonate with that: I can think of many walks I have taken where I felt no different or maybe even worse at the end.

The effect of walking can be similar to that of other repetitive habits, routines and rituals. The rhythm of equal-length steps, particularly along well-known paths, invites us to switch to autopilot. Safety in familiar physical movement can invite the reiteration of similarly comforting old beliefs, whether they serve us or not. The soothing rhythm of the regular footfall is an invitation for the mind to drift, to mull things over or to obsess about something. I could stride forwards with a sense of optimism and hope, enjoying an influx of new ideas, or I could let my steps confirm beliefs like 'I'll end up in a wheelchair'. What makes all the difference is whether or not there is an element of conscious intention, encouraging us to kindly watch the play of the mind without getting drawn into it. Or, similar to 'formless meditation', we may set out to walk with the 'abandonment of all specific ends'.

Creative Walking Meditation for a Group

In this walking meditation we are trying to keep our attention alert by directing it to a number of different aspects of walking and also by altering the way we walk. It is of course possible to stay interested while walking in the same way, up and down a stretch of ground, as in a traditional Buddhist practice, which can be particularly effective when done outside, where there is a rich input through our senses. This meditation has been developed for both indoor and outdoor situations and is very useful as a post-lunch activity on a day event, a time when the energy tends to be sluggish.

Start walking in your own way, at your own pace; walk where your feet are taking you.

Notice the sounds caused by the walking in the room: footsteps, rustling of clothes. Also other sounds, outside the room, sounds as expressions of life as it whirls around us.

Start taking note of the sensations in the soles of your feet, noticing the texture of the floor, hardness or softness, any unevenness.

Perhaps you are aware of a different temperature on different parts of the floor, where the sun has been shining or nearer the door, windows, radiators?

For a while, focus on your left foot. Which part of the heel first touches the ground? From which part of the ball of the foot do you feel propelled forwards to the next step? The middle part, the outer or nearer the big toe? Or maybe that's hard to feel? Is it possible to sense the pads of each toe on the ground? Now walk with your attention on both feet – do you feel a difference? Then focus on the right foot in a similar way. Perhaps you can detect a different pattern of walking.

Become aware of where you tend to walk: trailing the edges of the room or sauntering through the centre? Are you keeping your distance from others or staying close to them? Do you find yourself walking in the same direction as most people or against the stream? Just notice, without analysing or judging. Try what it is like to do it another way. Do you feel slightly less safe, exposed, free, bored, constrained? Is there perhaps a subtle change in the way you walk, letting your arms swing or keeping them in, letting your eyes roam or keeping them to the ground in front of you?

What would it be like to walk a little faster, to walk into the spaces between people, to take some risks? Do you feel more alert maybe, excited or a little weary? What does your body tell you about how you feel?

Stop. Close your eyes and become aware of your breath, your heartbeat, the heat of your body, the vibrancy of your skin, where it has felt the swish of clothes against it. Sense where you are in relation to the walls and to other bodies. Then open your eyes and compare the configuration of bodies in the room to what you imagined. Perhaps there is an aesthetic appreciation of this accidental pattern of bodies in space?

Now start walking again, but backwards. What would be a safe pace for that? Maybe you feel the need to keep turning your head to check where you are going – or maybe you can trust that it would be okay to gently bump into other bodies occasionally. Like microscopic one-cell organisms, sensing the electrical currents of other beings and altering their direction in response to contact. All our senses have evolved in relationship to specific environments. What sense of perception is coming alive in your back now? Notice the different walking pattern in your feet, a different part of the foot touching the earth first.

Stop again. How do you feel now – has anything changed in your body? Perhaps it can feel as if you are looking out from the back of your body, in a slightly softer way. Walk forwards again, with a sense of resting in the back of your body. A little less driven forwards, maybe? Less concerned with getting anywhere, but aware of the moment at each step?

Slow down and become aware of the way your soles touch the earth and how the earth touches them back. Be open to that contact as a mutuality, a mutual receptivity. Perhaps you feel your step slowing even more to allow for that tenderness of touch, a certain respectfulness.

Stand for a while, feel your breath, then coordinate your breath with your walking rhythm, lifting the back heel with the in-breath; take a small step forward with the out- breath, transfer your weight onto both legs. Wait for the next in-breath.

Finish by standing with the weight on both feet, absorbing the experience.

Playful Variations on Walking

Once we are familiar with walking in this way, anchored in our body, while aware of others and our surroundings, we can bring in more playfulness - there is no reason why creative fun should be excluded from mindfulness practice. In these variations, certain rules allow us to vary how we move, adding to the rich texture of experience and insight. Some people may feel a little awkward at first – we can take that as an invitation to bring acceptance to those feelings. Others may feel inclined to 'show off', trying to excel in inventiveness. In either case, there is 'selfing' in action, our 'small self', separate from others, making itself heard. The true spirit of improvisation is characterised by openness to emergence and allowing decisions to happen from a sense of interconnectedness.

For example, we may find ourselves standing, while others move around us, at different speeds, and at some point, we just know that this is the right time to start walking again. Something in us responds, not from a decision made in the head, but from a sense of participation in something bigger, and we trust that.

When debriefing after such a session, people often express amazement at the freedom and creativity they have experienced. They feel like part of a modern dance performance, without the performance anxiety; a sense of aesthetic appreciation. They enjoy the experience of being authentically 'themselves', while at the same time safe in belonging to the group.

Here are some possibilities to play with, at different times:

Walk through the room in curved lines, in and around each other.

Decide (or rather, let your body decide) when and where to stand, and for how long. When you start walking again, choose your tempo and stick to it till you stand again.

Include walking backwards in your options.

Walk in pairs without either leading. Don't look at each other, but let your bodies pick up subtle signals indicating pace, changes in direction, when to stand. Being aware of your heart connection – it's like walking with a good friend.

Do the same in threes, fours, or even the whole group. Like in a murmuration of starlings, in ways not completely understood, movement just happens.

This variation is particularly suitable to an indoor setting. To start with, stand in one line at one end of the room. Walk to the other end, turn around and walk back. Within this simple structure, you can play with the parameters already mentioned, introducing them gradually: standing, going backwards or forwards and speed.

If the group is large enough and has developed sufficient trust, it can be a wonderful learning experience to let half of the group watch the other half move.

~ Some Core Questions ~

What Really Matters?

If we engage in this simple practice long enough, we discover that our sense of being a separate, coherent, enduring self is actually a delusion maintained by our constant inner chatter, which generally features 'me' at its center. From mundane decisions ('I think I'll get the salmon with wilted spinach tonight') to existential fears ('What'll I do if the lump is malignant?'), this chatter fills our waking hours. Listening to it all day long, we come to believe that the hero of this drama must exist. But if we practice mindfulness long and often enough, this conventional sense of self can start to unravel. Ron Siegel[23]

The 2014 Reith Lecture by Dr Atul Gawande looked at 'how doctors fail'. Medicine has come to simply trying to prolong life, without asking why. There is a systemic lack of curiosity: in consultations, doctors tend not to ask questions but do most of the talking. Patients want their experience to be enquired into and want to do at least 50 per cent of the talking. Gawande suggests that good questions to ask the patient, particularly at the end of life, are:

What is your understanding of where you are at?
What is the worst possible scenario you fear?
What really matters to you?

Someone may say that watching the telly with a can of lager will do fine. One more day of that would be enough. Someone else wants to see their grandchildren get married. When their motivation is brought into the dialogue with the doctor, people actually live longer.

The question of what is really important is often asked in times of existential emergencies. The palliative care specialist Dr B. J. Miller, in his TED Talk 'What really matters at the end of life', tells how as a young man he had an accident that led to the loss of both his legs and an arm. He was in a windowless hospital room

[23] Assistant Clinical Professor of Psychology at Harvard Medical School.

on a snowy winter day, and a nurse brought him a little gift that changed his life: a snowball. As it was melting onto his burnt skin it became clear to him what mattered in the face of death and dying: the beauty of this moment of connection with the world, experienced through the senses.

I've noticed that synchronicity comes into play when I start to give passionate attention to something that matters to me. When I was in the last phase of my coaching training, I was thinking hard about how to describe what I wanted to offer to potential clients. Then I found a passage in the novel I was then reading, *A God in Ruins* by Kate Atkinson. Hugh is eighty-four and on a road trip with his granddaughter Bertie, visiting the graveyard his wife and other family members and friends are buried in:

> 'A woodland burial,' he said. 'No name, nothing, just a tree. An oak, if you can, but anything will do. Don't let your mother be in charge.'
>
> Death was the end. Sometimes it took a whole lifetime to understand that.... 'Promise me you'll make the most of your life,' he said to Bertie.
>
> 'I promise,' Bertie said, already at twenty-four knowing it was unlikely she would be able to do so.

I read and re-read that last sentence, with a sense of both sadness and determination. Am I really making the most of my life now? Are others? What does it take to be able to do so? In the middle of the night, I woke out of a dream where I was watching a mesmerising modern dance performance in a large Buddhist temple, organised by an old Buddhist teacher of mine. Thirty-five years ago we were both fired by a vision of the integration of creative expression and spirituality. My life has now moved in slightly different directions, being also concerned with healing, in the widest sense. And yet it seems vitally important to honour that dream of spiritual beauty through the arts, that early promise.

We promise ourselves at some point in our lives to make the most of it, to live our dreams. And then our lives unfold in the interplay of all kinds of different needs, including both safety and adventure. By middle age we are usually well set on our course – a course that may not be the north we had fixed our compass on, but perhaps veering towards east or north-east.

But what if it were possible to change course now and align ourselves once more with our deepest values? What if we didn't wait for that life crisis (like a major loss or a life-threatening illness) to make us stop in our tracks and reconsider our priorities? What if it was still in our reach to find that truly satisfying way to be in relationship, to engage in work that inspires us, to write that book, to make a difference to the world?

There are our dreams, and there are the parts of us that doubt our ability to realise them; the parts of us that are hanging on to what's familiar, even if it is limiting our potential (or maybe because it is doing that). We need to do both, clarify and develop our vision, and find ways to get to know and befriend what is holding us back. Frequent enquiry into the needs and values that motivate us as we go through our days is good practice. The small decisions we make shape who we become. Will I meditate this morning or read the paper? What's important about both of those options? The contemplation of impermanence can be a catalyst for staying curious and engaged in this process of becoming who we truly are.

How does it Serve Others?

If you want others to be happy, practice compassion. If you want to be happy, practice compassion. The Dalai Lama[24]

At the beginning of the year, email inboxes, social network pages and newspaper supplements are awash with good advice for self-improvement, usually covering diet, exercise, sleep, relationships and patterns of thinking. I notice, with a sense of cautious hope, that the environment features more liberally than usual: 'Avoid anything single-use', 'Explore flight-free holiday options', 'Let bugs live', the captions read. In an article on how to have more fun in the coming year, one line jumps out at me, an exhortation to ask ourselves 'Who does this help?'[25]

The well-being entrepreneur Nataly Kogan asserts that it is not possible to be a happy human being without an awareness of 'the bigger why'. She recommends viewing your to-do list, particularly tasks you find mundane or frustrating, through the lens

[24] From *The Art of Happiness*.

[25] 'The joy audit: how to have more fun in 2020', *The Guardian*, 1 January 2020.

of *Who does this help?* It can increase motivation, lift your mood and improve your ability to manage stress. And little gestures, she says, such as pulling out a chair for a colleague at work or enquiring after their well-being, release oxytocin in both giver and receiver and greatly improve job satisfaction.

We are seeing a flood of recent research corroborating the ancient wisdom that happiness, meaning and altruism are intrinsically connected. I do find that gives me hope, as it seems that people who experience reactivity against any overtly religious nudging towards 'being less selfish' show openness towards the idea of generosity when it is underpinned by research.

I am inspired to conduct a little action research myself. Rather than asking 'who does this help?' however, I am enquiring into 'how' others are served, since I am always interested in the detail, variety and beauty of values. So I will ask myself the question 'how does this serve others?' in relation to various kinds of actions I perform over a twenty-four-hour period and will journal my observations. Looking over the list, the actions seem to fall into certain categories.

First, the most obvious one: directly doing things for others. My four-year-old 'Buddha daughter' (equivalent of god-daughter) Willow has been longing for an Elsa doll, and I pop over to her house to present her with one I found at a recent swap party. When I spotted it among the medley of clothes, books and other toys, I thought of her, which definitely released some oxytocin, and more of it sweetens my bloodstream as I play with her. She wants to be partly Elsa and partly Peter Rabbit, and instructs me to be partly a reindeer and partly Mr McGregor. The game is clearly of mutual delight and benefit, until it comes to the point when my natural play span is exhausted, whereas she could go on for another few hours. I remember my research question, and defining the needs that are being met for her, namely fun, creativity, to matter and be loved, allows me to keep going wholeheartedly for a while longer, chasing Elsa Rabbit away from that carrot bed.

There are other activities in this category: cooking a meal for my husband Larry and me; asking the electrician who is rewiring our new home about his family; ringing my mum to tell her I am going away for a week's retreat. Connecting in this way, caring, taking an interest and letting people know they matter to me brings relaxation and openness into the relational fields, and taking this in consciously enhances the softening effect.

Second: chores. I am halfway through taking dry clothes off the pulley when I remember to ask myself how this serves others. It isn't a big deal at all, just folding up my and Larry's clothes, but it does contribute order and caring to our lives, and it means he has more time for other things. With that conscious acknowledgement a small inner change takes place, a brightening in the heart region, and my movements become a little more graceful, less goal-oriented. I enjoy the shades and juxtaposing textures of the current assortment of blue, white and grey clothes, taking my time. Much of mindfulness training consists in getting off autopilot and enjoying the present moment through the senses. But it can sometimes seem that it is all about 'me and my' experience. I am discovering that the orientation towards benefits for others seems to have the same, de-habituating effect.

Next is stripping the bed and getting a load of linen and bath towels into the washing machine for a slightly hotter cycle. I remember my question as I unbutton the duvet cover, and again, something shifts and softens internally, and I slow down. I admire the quality of the buttons, covered with sage-green, slightly shiny cotton material and sewn on in a way that ensures easy and repeated handling. With the next button the original question 'who is this helping?' returns, but with a difference. It dawns on me, with a shaft of clarity, that it really doesn't matter who I am doing this for, whose cover this is. Whether it is mine, Larry's or a stranger's are totally irrelevant distinctions: there is just open, loving awareness combined with attention to detail.

Third: when something gets in the way. As I approach the washing machine with my arms full of dirty linen, I notice that Larry has already filled most of the drum with his own clothes for a low-temperature wash. My spiritual realisation of non-duality experiences a little tremor of small-self upset, an almost imperceptible setting of the jaw, a familiar frown, giving way quite readily, however, when recalling the question. Who is being served, indeed, and the 'how' of the question fills the kitchen with a warm glow.

Fourth: self-care. I stand in the bay window and tap my body, down the inner arms, up the outer arms, following the meridian lines in Chinese medicine. How does doing chi kung serve others? A fierce south-westerly wind pushes against the windowpanes and needles its way in through minute gaps in the frame. Spreading my arms, I breathe it in; letting them flow back, fingertips facing, I breathe out. *Inhaling I take the world within me; exhaling I give myself to the world. Empty, I experience abundance; formless, I fulfil the form.*[26] Who knows how this might be serving others?

Fifth: indulgence. 'Really, how does it serve others to drink red wine and eat cheese on oatcakes one hour before going to bed?' My stern inner critic steps onto the stage with gusto and demands answers. When I was a little girl of two and a half, my two younger sisters needed our parents more than I did; I had to be reasonable, be the big girl who could look after herself. 'Don't be so selfish' was the difficult-to-hear message I grew up with, and even now, after many conversations between us, the inner critic hangs on to this parental voice from my childhood. But it is getting a little gentler, as his good intentions are recognised: wanting me to be loved and respected and part of the tribe. Basically, he wants me to enjoy life, so he and I surrender to savouring my late-evening snack.[27]

Sixth: silence. While making porridge I listen to classical music on the radio, Stravinsky most likely. There is a lot going on: the violin is struggling against the spinning of the washing machine and the hissing of the gas flame. I turn the music off and decide I don't need anything extra at the moment. Right now, less is more in serving a state of calm presence, which will benefit others, too.

Seventh: this piece of writing. While composing this piece of writing, I imagine others, you, receiving encouragement and inspiration from it. The effectiveness of this approach immediately shows itself in my experiencing greater ease, flow and clarity.

This focus on benefits for others is a marvellous mindfulness bell, chiming with insight and compassion. Perhaps you might give it a go, too, for twenty-four hours?

---

[26] Adapted from Lama Govinda.

[27] The habit of late-night snacking seems to have fallen away, I am happy to report, shortly after this was written.

Cleaning the Fridge: Getting out of Autopilot

First, I empty the top door-shelf: two 10 mg bottles of insulin and three GlucaGen pens, in bright orange cases, all of them out of date. (They are for emergencies, in case I fall unconscious due to a bad hypo, which luckily hasn't happened so far in my history of living with type 1 diabetes.) I discard the two oldest ones and make a mental note to order a new one. With some gentle tapping, the clear plastic compartment readily unhooks from the door. I clean it with soapy water in the sink and leave it to dry. It looks satisfyingly clear and sparkly. Next, the cheese and egg section – it really needs doing. So does the lowest shelf, which holds our three types of plant-based milk, a refillable sparkling water bottle and a bottle holding an inch of mulled winter cordial. (I realise these details tell you quite a lot about me, but never mind…)

I've got a system going now: clearing a shelf, cleaning it, letting it drip-dry while emptying and sponging the next one, working the previous shelf over with a tea towel, reslotting and restocking it to make room on the work surface for the next load of forgotten jams and pickles. The efficiency of the process, the repetitive pathways of my movements through the kitchen and the vision of the gleaming end result combine to keep me going without pausing, not exactly rushing but not exactly mindful either. There is a train of dimly aware thoughts: about how time-consuming this is; that we left it a bit long; dreaming about engaging a cleaner. And why is my husband not joining in with the cleaning, as he promised he would?

Before tackling the veg drawer, I put my head through Larry's study door, gauging whether he is interruptible. 'Can you ring a mindfulness bell for me?' I plead. He turns round from the computer and laughs. Sometimes we have 'work periods' together in the flat, like you have on residential group retreats. Every so often, one of us will sound our big singing bowl, and we stop in the middle of what we are doing, toilet brush or vacuum cleaner attachment in hand, for a mindful breathing space. I suppose it's quite funny that I should need a formal invitation to stop, that simply recognising the need for a break is not enough to make it happen.

I think we probably all know what it is like to push on with a task, overriding any mental and physical signs of tension, just wanting to cross the finishing line. Tick, done! Certainly, a sense of completion has its own reward, but we goal-oriented, clock-time-governed modern people are missing out on a whole lot of other satisfaction on the way – above all, the glorious experience of living life as it happens, this very moment. In fairness, even in the Buddha's pre-industrial times, human beings needed reminding to be mindful. As modern brain science confirms, the default setting of the mind is to go on autopilot and rehash past and future scenarios, which does of course have its uses. Sometimes we learn from past experience or pre-empt future mishaps. However, allowing anxious or overly critical thinking to run unchecked can be stress-inducing.

Seeds could germinate and take root in the layer of dirt in the bottom drawer of the fridge. We often buy organic vegetables from the farmers' market, and they tend to be covered in thick coats of soil. I am just about to shake the dirt into the compost bin when, finally, the bell finds me. Ahhh… With a great sigh of relief I put everything down and just stand. Deep in- and out- breaths, as the sound gradually subsides. Eagerly, my spine uncurls from its slightly curved stance to its full height; my chin draws back its forward-jutting determination, and my heart has space to expand again. 'I am cleaning the fridge for the benefit of all beings,' I surprise myself by pronouncing into the tiled kitchen.

I think I may have rediscovered the missing key to mindful presence: remembering my essential nature as interconnected and remembering that generosity is the natural expression of this truth. Love and mindfulness are close partners. Doing housework may not be of obvious benefit to more than the members of my household, particularly during Covid lockdown when we can't have any visitors. But the repeated intention of wanting to be of benefit takes hold and becomes a resource for better living for more people on earth. It's a training in eco-sattva-hood, and as such it will be a pleasure to recycle, to give careful attention to what I buy, to support campaigns, to devise mindfulness courses that address the pressing concerns of our times in appealing ways and to mindfully clean the windows, which are next on the list.

Home: Living with the Reality of Uncertainty

Graffiti-covered concrete motorway pillars and the roar of traffic beleaguer my senses as I stand at the bus stop waiting for the 60A to carry me home. Home! After a few hours of traversing the city on various errands, including viewing a potential new home, my weary body can't wait to unwind in a safe place, lie down and recuperate. I love our home; it's in a quiet street close to the River Kelvin and the Botanic Garden and breathes a relaxed, spacious and creative vibe. It is filled with yoga mats, meditation cushions, musical instruments, children's toys, Buddha figures, artwork, books and more books, art materials, pebbles, shells and other natural objects; some of it is properly displayed or tidied away and some of it isn't. There are several items of vague and/or infrequent use that claim their right to fill corners and adorn edges with their visible presence: a fist-size stone covered in green felt; a metre-long piece of ribbed plastic piping that makes a whistling sound when whirled fast in a circle; about a dozen wooden (walking?) sticks, spread over three different corners, next to rolled-up, used flipchart paper, rolls of gift-wrapping paper and empty (?) cardboard tubes. This is not a piece about decluttering, however (although there's an idea!).

We are going to leave this precious, familiar place, our home. For the first time, my husband and I find ourselves in a position to buy a place of our own. This brings with it a lot of uncertainty, and there is a lot to get our heads around. The Scottish property-sales system involves a process of blind competitive bidding based on a home evaluation report. We have only put in one offer so far, and in a bidding frenzy the property went to someone who paid 140 per cent above the home report figure. However uncomfortable we feel with the system, we have to play the game, it seems, if we want to enjoy the basic security of knowing that nobody can turn us out of our home. Staying where we are is not an option, as the landlady wants to move back in eventually. I have had the experience of being forced out of a beloved home several times before for the same reason. As anyone who has been in a similar situation will testify, it is highly stressful. On top of the general hassle of moving house, there are difficult feelings to deal with, related to the lack of agency and continuity. It is vexing that someone else should have the power to throw you out of your home. So there is no doubt that owning our own place will be the better option. But it doesn't mean the end of uncertainty, during the property search and beyond.

We have seen quite a number of places, which helps to clarify our respective priorities and what kinds of houses are available in our price range. We have had intriguing glimpses into other people's lives on the way. If not the dozen pictures of dogs, certainly the smell that hit us upon opening the front door of a lovely suburban villa gave a strong hint about the passion of the owners. Both my husband and I get readily drawn into conversations with people about their plans and hobbies, while forgetting to ask questions about damp treatment and roof insulation. We have viewed flats with TV screens in every room, or decorated in metal and black throughout or brimming with family photos and cute porcelain figures on every surface.

I was touched to hear the story of the youngest son of a large Irish family who moved in with his mother to care for her after her cancer diagnosis – there was rawness around his eyes when he told us she only lasted a few weeks. She was 'quite a character', had been working behind the bar in one of the big Glasgow theatres well into her seventies and kept beautiful roses in her front garden. But why am I telling you all this? Perhaps to find, in the midst of uncertainty, an anchor in detailed, concrete observations and a sense of shared humanity. All these homeowners are in a similar position to ourselves: in the process of moving house, with all the unknowns that entails.

So far, most places we have seen were either the wrong size (where to fit in the piano?), or had too many bathrooms (the thought of cleaning them all!), or were too near a busy road or motorway, or too far away from work, or didn't have a garden or at least some trees to look at. And the couple of properties that ticked most of the boxes went in the blink of an eye to people who were able to 'throw money at it'. When people ask me how the house search is going, I sometimes answer that I feel unsettled and resentful that it is taking so long and that I'd rather be doing other things in my life, such as writing and developing my teaching work. People usually empathise with that. But when I look a little deeper, I find that I don't really mind so much, and it is helpful to recognise that.

I am open to learning a lesson that, I intuit, is a useful one. My husband and I are in the privileged position of having a choice with regard to where we live, but even so, moving house is destabilising. We can all find ourselves in situations where the things that usually offer us a secure refuge, and in particular our home, are not under our control and are threatened by natural, political, financial or environmental disaster; by hackers, burglars or unpleasant neighbours. Looking ahead, there is a great likelihood of illness and the certainty of death, facts we usually avoid thinking about. Contemplating life's uncertainty invites me to find refuge in a larger place than one constructed of bricks and mortar: life itself, as it unfolds moment by moment.

The body is key to entering that expanded domain. I regularly interrupt the compulsion to get things done, the habitual fretting and drive to perfection, and ask the question: where in my body do I feel at home? In the belly, the chest, the feet? I encourage myself to be off-guard for a moment and to connect with the quality of trust. Resting. Breathing easy. Enjoying that relaxed, sweet, at-home feeling. It takes a little courage to surrender into it, to let go of the need to first have everything fixed and sorted in order to feel safe.

Learning to be at home in the body is becoming more vital as our continued safety on this earth is endangered. We are recipients of an intensifying stream of information about the precarious state of our home planet, which can draw us into an anxious, thinking-based existence that becomes increasingly fragmented. Mindfulness practice reminds us to stop, sit still and sense the points of connection with the earth through the body, the connection with a ground of being that is larger than the small, driven, everyday 'me'. Being at home in ourselves allows us to relax and feel whole, while embracing a sense of uncertainty and even enjoying it. Out of not knowing, moment by moment, the next course of action shapes itself, inspired by the felt sense of relationship with the family of beings we share our home with.

PART II

~ In the Midst of it ~

If you step into the street, and a car comes rushing by, you jump onto the curb to save your life – you care about your life. Every cell of your body carries this appreciation. Gratitude is loving attention that brings into the heart the sense that we belong here in this life. And, with each step, each smile, each gesture, we can add our gift and add our part in small and large ways. Jack Kornfield

Living with Diabetes: Waiting out a Hypo

In the seen, there is just the seen. In the heard just the heard... This alone is the end of suffering. The Buddha

Accident and Emergency on a weekday morning: a sizeable host of afflicted humanity in rows of metal chairs facing the reception desk. 'Estimated waiting time 2 hours,' a sign reads. On checking in I am classified as medium urgency. About two and a half hours later a nurse measures my blood sugar levels – they have dropped from the dangerous 40 mmol/L that had alerted my GP, to 26, which means less urgency and another two-hour wait. The only picture to look at, apart from the baby on the 'Spot meningitis' poster, is a black-and-white photo of Antarctica. Is it meant to help us keep a cool head? Normal blood sugar levels, my GP had informed me, are between 4 and 7 mmol/L, with occasional peaks up to 11 after food. '4 to 7 what?' I had asked, not really expecting to be able to make sense of the answer: milligrams per decilitre. Up to now I have not had cause to give the sweetness of my blood any thought. A friend arrives to provide company. We don't talk much, and I almost relax into this family of sick people, with the drone and occasional metal clunking of the soft drinks machine as the audio background. My eyes fasten onto the dark trolley marks on the double doors into the emergency room.

I am told to undress in a booth, which is separated from other booths by flimsy, calf-length white curtains. Hugging myself in a green paper gown, I glance at the ravaged ankles of the person to my left, his bandaged feet in tartan slippers; he must have left his house in them. I can't help overhearing the conversation: the doctor in charge used to be a student of the patient, an overweight, diabetic former university lecturer, suffering from a foot injury that won't heal. I avert my eyes and push away the half-formed thought of amputation.

The physician is in his late thirties, with tired-looking skin but an attractive brightness in his eye. He wants to know my story: two weeks of fatigue, extreme thirst, having to pee all the time, the urge to eat sweet things, drinking lots of smoothies and, despite that, rapid weight loss. 'I'm afraid you are a diabetic,' he says, matter-of-factly. He pauses for that to sink in. 'Type 1, insulin-dependent. You're forty-five? Usually it appears in younger people. There can be a genetic predisposition. Does anyone in your family have it?' I shake my head. 'The causes are not yet fully understood. You must have had an infection of some kind, maybe even without knowing it. Your immune system has destroyed the cells in the pancreas that produce insulin, mistaken them for invading viruses. Islets of Langerhans, these cells are called, in case you're interested.' I nod, feeling slightly spaced out. 'To explain it in a nutshell, body cells need insulin to be able to absorb the energy taken in by food. Without that hormone, the sugar level in the blood builds up and creates major problems, as you are experiencing.' He pauses and looks at me calmly. 'We need to get it down as soon as possible by injecting insulin. It used to be procured from animals, pigs and cattle, but most people inject lab-produced varieties these days. It's a bit of a process to work out the daily doses of insulin that are right for you. In the past people went to hospital for this, but I suggest you see a diabetic specialist nurse at the diabetes centre. She is very good, I know her. You don't want to stay here in hospital – the wards are full of demented old ladies.' He kind of enjoys saying that, perhaps reassuring us both of our relative youth and vitality. 'Do you have any questions?' Highly uncharacteristically, I don't.

Back home I scan the Diabetes UK website and spook myself with the possible long-term complications of the illness: increased danger of heart disease, stroke, kidney failure, blindness, nerve damage and loss of limbs. Feeling feeble, I lie down on my bed and give way to tears. It feels like a good thing to do, similar to when my dad died, basic and necessary. Reaching down to that big dark place of universal human grief and sorrow. Larry comes in quietly and lies close, holding me tight. He is bewildered too, I can tell; this is a major rupture of normality. After a while a few words come, through the sobs: 'Such a shock! What will it mean?'

Ten years later, I am teaching at the Holy Isle Centre for Peace, a three-day retreat called 'Coming to our Senses through Yoga and Meditation'. Lunch here is always excellent, fresh from the extensive vegetable garden and imaginatively prepared by a group of kitchen volunteers. Today it's brown rice with tofu stir-fry and a colourful salad, including marigold and nasturtium flowers. For dessert they bring in trays of succulent banana toffee cake, cut into generous squares. It is scarily sweet-looking, and I help myself to just half a portion. As I carry my plate back to the table, taking in the relaxed and animated atmosphere in the group after the morning session, I automatically compute how many carbohydrates I will be ingesting, how much vigorous exercise I have done and will do today, how much insulin I have recently taken and what will therefore be the correct dosage to go with the cake. There is a high guess factor with food I have not prepared myself. The women talk about mobile phones, how strange and liberating it is not to be using them for a couple of days. My insulin pump is the size of a mobile phone and discreetly hidden in my right trouser pocket, underneath the soft cotton tunic I wear for teaching yoga. Among the general chatter nobody notices as I press the button three times, for three units of NovoRapid. The pump bleeps once for each unit, in an ascending scale, and then once again before the delivery starts, to prompt another confirming push. There is no way to turn the sound off; I guess it's designed to work for blind people. On silent retreats people sometimes notice. My sister, who is a professional violinist, always notices.

I used to mention my diabetes at the beginning of a course so that people wouldn't be distracted or concerned if they saw me pricking my fingertip to measure my blood sugar levels, handling my pump or unwrapping glucose tablets during a class. I would assure them that I am fine and there is nothing for them to be concerned about. Being frank about it would also help me feel relaxed. But these days I sometimes choose to be more circumspect. I have grown weary of the question that inevitably follows when people hear about it: 'Do you have good control?' The issue is more complex than people assume, and going into it doesn't always seem appropriate. So for those interested, here is a little rundown of some of the medical and psychological implications, and how I use mindfulness approaches to work creatively with those challenges. To a large extent my experience is transferable to working with other long-term conditions, including simply being a human being, subject to ageing and mishaps.

Once a year I get seen by the medical team at the diabetes centre, where they perform a blood test called HbA1c. It indicates the average blood sugar level over the last eight to twelve weeks. This test is a looming presence in a diabetic's life, comparable to the Last Judgement: all your sins will be revealed, and you know you will suffer for them. The discussions with the doctor hinge around the test and how to get the figure down. There don't seem to be categories for the things I would appreciate talking about, such as the challenge of living with the inescapable lack of control you have as someone living with type 1 diabetes. You can do all the right things, and still your blood sugar levels can shoot way up or down without any obvious reason. It could be a latent illness, an over-used injection site, an air bubble in the insulin reservoir or any other unknown factor. It is so easy to feel like a failure, to blame oneself and/or get depressed. The risk of depression among diabetics, with both types 1 and 2, is twice as high as the average. I recognise all the reasons for depression in type 1 patients given in a recent study: feeling different from others, overwhelmed by the complexity of managing it, worrying about complications, loss of a sense of control when sugar levels fluctuate wildly, tension between you and your doctor. I feel quite gratified to note this last reason. Among the recommendations on how to deal with these trials are yoga and relaxation. I have often counted my blessings, feeling fortunate that I was already firmly rooted in these disciplines at the time of the diagnosis. And it was then that my personal and professional exploration of Mindfulness-Based Stress Reduction and Mindfulness-Based Cognitive Therapy began.

Over the past eight or nine years I've been teaching on Holy Isle, it has become something of a ritual to go for a solitary walk up the hill after lunch. Weather permitting, I will find a quiet spot away from the (one) beaten track across the island and lie down in the grass, with a view of the hills and the sea, and will let go into a sense of being embraced by the earth. Holy Isle is a protected wildlife haven; there may be Eriskay ponies grazing nearby as I fall blissfully asleep for a while, refuelling for the next teaching session.

The low October sun still has some warmth, and I enjoy breathing in the scent of the tangled biodiversity on either side of the narrow path. The native trees that were planted fifteen years ago are just mature enough to have an air of forest about them. I have been striding uphill for ten minutes, picking some of the last blackberries, when I start feeling uneasy. My heart is beating heavily and erratically, more than I would expect as a result of the climbing. Sweat is suddenly issuing forth from all the pores of my skin, and I am flushed with a mixture of alarm and weakness. This is all very familiar: I am having a 'hypo', an episode of hypoglycaemia, low blood sugar. Just to make sure that I read the signals correctly I test my levels: 2.2. This is the lowest I have measured for a while, and I look around for somewhere to sit down. I spot a flat stone a few feet further up and stagger towards it, feeling rather dizzy. Yes, this is worse than usual; my early-warning signs normally kick in at about 3.6. I rummage in my bag for the glucose tablets I always have with me, and as I unwrap the packet I notice my fingers trembling. The sweetness of the tablets is intense, overpowering any memory of the warm, subtle taste of the banana toffee cake I enjoyed not so long ago. I eat a piece of chocolate as well for a more palatable aftertaste. It's always such a shame, though, being forced to eat more sweet things so soon after a satisfying meal, particularly when trying to lose weight. (I have a hypo about once a week on average, luckily not always as dramatic. The closer you sail to a low HbA1c, the more risk of hypos, which happen as a result of having injected too much insulin.) Now I need to wait it out. Following the urge to be horizontal, I spread my waterproofs on a small, sun-dappled area of relatively flat, mossy ground and nestle down.

After the morning activities of yoga and meditation, I still feel all wrapped in well-being and am gently determined not to let this hypo get me all frazzled. I know that I must watch grumbling thoughts like the ones I was just having about the taste of glucose tablets and not let them run unchecked. I put a hand on my heart area and sense the breath as a warm, compassionate influence, filling and leaving the chest. Quite intuitively I go through stages of a 'compassion break' (as devised by Kristin Neff[28] and Chris Germer): recognising this as a moment of suffering, reminding myself that suffering is universal and the experience of a hypo, in particular, is shared by many others. I endeavour to meet it with acceptance and compassion. Breathing in… breathing out. Being in touch with some measure of kindness, I let the gentle breath guide me towards experiencing the physical effects of the hypo with a greater sense of spaciousness. My heart is still thumping in strange ways, and I have the urge to devour the rest of the chocolate. Essentially a hypo is an automatic stress response, I remind myself. My sugar-deprived body is pumping out adrenalin, sending waves of alarm through the system, trying to get me to act in the interest of survival. Eat, in this case. But I know it is very common to over-medicate and end up with blood sugars shooting through the roof, so I resist the urge. I just allow the sensations in the body to be there. Breathing in… breathing out. Breathing in ease, kindness and reassurance, which is what I need right now, and letting those qualities pervade my whole body/mind.

Part of taking care of myself is awareness of my thought patterns: there is a degree of catastrophising (what if I pass out?) and criticising (I should have injected less insulin at lunchtime). What is happening here is very understandable: sparked by the old-brain, knee-jerk fear reaction, the prefrontal cortex-based thinking mind slots into ways of operating that are supposedly helpful and life-saving. In mindfulness training we learn not to buy into such anxious thoughts, as they rarely have any connection to reality, but have a strong adverse effect on mood. The interesting twist here is that some version of such thoughts is actually necessary; I can't afford to be too laid back, blissing out in the 'here and now'. Control is of the essence. More than once I have got myself into a situation where I didn't have any test strips for my glucose meter because I hadn't taken note, with a sufficient degree of urgency, of my supply running low.

Another way of conceptualising these psychological processes is to think of them as a system of different inner parts (as described by Schwartz in his Internal Family Systems approach). The part that will serve me best here is a firm and compassionate inner

[28] https://self-compassion.org

mentor, instead of an unforgiving inner critic. The critic is a part of the psyche that was formed in my childhood, and it has some outdated ways of trying to serve my well-being and safety. The inner mentor has a more up-to-date understanding of how to achieve that. She is informed by neuroscientific knowledge of the territory, as well as some spiritual insights, such as awareness of the changing nature of everything and the universality of suffering. She also reflects with some composure about what I could have done differently to avoid the hypo. These considerations help me regain my equilibrium as I am slowly recuperating in my supine position on a Scottish hillside. The most important piece in the whole process is doing my best to keep a strong foothold on the safe ground of open-hearted, compassionate awareness. 'Taking Refuge' in awareness, as Tara Brach and other Buddhists call it.

Like me, many other meditators have found the teachings of neuroscientists such as Rick Hanson invaluable in supporting a more compassionate attitude to suffering. Rather than berating ourselves for not overcoming our hindrances and distractions more heroically, we can take solace from knowing that these ways of functioning are hard-wired into our genes. It doesn't mean that we don't have any choice. But it is useful to understand that in terms of the survival of our species, alarmist thinking has proven to be advantageous. Those human beings that learned from dangerous situations by rehearsing the circumstances and implications in their minds are the ones that became our ancestors, not the ones who just shook it off. The laid-back people are more likely to have perished before being able to rear children. But these days it may be the other way round. Living longer and in very different worlds, many of us experience levels of stress that are damaging to our mental and physical health. Apart from the direct detrimental effects of chronic stress, it is probably true to say that most of us nurture some form of addiction in order to escape pressure and dissatisfaction. I often think of all those media-obsessed, increasingly obese children – how successful will they be in finding partners and raising families, passing on their genes?

Now my heartbeat is less noticeable, and my fingers have stopped trembling. A gentle breeze cools my damp forehead and rustles nearby birch leaves. I am aware of the ubiquitous seabird calls sifting through into consciousness. Now that the immediate danger is over, my senses are waking to a wider reality, and I feel at peace. Following the slow progress of a couple of sailing boats crossing the clear blueness between the island and the Ayrshire coast, another thread of reflections unspools in my mind, to do with gratitude. I am lucky to live in a country and a time where having type 1 diabetes doesn't imply a death sentence. Diabetes has been recognised for a long time, but before 1921, when insulin was discovered, its treatment was largely ineffective. The Egyptians applied a combination of ground earth, water, bones, wheat and lead; in the nineteenth century the treatments of choice were bleeding, cupping or blistering, and opium was prescribed to reduce the despair of dying patients. Before 1921, diabetic children rarely lived a year after diagnosis, 5 per cent of adults died within two years, and less than 20 per cent lived more than ten. The only method that had some chance of slowing down patients' decline was a near-starvation diet. During those long stretches of human history, till about a hundred years ago, people with this disease just wasted away.

Another thing I am grateful for is the modern insulin pump. In 1963 the first apparatus that delivered insulin continuously into the subcutaneous layer of the skin was the size of a backpack. It would have been hard to perform sun salutations attached to one of those. Pumps generally give better control than manual injections, but they are expensive and hard to get on the NHS. By far the majority of people in this country with type 1 diabetes inject insulin three to four times a day, with a mix of fast- and slow-acting types of the substance. Here is a heart-warming, gratitude-invoking story of how I became one of the fortunate pump wearers.

I was leading a retreat at Dhanakosa Retreat Centre about a year after my diagnosis and was struggling to make the daily injections work for me. Whatever method and type of insulin I used, my blood sugar levels would be too high in the mornings, making me feel sluggish, followed by a hypo around lunchtime. I happened to have a conversation with a retreat participant about it and mentioned that a pump would probably solve the issue, because it adjusts the flow of fast-acting insulin over twenty-four hours to match the individual's fluctuating absorption rates. I would be able to compensate for my extreme insulin resistance in the early morning hours. I mentioned that I wasn't able to afford a pump (which at that time cost £2,000) and was unlikely to receive it from the NHS. At the end of the retreat, the woman approached me and said that she would like to give me the money for a pump. She regularly donated a proportion of her sizeable income to a charity anyway and felt that by giving it to me instead she would also serve the wider community. I was bowled over by her generosity and at first was reluctant to accept it. I said to her that being on retreat can sometimes change the way we feel and think about things, and suggested she went home and let it settle. A few days afterwards she repeated her offer and then kept it alive for a year, while I went through a process to get the NHS to pay for the costly 'consumables' (the disposable 'set' and 'reservoir' that have to be replaced every three days). Every time this story comes to mind, I feel uplifted and inspired by this example of human generosity.

Having fully recovered from my hypo, I walk a bit further up the hill and, to my delight, encounter the wild ponies. I love immersing myself in relatively wild nature and have been on many solitary retreats, staying for one to four weeks without meeting other people and preferably out of sight of phone masts and machine sounds. For many years it has been an essential part of my spiritual and personal development. The consultant at the diabetes centre doesn't like it. 'You go away and do these strange things on your own, don't you?' He thinks I put myself at risk. And he is right – there have been a few nail-biting episodes (which I haven't shared with him). Just a few weeks after that life-changing visit to A&E, I went on a previously planned solitary retreat on the Isle of Skye. The crucial importance of always carrying concentrated carbohydrates with me hadn't sunk in yet. I was caught out by a hypo in the middle of what felt like nowhere, at least two miles from the house I was staying in. I didn't even own a mobile phone at that time and carried not a morsel of food. I knew that one could pass out during a hypo (which has actually not happened to me so far), fall into a coma and suffer brain damage, so I was truly scared, on top of the other alarming symptoms. Luckily my bad sense of orientation had worked in my favour for once. When I got to the top of a small hillock, I saw my abode not too far away.

Another time, staying in a cottage in a remote part of the

Cairngorms, I dropped my blood-testing equipment irretrievably down a steep gully. In a complicated arrangement involving using the phone of distant neighbours (I still didn't have a mobile phone) and an expensive taxi ride, I had to get myself to the nearest surgery and chemist twenty miles away to buy a replacement. And there was that scary moment in the Pyrenees, where I stayed for a month-long solitary retreat, when I got so hot and sweaty during a long hike that the injection cannula of my pump got dislodged and I had no other means to get insulin into my body. Adding to the drama, at that moment I found myself in one of those precarious situations on a rocky cliff face where you can't find the next foothold. It took several hours to get back home into the coolness of my beautiful straw-bale eco-cabin and the next insulin fix. That taught me to always carry a spare.

My Buddha daughter Willow (two years old at that period in my life) has cottoned on to the fact that I always have sweets in my little backpack. 'What have you got in your bag?' she asks, and won't be side-tracked for long by an offer of pen and paper for some drawing. 'Do that thing,' she says, starting to unzip the compartment where I keep my glucose meter. She is fascinated by the pricking of my finger to obtain a drop of blood. 'Again!' she demands. Then she points at my belly: 'Show me!' We are in a public playground. Surreptitiously I peel off my layers to let her have a look at the infusion site on my belly, covered by a small white adhesive patch. 'Why?' she asks. 'Because I need insulin.' 'Why?' And so on.

So these are some of my ways to meet the challenges involved in living with a chronic, life-threatening illness: not letting it get in the way of adventure; doing my best to control my blood sugar levels with the help of a wise and firm inner mentor; meeting the inevitable moments of alarm with compassion and mindful presence, and consciously cultivating gratitude. Oh, and always carrying chocolate.

Haircut

I've been standing in front of my wardrobe mirror for the last ten minutes, inspecting my new haircut, willing it to look different. I hold the small mirror in one hand, gazing sideways at the reflection of the sides and back of my head in the large mirror, and try to pull some strands forwards to cover my ear, but there is no hiding the pink flesh peeping through my dark hair: shiny, naked, exposed. I have felt self-conscious about my ears ever since being teased as a child. They are big, floppy and stick out at an angle that has given rise to comparisons with aeroplane wings and sails. 'I explained to her exactly what I wanted,' I say to myself, full of indignation. 'She even said she knew how I feel because she has the same problem and has been agonising for months whether or not to pin her hair up for her wedding. And now look at this big gap. She just didn't take care.' I turn round to have another look at the other ear, hoping for some new point of view, a change in my perception. But my aggrieved inner dialogue continues unabated. 'This doesn't look like a bob at all, not to speak of the "funky bob" she promised me. I should go back and complain, let the manager sort it out, as he has done before. They'll probably ban me from the premises as a nagging costumer who is impossible to please.'

I know I have got into one of my well-worn grooves of mental reactivity. It's both painful and strangely comforting, like running your tongue over a fresh break in the enamel of a tooth, again and again, despite the increasing soreness. No, that's too small a gesture. An image from my childhood presents itself: we used to heat with coal, and every couple of months in the winter there would be a delivery. Bag after bag of coal rumbled down the shoot into the cellar, landing on the growing heap with a satisfying crash. Enough fuel to keep going for a long time. Here it goes, another load descends, compounding the tightness in the pit of my stomach. 'She is an experienced hairdresser and I paid a lot of money. What did she think she was doing?'

I must change tack, get some perspective. Larry is in the kitchen preparing lunch. I stand in the door.

'I feel disappointed by my haircut,' I say, in a neutral voice. He looks up from cutting tomatoes. 'Look at the sides.' I turn my head and adopt an exaggerated childlike tone, so he knows I am play-acting. 'How my ears poke out.' I point at my right ear for emphasis, then at the left. He puts the knife down, comes over and takes me into his arms. 'I am sorry you don't like your haircut. Are you going to do something about it?'

'Well, what do you think about it – how does it look, here at the sides?' I know what he is going to say. He doesn't notice these kinds of things. He used to get off-the-peg haircuts for around £4.50 that were totally insensitive to his particular type of hair, shape of head and degree of, let's say it, balding. Then I offered to cut his hair, which has since become a pleasurable new routine. He seems to enjoy the attention, the grooming, going into a semi-trance state. When I have finished the careful sculpting, a last snip to smooth the line above his ears (which are beautiful, neat, close to the head), he shakes the hair off the towel, gets a brush and dustpan to gather it off the floor, adds it to the compost and gets on with his work. He doesn't even think of checking his new haircut in the mirror.

Later that day a friend comes to meditate together, as we do once a fortnight. We sit in front of the picture of an old standing Chinese Buddha, his robes flowing in simple, arresting lines, his sandstone lips curved into a subtle smile that speaks of contentment, of having seen through the folly of caring for appearances, of compassion for the pain we cause ourselves and others when looking for happiness in the wrong places. While kneeling to light the candle and a stick of amber incense, I gaze longingly at his serene features then settle into my cushions, paying attention to the sense of my body supported by the earth. It's V's turn to read a few inspirational lines to get us into the mood.

'In order to achieve autonomy, listen to the silence between the thoughts.'

She rings the bell, and my mind goes straight to the haircut, as I knew it would. There is a twitch, a twisting in my torso; I want to look in the mirror again, confirm the terrible truth. There is another round of indignant complaining, more coal rolling down that shoot, and then I am ready to apply myself to what needs doing: tenderly tracing the feelings in my body, without judgement, breathing with them, into them. In a kinder voice I reassure myself: 'This goes back to my relationship with my mother, my needs not being met fully enough. In the hands of a hairstylist one is as helpless as a baby.' I start listening to the silence between the thoughts, a compassionate smile hovering in that silence.

Clutter of thought, swishing of scissors, surrounded by awareness.

Solitary Retreat on Eigg

Knowing there won't be any shops for miles, I've brought with me a packet of flour to make my own bread, a wholewheat mix with 20 per cent rye and various seeds. It's a lovely mellow day, ideal rising conditions. Kneading the dough with sleeves folded back, I sense the touch of warm air on bare skin from the wide-open window, such a rare delight in Scotland. The scent of yeast blends with that of the meadowsweet that surrounds the wooden shack in profusion, plus a hint of sheep and chicken droppings. A homely smell; I can almost imagine growing up with it. At home I would listen to the radio while being industrious like this, but there isn't one here, and anyway, I am on retreat. The sound of birds and insects is fine enough company. During the first rising I scythe what Ellie called in her letter of instructions the 'laundry green': a rough square of wily tufts of grass barely claimed from a jungle of bracken. One end of the low-hanging washing line is attached to the woodshed, the other to a wobbly gatepost, from where one walks down to the beach. The shack, the caravan, the woodshed, a toolshed, a trampoline, four chickens and a couple of rows of potatoes – this is the 'croft' on the Isle of Eigg my friends have inhabited for a year. They have now moved back to Glasgow, with their two children and cat, and I am 'hen-sitting' for three weeks before the next occupant arrives.

I am quite pleased with how the scything is going, given I last did it twenty-five years ago when living at Taraloka Retreat Centre. I only get the blade stuck in the grass a couple of times, and the grass is flying off in bushels. I try to swing from the legs, minimising the strain in the arms. This is rather fun, this countryside living. I knead the dough again and press it into a couple of oiled tins for the second rising, which shouldn't take more than half an hour, I reckon. I light the gas oven to pre-heat it and see to the hens. They have been pecking at the door and squawking vociferously, demanding their feeder be replenished. The food is disappearing at a fast rate, I have noticed, with quite a bit of wildlife taking their share: pigeons in particular, also crows and a number of small birds that fly too fast for me to see what they are. If the feeder is not full in the mornings, the chickens wake me up at 5.30 with a rather shrieking style of clucking. I am starting to get to know how things are run here. At mid-morning and early evening they expect a handful of grains at the top of the wooden stairs. They adore leftovers of cooked food, apparently, which I am strongly conditioned not to produce, so not much joy there for them so far. I tried a couple of spoonfuls of porridge the other day, calling them with a high-pitched 'tock tock tock tock', as instructed. (I had rung up to ask for an explanation: 'what do you mean, "calling the chickens"?') It worked, and they came running excitedly with feathers flying (literally), only to pick at the porridge rather half-heartedly, like well-behaved guests humouring their hosts and their pitiful culinary efforts, then wiping their smudged beaks from side to side on some leaves, rather like using napkins, only more vigorously.

Soon it is time for the bread to go into the oven; the loaves have risen to an impressive, quivering fullness, but here is where things stop being quite so idyllic. The oven is only just warm, and there is no hissing of gas. Rocking the tall, red gas cylinder at the back of the wee house confirms that it's run out. I turn the switch to 'off' and stand there for a moment, feeling the sun on my slightly sweaty skin, wiping off a few flies. What to do? And of equal importance: how to be? I am aware that the hiatus in the smooth running of things could have a detrimental effect on my state of mind if I don't watch it. I take the opportunity for a few conscious breaths. Then I call Ellie, and luckily she is at home.

'There is a spare cylinder by the gate, lying on the ground, but you will need help getting it into place; it's very heavy. Ask Scout from the house further up the track, or if he is not in, Ben from the nearest house in the other direction. They may need to do it together; it is very awkward to get it over the uneven ground around the house.' I have indeed noticed the precariousness of the immediate surroundings of the shack, which they built last year and obviously didn't manage to quite finish. There is a kind of double draining ditch surrounding it, and one balances on the untidy wall of earth in between to get to the toolshed.

I find Margot at home, her husband not due back till later in the afternoon. I explain about the loaves ready to go in, and she says she would take them but her oven is full. She says the cylinders are definitely too heavy for the two of us to move on our own. 'They should have left it in place for you. How are they living, anyway, leaving things unfinished like this! They are dizzy, these people, too many projects. Anyway, I'll send Scout over when he comes home later this afternoon.'

On the way down the dusty track to the other neighbour, I am aware of the crunchy rhythm of my sandals on the dusty track. Keeping time with the familiar, regular swing of the body, thoughts cue themselves in. How this kind of situation is probably very much part of living in the countryside. Emergencies leading to mutual help and critical gossip in equal share. Ben isn't there either, but Sue says it shouldn't be too difficult to move the thing, she does it all the time. I explain how awkward the terrain is and say I'd rather wait for Scout to come back later in the afternoon. At home I look at the hopeful loaves and ring her with the afterthought that she may have space in her oven.

'You can't move bread once it has risen; it would collapse.' A sound piece of advice from a woman experienced in many aspects of countryside survival. I make myself a cup of tea and sit on an upturned crate, careful to avoid any of the hazardous chicken droppings I have learned to navigate. Watching a few wispy clouds over the Cuillins on the island of Rum in the distance, blue sky, calm sea, it is easy to let go of plans and projects. I feel like the dough, soft and expanded in all directions and not in imminent danger of collapsing, although Margot's judgemental comments do go through my mind occasionally. I wouldn't expect it to be otherwise. Our genes and conditioning make it hard to drop the habit of checking and re-checking that we are safe in a group and whether our behaviour is acceptable. I replay my answer to Margot: 'Yes, it would have been helpful to have the cylinder in place, but I feel so grateful to be here.' I can't find any fault with it. But did I ask for too much when I rang Sue about the bread? Actually, our exchange gives me a sense of womanly alliance; here we are, on a stretch of gently sloping fertile land on a small island, sharing practical housekeeping experience in ways that would not have been out of place two centuries ago. Or among two women in Africa now. Ten minutes later Sue is at the gate, wielding a spanner.

'How's your bread doing?' Sue must be in her sixties, a little overweight and moving somewhat stiffly, as if trying to minimise joint pain. She is wearing a comfortably cut cotton blouse over clean black trousers. Is she really going to tackle this beast of a metal container? I had pushed my weight against it to get the measure of it, and it didn't budge an inch. It doesn't seem a fitting match for a human body at all; just the memory of it makes my sandal-clad feet and naked shin bones shrink. Sue, however, leans in and with minimum intervention from me swings this monster round, drags it along the dirt, lets it smoothly slide down the flimsy steps made of wooden pallets, twists it, dances it around the shack, without a moment of hesitation. Her body just knows how to respond to angle, gradient, consistency of ground.

'Thirty-seven years of living in the countryside,' she responds to my admiring comments. 'After a few years my arms didn't fit into the sleeves of my shirts any more.' She puts the spanner around the bolt and frowns, unsure which way to loosen it. I mime how I would unscrew a lid, then go the opposite way. 'Right, definitely,' I offer, glad to be able to make some contribution.

I am enjoying a slice of my freshly baked bread, with tahini and honey, aware of the hens' contented gurgling sounds in the quiet of the afternoon, when it suddenly occurs to me that I haven't heard the sound of the water pump at the back of the shack for quite some time. Normally it comes on every few hours and when I open the taps or flush the loo. I try the cold-water tap, and sure enough, there is barely a trickle. The water gets pumped into the tank on the bed platform inside the shack. I remove the giant teddy bear that sits on top of it and have a peep inside: the water level is several inches below the mark. Normally I have a lot less human contact on solitary retreats, but I do need help with this. Another phone call to Ellie sends me across to the neighbours again. Apparently Scout put in the pump and should be able to help. He is a compact man of medium height with unkempt fine hair, his upper body tight and muscly in a way that makes me wonder whether he suffers from frequent coughs. He sets to work disconnecting and reconnecting various parts of the plumbing, but not without coming out with disparaging remarks similar to those I had heard from his wife earlier. In fact these comments burst force with the pent-up pressure we are expecting from the water pipe, from which, however, appears only a mere trickle.

'I knew when they came off the boat that they were not the kind of people to make it here. These "green" people, all they do is sit in front of their computers. When I came here thirty-seven years ago, I had my hands and a shovel, and I set to work. That's what you need to do here, work the land. I tried to help him, I really did, showed him how to do things. I told him three times he should move the gas cylinder to the back of the house. He never tried.' He angrily flings away a piece of blue pipe, then pokes about in the mud that is forming around the pump, looking for a nut he has dropped. 'This happens when you don't finish things. Just sitting on their butts with their computers all day long.'

'Does it have to be someone's fault?' I think, but don't say. I am reminded of my father's tirades and the way I would hook into arguments that went on and on. I feel the stirring of the habit, the defensive, pugnacious tightening of the gut, and I am also aware of a spaciousness around it. I am on retreat here, and anything that happens is simply what happens – it doesn't get in the way of something else that's more important. Maybe the problem won't get sorted, and that's okay. I picture myself carrying buckets of water from the nearby burn for the rest of my stay here.

'Sounds like something about Gus really irks you,' I try. I haven't actually used that word before, 'irk', one of those words that you read and don't say, particularly when you come from a different country. But it fits; the very sound of it corresponds to the irritated quality of his movements, and my attempt at empathy does seem to have a softening effect. He straightens up and looks at me – his eyes are kind and sparkly. 'I like Gus, but he wouldn't listen to me,' he reiterates in a softer tone.

It turns out the fault is a disconnected hose further down by the caravan ('the guy who worked on it didn't have a clue'), and soon the pump is pumping away again. We end up conversing amiably for another half hour, him sitting on the steps in the sun, doing most of the talking, me standing in the door in the shade, mainly listening. We cover the island's buy-out, climate change and my mindfulness work with depression, which he says he suffers from. I manage to say at some point, and am surprised by the emotion in my throat, that these are very difficult times, knowing as we do about the destruction of the planet's habitability for future generations, and it is hard for anyone to know what a good way of living one's life is.

I wonder how I can repay my neighbours' helpfulness. Have I

got anything they would like? Incense? Roasted sunflower seeds? Gus had described the community here as 'not very hippy, but not unhappy'. The frozen steak comes to mind. I ring Sue. 'Do you eat meat or are you vegetarian? I'll tell you why. I stayed in a B & B in Mallaig on the way here, and the landlord kindly let me put a lot of the perishable food I had brought in his fridge. When I left, I took this steak by mistake and left behind a vegetarian quiche. Would you like it? It is frozen so should be okay.' She and her husband do indeed enjoy meat, and I drop the steak by on my walk later on – a perfect ending to a chain of events.

I could bake something for Margot and Scout, I decide. Eggs have become a plentiful natural resource. During my first week here I couldn't find any of the very free-range eggs the hens were presumably laying. There were so many potential hiding places in the surrounding bracken. Feeling a little defeated, I had even bought a couple of eggs from an organic farm down the track. Then one morning I heard the soft, chuffed clucking I was told to listen out for, and there they were, three hens huddled close on a nest with five eggs. When they left the nest, I carefully lifted the eggs. I was taken by surprise and touched by the feeling of aliveness from the warmth of the hens' bodies, so different from taking an egg out of the fridge.

Margot's apron reads 'I am gorgeous', pink on grey, and so she is, a fine figure with dark eyes that light up as she receives the cake. She holds it with care, as if it were made of something precious and breakable. There is something very womanly about this holding, this fussing with the plastic cover. 'I hope it's alright, I made it without a recipe, with what was around.' I am aware that I am putting myself or the gift down a little; this is all part of the dance, this very particular British dance I have learned over the years. The receiver of a gift could easily feel uncomfortable if the offering is too precious or the giver too smug. The giving could backfire. 'I am sure it will be delicious. What kind of cake is it?' 'It's made with plums I brought from the mainland. They needed using.'

Margot plays her part of the game, saying something like it's too much, but her genuine delight stays with me as I walk back home. The exchange has made us both that little bit more at ease about being neighbours for these few weeks, I sense. She knows that I am here to be quiet and get on with meditation, writing and artwork, and I know that she makes felted hats and bags that she sometimes sells at the fair but has not enough time for. We will keep each other in mind, which is lovely to know.

Spiral Fracture

I had noticed, even aesthetically admired, the hefty anchor chain on the exposed sea floor of the harbour. Its rusty orange contrasted with the shades of grey that are everywhere on Easdale Island: rocks, walls, the walkways among the former quarry workers' cottages. And I saw it again as we took advantage of the low tide and took a shortcut to go for a swim in one of the flooded slate quarries, where the water is a little warmer and less salty than the open sea. It is a mystery to me why I still fell over it. I must have got my foot hooked in one of the chain links. I felt the torque in my bone a fraction of a second before my body hit the ground. The onset of pain was immediate, as was the swelling, like a balloon being inflated, bulbously, irregular at first, squeezing through the spaces between the ankle bones, muscles and ligaments, about to form itself into a thick, throbbing cushion of protection.

Luckily I wasn't on my own, and it wasn't far to shuffle back to the Old School House, where we were staying for a writing holiday. I was leaning heavily on Larry's shoulder and letting out moans and groans with every step to help with the pain. Then it was phone calls, a ferry to the mainland, examination by the kind doctor in the local surgery, a drive to Oban hospital for further diagnostics. The X-rays showed a diagonal fracture of my right fibula bone, just above the ankle. A 'spiral fracture', a poetic term for something potentially 'complicated', as the doctor said. We had to wait to get news from the next biggest hospital in Paisley about how to stabilise the leg. Two German families occupied the small waiting area. A boy who had injured his ankle jumping from a sand dune on the Isle of Mull seemed to be rather enjoying the swing of his crutches; his two brothers were a little envious, perhaps? They didn't talk much, the five of them, and there was a patient hum in their collective waiting, the containment and security of being part of a family unit. A woman had her bent arm in a sling – broken in two places, it turned out, and they wouldn't be able to get the last ferry back to Jura; her husband managed to secure the last room in Oban for the night. We all took an interest in each other's calamities and appreciated the comfort of our mother tongue. The staff were calm and professional, but their freezer was broken and we weren't able to re-freeze our bag of peas to help keep the swelling down. A taste of NHS money-saving policies; it 'drives me nuts', the nurse said. The radiologist readily complied with my request to obtain a copy of the X-ray; she took a photo with my phone.

Having bemoaned the inexorable rise of the smartphone many times, I now appreciated being able to send the ghostly picture of my ankle, with those long, ominous crack lines, and then an image of the pristine plaster cast to friends and family, straightaway from the hospital. And I enjoyed the sweetness of receiving their condolences almost instantaneously, in some cases. I was reminding myself to let this positive experience linger, taking it inside myself like another form of medicine, the healing balm of belonging and friendship. This is using brain plasticity to its advantage; my bones may be getting thinner with age, but cells in areas of the brain connected with wellness can spread and thicken in response to my conscious choices about where I put my attention. I am 'letting in the good', to use Rick Hanson's term, and counting my blessings. My back is not giving me any trouble; how wonderful. My shoulders are in good shape and getting stronger by the hour from using the crutches.

People send me emails and text messages telling their own stories of calamities, trapped nerves, chronic pain, which opens my heart to the universality of human suffering a bit more readily than usual. The most common and avoidable form of suffering is focussing on pain in a way that leads to more of it by getting stuck in resistance to it. We are all prone to this, trying to push away our unpleasant experience only to get more entangled in it. And we are also all prone to skimming over the many, many often inconspicuous pleasant experiences every day offers.

The average person has two bone fractures in their lifetime, but even if that's not you, it is likely there will be other accidents that have the potential to disrupt your life and equanimity. Or could they be an opportunity to enhance your quality of life in surprising ways? Three days after the incident, I would honestly say that I had a good holiday, and a lot of that is due to my mindfulness practice, imperfect as it may be.

As I am meditating propped up in my bed, leg raised on the cushions I would usually use to sit cross-legged on the floor, I am feeling pain in my ankle. I am thinking of my mother who is in 'constant pain' since a similar ankle injury a few years ago, falling off her bike. It is not easy to keep empathising with 'constant'; it leads to compassion fatigue. But 'constant' is just a concept that doesn't withstand careful investigation. When my friend Vidyamala was in agony after an accident that led to a lifetime of chronic back pain, she had a breakthrough experience: 'I knew, not intellectually but in the marrow of my bones, that life can only unfold one moment at a time; I saw that the present moment is always bearable and I tasted the confidence that knowledge brings. Fear drained out of me and I relaxed.'[29] So I decide to explore this for myself, for a while anyway. After relaxing into the support of the cushions and letting my heart soften, I focus in on the sensations emanating from under that big white cast that still looks a little alien. There is pulsing, tearing, rippling, a layering of sensations, subtly different from moment to moment. For a while it seems that focussing on it makes it more edgy, intense, but I try to relax into it, to trust the process, just for this moment. Letting the sensations float in a larger space of relaxed, loving attentiveness. Being open to what happens, not expecting anything. Yes, this seems possible, and it gives some peace.

Sometimes I work with pain in this way, sometimes I shift position, take painkillers or distract myself by immersing myself in something compelling like painting or watching a movie, letting the pain be a smaller part of the overall picture. Both approaches are valid and important; there is no need to be a spiritual superhero of endurance. Sometimes I feel impatient with the lack of mobility and weary with pain. But overall, having a broken ankle seems to have become a quietly normal experience. It is simple, even if I will probably have to cancel some work and it takes four times as long to get down the stairs. 'Throw the crutches down the stairs, then slide down on your bottom,' the nurse had advised. 'And here she comes.' Larry welcomes the clanking and clutter of aluminium on wood. I mentally rehearse getting up to our second-

[29] Vidyamala Burch, *Living Well with Pain and Illness*

floor flat in Glasgow. Meeting the neighbours on the way, the kids having fun seeing a grown-up in this ignoble position.

So this is it, really, it's simple. Mainly, remembering what kindness feels like, again and again, which is not difficult when on the receiving end of so much generosity. The young ferryman giving me a ride to the pier in the only electric vehicle on the island and standing ready to catch me in case I should fall while levering myself onto the boat. (It turned out he had broken his hand the previous year, which perhaps explained his patience and kindly encouragement.) The careful, gently exploratory touch and kindly eyes of the doctor in the local surgery. The building-savvy neighbour who came over to see whether the chairlift that had been fitted for our dear friend Kay, who owned the house, could be made to work (sadly not). Before Larry goes out for a swim, he asks if I need anything. It's tricky carrying a cup of tea when you need both hands for crutches. When he returns his eyes are full of sun, wind and shimmering waves. I have a choice here: to envy him or to join in with his pleasure in my imagination, dive with him from a three-metre-high slate ridge into the deep, cool, soft, indigo-blue sea.

Beyond Ideas of Wrongdoing and Rightdoing: Incidents on a Building Site

From our second-floor Glasgow tenement flat, I am in a perfect position to survey the comings and goings of the various tradesmen involved in the extensive renovation of our new ground-floor flat next door. Eddie's van is blue, with white and red writing: MARYHILL BUILDERS. When I see it parked outside, I feel reassured. He is our main builder, and he coordinates joiner, plumber, electrician, glazier, kitchen fitter, tiler, stove installer and painter. Most of them know each other, some of them are each other's in-laws, and they all talk in fast, broad Glaswegian. I, the German client and supervisor of the project, understand about half of what they say, which, together with the fact that I don't know much about building work, is a challenge for all of us. However, in my early thirties I spent a couple of years as part of a team of women converting a farm into a retreat centre (Taraloka Retreat Centre for Women), and while this seems a long time ago, there is still some residue of confidence lodged in my bones, an understanding of masonry and timber and how they respond to tools, a sense of how a project evolves organically from plans, unexpected findings, circumstances and mistakes – many of them.

There are also accidents and deaths: just as we were returning to work after three months of Covid-19 lockdown, the plumber's dad died of an unexpected heart attack after a fall. So the plumber took another week off, understandably. The glazier had recently suffered a stroke and had forgotten everything that had been agreed upon about the replacement of window panels. The electrician hurt his back falling off a ladder and needed to rest. I pray that Eddie, who is probably in his late sixties, will take good care of himself. He sometimes doesn't eat anything until mid-afternoon, and he smokes.

Eddie is the kind of person you'd want for your grandfather: calm and courteous even under trying circumstances, a twinkle in his eye when he greets you, a wink when you leave and in charge without seeming to be. He is wiry and strong, despite arthritic joints, with dry skin toughened by decades of exposure to dust and fumes from all kinds of noxious substances. We are of similar height, our heads leaning towards each other as we try to decipher each other's accent while preserving social distancing. 'Say that again?' 'Do ye want a facin' tae cover that joint?' 'What's a facin'?'

Awareness of possible infection from Covid-19 is ubiquitous. I wash my hands when returning from my daily check-ins with the builders and remind myself to relax; that life is not a rehearsal for a future moving-in date. After all this time spent researching the 'best-buy' washing machine, fridge freezer and dishwasher, the most fitting bathroom tiles and engineered wood floorboards to cover our underfloor heating, there is no guarantee that my husband and I will actually be there to enjoy it or to do so for very long. Whatever enjoyment life, or our own hearts, might offer us, it had better be happening now. No point in getting all tense about missed deadlines or deliveries of items that I never ordered, like a large shower basin and glass door panels that are cluttering the space and that it seems to be impossible to get picked up for return, despite dozens of phone calls, emails and text messages.

Being left hanging on the phone with some tinny muzak grinds away at my emotional resilience, despite my best intentions to remain grounded and calm.

My daily practice of mindful movement and meditation is absolutely essential, but even so, there have been some fraught and sleepless nights. 'I spent a couple of hours imagining worst-case scenarios,' I tell Eddie in our mid-morning check-in. He smiles encouragingly at me. 'I was wondering whether rats and mice might build nests from the mineral wool we put in between the joists.' Eddie tells me he's had problems with mice in his own house and put down some concrete with embedded glass splinters to deter them. Or something like that; I don't understand all of the story and am not too sure how it relates to my question. But never mind. I decided right at the beginning to basically trust him, while keeping an eye on things – a sensitive and delicate balance. For example, the tiler was just about to attach tiles to a section of the bathroom wall when I noticed that a waste pipe had been boxed in a way that would not allow enough space for the cabinet I had already bought. 'Eddie, do you have a minute to have a look at something in the bathroom? And bring your tape measure?' He is easy about admitting and correcting mistakes that he or his men have made, and maybe my practice of non-blaming helps. Or maybe it's the profiteroles I offer them occasionally.

After a few weeks of being on call in this way, I decide to partake in an online meditation retreat. I will still need to be involved with the building work, and part of the intention is to gain more insight into the dynamics of *being* and *doing* – how to enable more of a continuity of awareness. The retreat is structured around this excerpt from a famous poem by Rumi:

Out beyond ideas of wrongdoing and rightdoing,
there is a field. I will meet you there.

When the soul lies down in that grass,
the world is too full to speak of.
Ideas, language, even the notion 'one another'
make no sense.

The retreat leader, Paramananda, is skilled at establishing a felt sense of connection between the sixty of us joining through our screens from all over the world. 'Imagine we are all sitting in the same room together,' he says in his deep, mumbling growl, which I also struggle to entirely understand. 'Soften your face, and imagine the faces of everyone else softening.' In my meditations I bring to mind Eddie, who has never meditated but didn't bat an eyelid when I explained to him that I wanted him to build a meditation platform above my bed. Paramananda likens the current pandemic to a *bardo*, a gap or interruption of normal consciousness. The conditions that have led to the outbreak of Covid-19 show up the hubris of humankind, the way we have become intoxicated with our power to dominate and exploit the natural world. What can we make of this interruption? 'What needs to happen is a simple change of heart,' he suggests. 'We need to become comfortable with our own vulnerability and weave feelings of love between us.'

When I check my mobile phone after the morning session, there is a message from Eddie: 'Can you come down? I have run into a problem.' I descend the stairs feeling calm and curious. Eddie points to a section of the continuous underfloor heating coil that loops warm water through the whole flat. He had fixed foam underlay onto it the day before, in preparation for the floorboards being laid. 'Ah pit a staple intae the coil. Ah wis bumpin' ma gums tae the stove fitters, no payin' attention. Took ma eye aff the ball. Ah'm a right eejit.'

Eddie looks crestfallen. He raises his hands, palms facing me, as if to say: 'I'm guilty.' What to do now? Do I want the whole section replaced, which would mean several days' delay as we wait for new materials to arrive and undoing the floor coverings already put in place, or would I accept a joint repair? I don't want to decide on my own, so I ask Larry to come down and have the situation explained to him as well. I'm aware that this is a decision that will affect not only us, but also future inhabitants of this flat, who may not be aware of a possible weak spot in the system. After some discussion, we decide to put in a joint and make sure that it can easily be monitored, with removable floorboards and an explanatory label.

Predictably, the situation replays itself in my mind during the next meditation, and I notice that I don't feel any anger or blame towards Eddie, just compassion for him feeling bad about what happened. And I enjoy a rich and subtle sense of connection with him, Paramananda and the other retreatants, a connection that doesn't depend at all on understanding every word that is spoken.

~ Living Through a Pandemic ~

The Anxietatem Virus

In March 2020 I co-led a tai chi, writing and meditation retreat at Dhanakosa Retreat Centre in the Trossachs, the last one for eighteen months, as it turned out. During that week, life in the UK (and all over the world) changed in ways that would have profound effects on all aspects of our reality. We had been without our phones, and a few days before our departure, the centre director briefed the retreat team on the developments in the outside world. Lockdown was imminent, and it was that time of widespread panic-buying and general mask-wearing. Preparing retreatants for re-entry into 'normal' life is important at the best of times, and it was vital for this situation. Since it was a writing retreat, I composed this satirical piece, initially for our participants:

This is your inner prime minister speaking. After in-depth consultation with my trusted advisers, I want to address you with regard to the current health crisis: the pandemic spread of the anxietatem virus. Thank you for listening and thank you for voting for me and the values our party stands for: Consciousness, Calm, Compassion, Curiosity, Clarity, Contentment, Creativity, Connectedness, Confidence and Cheerfulness.[30] *As you know, the 10 C party has been successful in containing similar outbreaks in the past, and we are confident that we will, with your cooperation, do so again.*

It is important to recognise the urgency of the situation. We are seeing the effects on the stock market, and outbreaks of panic-driven behaviour have led to empty shop shelves and the disruption of civil order and peace.

Early detection of the anxietatem virus is of the essence, and it is easy to self-diagnose, without any special kit or experience. All you need is awareness, which should be in plentiful supply under the current administration. The most common physical symptoms are tight jaws, clenched stomach, hunched shoulders, clammy hands and a general jitteriness, going hand in hand with a raised heartbeat and elevated blood pressure. Among mental manifestations is repetitive, alarmist thinking that tends

[30] This is a play on Rick Schwartz's '8 C Self', which I had mentioned on the retreat.

to spin out of control and can lead to depression. Infected people can easily be spotted by their behaviour: compulsive buying of pasta and toilet rolls, restlessness, erratic decision-making and obsessive social media activity, spreading messages of doom and gloom.

Our scientists think it may be helpful for you to have some information about the nature and behaviour of the virus. It is present in all human beings and can lie dormant for some period of time. Some people have developed a high degree of immunity through the systematic cultivation of awareness antibodies. Denial can be mistaken for immunity – it suppresses the virus for a limited period of time, only for it to erupt with greater force later.

The virus seems to have formed a highly successful alliance with Covid-19, a new form of flu. Information about this coronavirus enters the host through news and social media outlets and activates the fight, flight, freeze or flock parts of the brain, which are the oldest, survival-linked parts of the organism. The amygdala fires messages of danger to related brain networks, adrenalin is released and the victim starts thinking in anxious ways. Typical forms of mental activity involve imagining worst-case scenarios, shortness of supplies and death. The immediate fatality rate of the illness is actually negligible, but long-term effects are likely, as the prolonged presence of adrenalin undermines the immune system and affects cardiovascular health. The apparent aim of the virus is to overturn the host's elected government and take over by saturating the system with trembling, jelly-like or rigidifying fear, blind resentment, paranoia, blame and the urge to join group trends, a form of flocking. Make no mistake about the severity of the situation: the virus is highly infectious. It has the insidious ability to masquerade as ordinary problem-solving. A conversation may start harmlessly enough, but before you know it you have succumbed to the virus.

The government has put together a list of recommendations based on our 10 C values. We hope that this will help you not just to survive, but thrive in these extraordinary times.

1. Be conscious and mindful of the first signs of the virus. The sooner you spot physical tension, obsessive thinking and the urge to join collective panic behaviour, the higher the chances of recovery. When you notice thoughts accompanied by a sinking feeling, attend to the sinking feeling first. Feel the physical sensations and breathe into them, embrace them with kindly awareness. Contrary to lifelong beliefs, anxious thinking does not help, but exacerbates the spread of the disease. Focus on present-moment sensory experiences, such as the feel of the water and the scent of the soap when you wash your hands.

2. Be calm. Yoga, tai chi, dance and other forms of movement stimulate the soothing system of your organism, as does sitting meditation and even just regularly taking some long, deep, conscious breaths. Slow down and do one thing at a time.

3. Coping with the radical changes in lifestyle and loss of income connected with the Covid pandemic is not easy. Remind yourself of the natural human inclination towards caring. The virus shrivels in an atmosphere of kindness, and smiling works wonders.

4. Be curious and enter into a friendly conversation with the virus. Find out its true, underlying intention, which is to keep you alive and safe. Anxietatem is not used to being listened to in this respectful way and will sometimes spontaneously mutate into more benign forms. It can even turn into an ally in the pursuit of safety and happiness.

5. Be clear about the dangers of feeding the virus and letting it roam unchecked. It is trying to get you to share stories it is embedded in. Curtail its multiplication by resisting this lure. Also be clear who you want to be in charge – anxietatem virus or the 10 C party and its prime minister. Remember, you are not your anxious thoughts. Ultimately, you are not your wise thoughts either, but something altogether more mysterious and wonderful.

6. Be content. Covid-19 containment strategies involve self-isolation and curtailing social interaction. This is an opportunity to let go of the stressful striving and craving that are a breeding ground for the anxietatem disease. Accept the limitations, relax into a simpler life of 'being' rather than 'doing'. Savour simple pleasures, such as your breakfast when you don't have to rush to work.

7. Be creative. If you are self-isolating, re-frame the situation into one that emphasises opportunities for self-expression. It will give you a healthy sense of agency. Try writing about your symptoms of worry – this can be an excellent way of unblending from it and keeping the 10 C government in charge.

8. Stay connected with your fellow human beings but beware of contagion. Talking **about** *your anxiety rather than* **from** *it is usually an effective way of disabling it. Share your success stories. Useful as your phone and social media are for staying in touch with your community, we strongly recommend you give yourself regular breaks from them. This allows you to connect with yourself and your own resourcefulness, and in particular with me, your calm inner prime minister, who has your very best interests at heart.*

9. Be confident and trust these awareness- and compassion-based methods for containing the spread of the virus. Stay rooted, grounded and connected with your deeper wisdom. This will allow you to use your thinking faculties in the most effective way and make clear decisions.

10. Be cheerful. Humour and laughter are as infectious as worry and anxiety and an excellent antidote.

Thank you for your attention. For now, I will leave you with the words of Robin Wall Kimmerer: 'I choose joy over despair. Not because I have my head in the sand but because joy is what the earth gives me daily and I wish to return the gift.'

What Helps us Through this? A Collaborative Enquiry

Something was holding me back from penning any further mindfulness-related contributions about the Covid-19 situation. It would seem the obvious thing to do for a publication on 'bringing mindfulness to life'. I've come to the realisation that I have mixed feelings about giving advice. As a trained coach and mindfulness teacher, I practise biting my tongue when I feel the urge to try to fix another person's problems. Too often, giving advice disguises unacknowledged discomfort with the issue at stake, and maybe more is to be gained, for both of us, from allowing the reality of the pain to be felt, at least initially. Empathy and curiosity can create some space around the problem, in which unforeseen insights can come to light. I don't want to take away the satisfaction a person can derive from accessing their own wisdom.

Then it came to me: why not simply ask a few people how they are faring in these difficult times? I would enjoy the back and forth of emails, knowing what is going on for people, a sense of mutual respect and discovery. With connection, or the lack of it, as perhaps the main issue experienced during this time of lockdown, what better way to approach the theme?

So in that spirit I sent out three questions to about twenty people, taken from my circle of friends, family, neighbours and work, covering a range of different circumstances and experience of mindfulness:

1. What do you find most difficult in this time of Covid-19 restrictions?

2. What is helping you through this period?

3. How is it for you, reflecting on these questions?

I received a heart-warming influx of replies. As predicted, one of the most often-cited difficulties, particularly for those with small children, is the lack of contact with extended family. On the theme of connection, lack of physical contact is mentioned, not recognising faces behind masks and living in an atmosphere of fear. *'I've become so wary of others – my hand brushed against the Amazon delivery driver's hand the other day and I recoiled in shock!'* someone shared.

The other common cause of distress is *'doing the same local walks again and again'* and not being able to get out of the city. Not being able to work is also mentioned. For a couple of people, what has been most difficult is regarding the extent of restrictions as *'nonsensical'* and *'damaging to the well-being of so many people'*, particularly children. One person described the *'ominous feeling that instead of Covid being recognised as another sign that a wholesale change is needed in the way we are relating to one another and the planet, it's diverting attention from environmental issues and being used to justify destructive steps.'* I appreciated the honesty of one participant in naming as challenging *'the way in which I'm confronted by myself so much!'*

Moving on to what is helping, it seems to me that it is often directly related to and stimulated by what is difficult. Again, connection is often cited: *'maximising on the hugs that ARE possible'*, *'finding a different channel in the brain'* to connect effectively on Zoom and valuing any kind of meetings, *'with whatever means available and as much heart as possible'*, enjoying the support and fun gained from them. One person mentions writing more actual letters or cards, and even sending small gifts. This reminds me of a satisfying exchange I started with my five-year-old 'Buddha daughter'. I sent her a handmade booklet made of thick cartridge paper and the start of an illustrated story, which we take turns continuing.

Almost everyone writes about contact with nature, feeling *'nourished and recharged'* by it. The monotony of the same walks is alleviated by *'noticing and photographing the things I might otherwise walk past'*. *'If we are willing to lower our expectations (or perhaps our sense of entitlement), this can't but create greater possibilities, in that what we may have overlooked before suddenly becomes something we can find interest in.'*

Lack of control and uncertainty are relieved by keeping up the *'reassuring sense of familiarity'* that comes with establishing some structure and routine. I have a long-standing fascination with the dynamic between sameness and difference, theme and variation, and it seems more people are discovering the inherent opportunities for depth and contentment. I think this is the playing field for any creative endeavour, in the arts, meditation and life generally.

I am particularly interested in several people's struggles and insights with regard to experiencing themselves as less effective in what they can achieve. One woman who had just set herself up in business as a designer found her plans put on hold by the crisis. She wrote:

'The positive is that it has highlighted how I worked too hard at doing things I wasn't invested in, and it gave me the confidence to make a change. It also highlighted how my identity was very much wrapped up in what I did instead of who I am… I have made a conscious decision to change my pace and approach to life and will never go back to the constant rushing around again. The focus now is on what human contact we can have and noticing more what is going on around us, on our own doorstep….'

Another contribution was from a retired psychologist who usually leads a busy life: *'Allowing my life to become simpler and slowing down – though this is also a bit scary – as it feels like I achieve so little. I am resisting the need to justify myself and my inaction – we need to recognise the trauma of it and use a bit of self-care.'* And in the same vein, an artist whose time is caught up with homeschooling: *'not allowing myself to feel guilty when I don't achieve or create as I normally would.'*

The people who have an established mindfulness practice mention how invaluable it is, even if the time for it may be limited: *'Mindfulness practice, including mindful walking, and my mindfulness meetings are helpful. Some online things work so well I want to carry on with them after.'*

My third question within this very small-scale research project was related to the effects of reflecting on these matters. For a few people this is nothing new but something they do 'on a daily basis'. Some mention they enjoyed 'being helpful', which is interesting to me, as making a contribution to others is recognised as having a positive effect on mental well-being. For some people, the process of answering my questions seems to have been valued as an opportunity for deeper reflection. *'I feel guilty because I think of myself as a citizen of the world and always try and educate myself on what is happening to people everywhere. I have been doing this less because I find it overwhelming.'*

I can relate to this dilemma, having felt, during these late winter months in the northern hemisphere, a bit like a bear in a den, wanting to wait it all out. And there is another part in me that can't quite allow that, nudging me on to be informed and active. To keep engaging, as with this little project that brought me closer to the people who participated. I bow in gratitude to our collective wisdom.

Being Fully Alive: Enjoying the Small Things

The same stream of life that runs through my veins night and day
runs through the world and dances in rhythmic measures.

It is the same life that shoots in joy through the dust of the earth
in numberless blades of grass
and breaks into tumultuous waves of leaves and flowers.

It is the same life that is rocked in the ocean-cradle of birth
and of death, in ebb and in flow.

I feel my limbs are made glorious by the touch of this world of life.
And my pride is from the life-throb of ages dancing in my blood
this moment. Rabindranath Tagore

In your own mind, what do you usually think about at the end of the day? The fifty things that went right, or the one that went wrong?... The brain is like Velcro for negative experiences, but Teflon for positive ones. Rick Hanson

I've pulled this Tagore poem out of my mindfulness poetry folder a few times recently, weighing up whether or not to use it for some online day retreat or meditation practice session. Each time I've put it back, thinking it's a bit over the top, inappropriately exuberant for these dark and troubled Covid times, too much of a contrast. People may take offence. Who wants to hear about limbs being 'made glorious' when there is rising unemployment and depression, not to speak of death rates, both directly Covid-related and as a result of postponed or cancelled operations for other conditions, and when the UK's current economic slump is as low as it was during the Great Frost of 1708–9?

It seems easier and more in line with the tone of the times to write about pandemic-related suffering, plastic pollution, global warming, conflict or broken bones. However, if I am honest, I have to admit that I am feeling happy and content overall, and have done so for some time. Yes, the news of what is happening in the world touches my heart, and sometimes I do feel sad that we can't see friends more freely and can't invite them to our new home. But personally, the current tier-4 lockdown restrictions don't really bother me that much. The pared-down lifestyle reminds me of being on retreat; everything is slower and simpler, there is less restlessness, less drive to want to achieve things. Some of my happiness relates to my fortunate conditions, such as relatively good health, a stable and nurturing marriage, finally enjoying the safety of owning our own home and living in a country that allows a large degree of freedom of expression. But more importantly, over the years I have learned how to actually enjoy the good things when they happen, absorbing them into my blood and bones, allowing myself to be changed by them.

There is an art to 'enjoying the small things'. It's not just making a daily gratitude list, although that is undoubtedly a good thing to do. Not just cultivating loving kindness and related states in sitting meditation, although that creates an invaluable base for positive emotion. Not even reflecting on existential truths such as impermanence and interconnectedness, however meaningful and perspective-creating that can be. Tagore's poem pulses with the joy of deep insight, but for most of us such states can perhaps seem a little elusive and esoteric. What has probably had the biggest, practical, everyday impact for me in learning to become happier has come from the practice of NVC (Nonviolent or Compassionate Communication). It's recognising the needs present in any situation, whether they are met or unmet, and feeling tangibly nourished by them in the moment.

For example, as I am writing this, I am thinking of my potential readers and feel all warm and buoyant because my needs for connection and for making a contribution are being met. In crafting these sentences, my needs for creative expression and for meaning are also met. As I bring my curiosity to bear on the qualities of these needs, I sense them as exquisite aliveness, particularly in my heart and belly, as a process of probing, playing and intuiting. I pause for a moment and let these states percolate more fully, allowing them to attract similar qualities. Some joy is lingering just at the entrance to awareness, and I invite it in. And for you, what is it like reading this? Whether you agree with me or not, what needs are being met? Perhaps for learning and discovery, for meaning-making and connection? How is that felt in your body? How is it colouring this moment of aliveness? Take some time to explore – it's worth it! Pause and breathe with it.

We probably all need some encouragement to frequently dwell on positive states, as we have evolved with an inbuilt negativity bias: we simply don't pay as much attention to happy experiences as to difficult ones. Or we are suspicious of too much happiness, as it could make us dangerously complacent or invite the wrath of some jealous gods or neighbours. 'It can't last,' we tell ourselves, 'so better not get used to it.' Doesn't the art of happiness lie in enjoying it without attachment, as William Blake wrote so memorably in 'Eternity'?

He who binds to himself a joy
Does the winged life destroy;
He who kisses the joy as it flies
Lives in eternity's sunrise.

Letting a joy fully in is different from trying to hold onto it, and is an art we can learn to master. The more practice opportunities for 'kissing the joy' we create, the better. Not just for us, but for everyone else and for the planet.

A recent study looking at views on the future of the planet and reproductive choices found that among six hundred people in the US aged 27 to 45, 96 per cent were very or extremely concerned about the well-being of their potential children. Only 0.6 per cent felt positive.[31] Interestingly, these people were not as emotional

[31] https://www.theguardian.com/environment/2020/nov/27/climate-apocalypse-fears-stopping-people-having-children-study

about the carbon footprint of simply having children as they were about their possible fate in a 'hot-house hell, with wars over limited resources, collapsing civilisation, failing agriculture, rising seas', as a forty-two-year-old father wrote.

We can be very concerned about these problems and still contribute to them just because we want to be happy and enjoy life now. If only we could learn how to be truly happy in ways that don't cost the earth, be more modest in our ambitions, more content with what we have. I am in my sixties, and perhaps me harping on about contentment reflects the views of someone who has left behind some of the ambitions natural for a younger person. And yet do we not collectively have to wise up in order to have a future together? We must talk about these matters and encourage each other.

So many healthy sources for happiness remain unmined because we miss them. Some of the greatest pleasure I receive comes from communication with the mindfulness teachers I supervise, all online at present. I relish giving them the stage and tuning in deeply to what they want to express. Mhairi has been teaching mindfulness and compassion courses for many years and said she was a little fed up with what typically comes back from her students: 'I felt so calm, I loved your soothing voice.' She felt tired of playing it safe and wanted to feel the presence of her 'vibrant self' in the present moment, but felt scared of it. 'What is the scariest thing you could do in class?' I asked her. She threw her head back in laughter, and I could sense the sparkle in our eyes dance across cyberspace. She paused and then talked about being less prepared for class and disclosing more of herself. I replayed that moment in my gratitude practice that evening: having the courage to allow ourselves to be ecstatically alive, to live fully connected.

Just making a mental note that something is pleasant, uplifting or beautiful can be helpful. By further training ourselves to stay with that experience, letting the positive thoughts, feelings and body sensations linger, marinating in them, 'we turn good facts into good experiences', as the neuropsychologist Rick Hanson says. One way of doing that is to ask ourselves the question: **what needs have been met by the thing I am grateful for?** This will lead us to qualities such as appreciation or closeness that enrich this very moment of practising. Appreciation and gratitude for these enjoyable moments deepen, and we are less likely to be thrown into reactivity.

Meditation: Ten-Finger Gratitude Practice

Holding one finger at a time, bring to mind something uplifting and nourishing you have recently experienced or that forms the background to your life: your relationship with people important to you, circumstances that give you stability, a piece of good news, a particularly delicious meal, etc.

While you let your finger and your whole being absorb the warmth of the touch, notice what's alive in you associated with the event or circumstance, and allow yourself to dwell in gratitude.

Then ask yourself which needs[32] have been met, and let yourself enjoy the qualities that suggest themselves (perhaps 'belonging' or 'ease'), absorbing yourself in them. Let the breath suffuse your body/mind with those qualities, so that they are felt in every cell.

When you feel you have basked in that goodness enough for now, move onto the next finger. The quality of the experience is more important than reaching ten. There can be some resistance to this practice, and simply acknowledging that can help.

[32] See the Appendix for a list of universal human needs you may want to browse through to help identify the ones that resonate for you.

~ Engaged Mindfulness ~

What we are capable of loving from moral duty is limited, but when we widen and deepen our sense of self... then our protection of nature is felt and conceived of as protection of our very selves.
Arne Naess

Wood Wind: Voicing Our Sorrow for the World

Warmed by autumn light streaming over our allotment garden, I sat in front of the rain shelter, shelling runner beans. It was a particularly delicious and bountiful variety, sweet and stringless, and we'd left a few maturing on the stems to save for sowing next summer. Inside the tough, long pod, each pink-red bean was encased in a delicate white crêpe sheath; it was like opening layers of gift wrappings.

There is always so much to be concerned about and to think about, but right now I was choosing to simply be aware: letting myself be captivated by the moist shine of these precious ovals. I was also aware of listening to the wind rustling through the little wood bordering our plot. The leaves were that much drier from the frost last night, the first of the year, providing a rough texture to that 'wood wind' in the middle of the city.

My mood of appreciation was laced with sadness, most likely linked to a ritual called the 'truth mandala' we had performed in our mindfulness meditation group the night before. Over a couple of months we were taking Joanna Macy's 'Work That Reconnects' (WTR) as inspiration for meditations and exercises helping us to deal with the precarious state of the world. Only one decade left to get our act together, so the IPCC (the Intergovernmental Panel on Climate Change) experts tell us, before runaway climate change becomes inevitable. The curves describing the melting of the Greenland ice sheet are already off the charts.

I wonder, what kinds of thoughts arise in you when reading this? Are you tempted to skip this bit and move on to the next chapter? Do you want mindfulness to give you respite from such worries? Are there parts in you murmuring 'it's too late anyway,' or 'individual efforts don't matter,' or 'it's too difficult to contemplate'?

Such reactions are common and understandable, and they are all fulfilling some purpose, perhaps to protect us from feelings of overwhelm, guilt and impotence. But long before the advent of the mindfulness boom, Kafka said: 'You can hold yourself back from the suffering of the world: this is something you are free to do… but perhaps precisely this holding back is the only suffering you might be able to avoid.' Denying our feelings comes with a price – it leads to depression and passivity, when it is so obvious that humanity needs to pull out all the stops to avert climate disaster.

In our meditation group we are exploring what 'engaged mindfulness' could look like. Steve Kretzmann, the long-time director of the climate policy and action group Oil Change, suggests two approaches to climate action: changing consumption and changing production. It is easy to see how mindfulness training can play a part in changing consumption. We are training ourselves to embrace the more difficult aspects of our inner experience with openness, curiosity and kindness, allowing ourselves to feel sensations in the body and ride out our urges. Together with an encouragement to enjoy the simple pleasures of life, this approach engenders contentment: happily consuming less.

Is there also a place for mindfulness in 'changing production'? For example, what is the part it may play in the worldwide rise of grassroots activist groups such as Extinction Rebellion, who are taking an active, nonviolent stance against fracking, among other government-supported, climate-wrecking schemes? A couple of weekends ago I sang with a choir called 'Protest in Harmony' at an Extinction Rebellion rally in Edinburgh, where I was very pleased to see the speakers include pauses. They allowed silence for the mindful experiencing of feelings such as sorrow and fear in the face of the accelerating deterioration of habitats for millions of species, including ourselves. Such emotional honesty provides the best chance to avoid counterproductive, reactive behaviour.

Giving space for our feelings is an integral part of the 'Work That Reconnects'.[33] The first stage is 'gratitude', then 'honouring our pain for the world', followed by 'seeing with new eyes' (embracing interconnectedness) and lastly, 'going forth' (commitment to action).

[33] See the next chapter for a fuller description of the Work That Reconnects.

The 'truth mandala' provides a ritual space to 'honour our pain for the world'. We had four natural objects laid out in the middle of the group circle: a stick for anger, a stone for fear, dry leaves for sadness and an empty bowl for numbness and bewilderment. One by one, we stepped into the centre, holding one of the objects while allowing ourselves to get in touch with and express our feelings. Held in the safety and acceptance of the group, people spoke with moving sincerity and frankness.

Social acceptance plays a pivotal part in how much choice we feel we have with regard to our environmental actions. My friend Barbara's teenage daughter Iris was taken home one night by a couple of friends, and when they arrived, the house was dark. The friends thought that nobody was at home, but Iris explained that her mum only had lights on in the room she was using at any particular time. 'My mum is weird. She's a vegan,' she added. Barbara often feels on her own with regard to her environmental values and actions, and it is obvious how much she values being able to talk about these matters when we meet. She minimises car use and will cycle the thirty minutes to our house, even if it's raining. Rather than buying Christmas presents, she plans to give books from her shelves.

I think of her when I turn down the radiator and put on another warm layer of clothing – her house is usually a few degrees colder than ours and her family have got used to it. It is all a matter of degrees… The atmosphere is 1 per cent warmer than before the Industrial Revolution, and even 1.5 per cent warmer will bring unprecedented shockwaves of disaster. However, every little action counts – or does it? 'Personal virtue only matters if it scales up,' writes the human rights activist and journalist Rebecca Solnit.[34]

One upscaling method is to speak up, not just politically but with friends and family. I am frequently at a loss about what to do with the huge environmental elephant in the room in conversations with friends. I am getting dissatisfied with general, politely pessimistic discussions about the state of the world. Encouraged by the open-hearted, non-blaming atmosphere of the mindfulness group, I decided to take a risk and open up the subject of flying with another friend who spoke about the fun he had on his recent holiday trips to Canada and Cologne.

I also fly about once a year to Germany to see my family and

[34] https://www.theguardian.com/commentisfree/2018/oct/14/climate-change-taking-action-rebecca-solnit

was sharing my quandary. We had a fairly non-reactive discussion around the complexities of the issue, including the power of consumers to affect change (no new runways without customer demand), and at the end he said: 'But let's face it, I am not going to change my flying habits any time soon.' I decided to push a little further and asked: 'What do you think it would take?' After some silence he said it needed to become more socially unacceptable to fly. History has shown that dramatic circumstances can lead to significant change in what is seen as acceptable behaviour, he said. The Second World War, for example, led to many more women entering paid employment.

Most people don't relish the thought of sacrifice, and one of the most powerful and quietly revolutionary contributions of mindfulness practice is also very enjoyable and grounding: deliberately and wholeheartedly homing in on pleasure, without hanging onto it. If we can make a habit of truly savouring simple pleasures, such as the sun on our face or the smile of a child, we are less driven to fulfil our desires in ways that cost the earth. This attitude of appreciation goes hand in hand with treasuring and expressing more difficult feelings, such as sadness or fear. Avoidance of those darker shades of life blunts our capacity for joy. 'Don't turn away, keep your gaze on the bandaged place; that's where the light enters,' Rumi famously said. Or what about Rilke: 'Quiet friend who has come so far, feel how your breathing makes more space around you. Let this darkness be a bell tower and you the bell. As you ring, what batters you becomes your strength.'[35]

At that time of sadness at the allotment when shelling those beans, I asked myself: 'If this emotional state was a piece of music, what instrument would play it?' It would have been the heart-rending, reedy sound of an oboe, probably an oboe d'amore or a cor anglais, the lower range of the family. The timbre is intense and focussed, yet mellow and subdued, the perfect voice to lament the passing of the good days on earth, the disappearance of species, the loss of plastic-free oceans, the loss of the right to save seeds, the thousands of daily needless deaths caused by economic injustice.

On another day my choice of instrument might be a violin, flowing along bright and easy with the other strings. When allowing the full orchestral range of our emotions, we live through these

[35] From 'Let this Darkness be a Bell Tower', transl. by Joanna Macy.

difficult times with resilience, beauty and integrity. At the end of a concert, the conductor will often ask individual woodwind players to rise and take a bow. Oboists, flautists and clarinettists are soloists who cannot hide in the masses; it takes a particular strength of personality to risk this kind of exposure. Relaxation and confidence arise when we realise, like the woodwind players, that we are always carried by the whole. Imagine a world where more of us make our voices heard, with courage and creativity: speaking without blame, sharing our sorrow and hope for the world.

Hope just means another world might be possible, not promised, not guaranteed. Hope calls for action; action is impossible without hope. Rebecca Solnit

If You Think of the Dark

If you think of the dark
as a black park
and the moon as a bounced ball,
then there's nothing to be frightened of
at all.

(Except for aliens…)

I see this poem by Carol Ann Duffy, the former UK poet laureate, on our bathroom wall every day; it helps me to keep my cool when faced with the many concerns of twenty-first-century living that could easily spark fear. (For example, at the time of writing this, the presidential election of Donald Trump.) In a delightfully whimsical tone the poet counsels us on how to deal with fear: you simply change the way you look at things. There is no absolute reality out there called 'the dark' – why not see it as a 'park'? Similar sound, and still pitch-black, but it is transformed into more familiar, manageable territory, particularly in the light of the moon. We've bounced it up there ourselves, in fact; we've made use of our ingenious magical powers, fortified by rhyme (*ball, at all*).

And then there is a pause, where we hold our breath: has it worked?

It is followed by the caveat *'except for aliens'*, which makes us smile. We find one of our most enduring human traits exposed: how our minds scan for the source of possible danger, more likely than not finding it (even in the most outlandish forms), fixing the thoughts through repetition and believing those thoughts, identifying with them. The fact that we have had some success in using our minds more creatively doesn't mean we have cracked the habit.

Followers of the Buddhist path are familiar with this way of thinking: to the extent we have insight into the construction of our own reality, we enjoy freedom from pain and fear. This can liberate more resources for wise and compassionate action. One way of accessing this wiser perspective is to recognise how we keep our 'self' in a state of painful tension by sticking vehemently to our views and opinions. The more fear, the stronger the views, it seems.

'How are these wise words going to save the world from Trump?' I hear incensed voices saying: 'He is going to destroy the ecosphere in blind, self-interested denial of climate change; encourage racial and religious divisiveness and violence; make the rich richer and the poor poorer. He is far too unpredictable in temperament to be in charge of nuclear weapons!' Can you sense the non-spoken fear behind those words?

The modern global situation is so complex and ambiguous that it is very difficult for anyone to see what's going on and what the right course of action might be. No wonder we are confused and frightened. Politicians seem as helpless as we are to deal with wars in the Middle East, random bomb attacks and so on. According to the documentary film-maker Adam Curtis, we isolate ourselves in 'hypernormalisation'[36]; we 'retreat into a simplified and often completely fake version of the world. But because it is all around us we accept it as normal.' Demonising Trump is part of that. Have a look at Curtis's film, and also the three-part episode 'Imaginationland' from *South Park*, which is a humorous take on the imagination, and questions what is real.

I was talking about the presidential election with a friend, and we were both using our best awareness skills to avoid reinforcement of views and stereotyping. What emerged out of the discussion was that Trump reminds me of my father, who died about

[36] The title of a 2016 BBC documentary by Adam Curtis.

fifteen years ago. He would have said: 'Global warming? Don't see any evidence of it: it's bloomin' freezing! This is a conspiracy led by the Chinese government. I'm not taking any bullshit from anyone. Nobody is stopping me from flying as much as I like.' Does Trump remind you of someone you know?

It would be easy to judge my dad as a bully – and I certainly have done so in the past. And yet his family stood up against Hitler. Being a relatively uneducated man, he prided himself in his 'civil courage' in dealing with the educated establishment. As a teenager I exhausted myself in endless, angry arguments with him where neither of us listened to the other. I like to think that if we were to talk now, I would go about it differently. I would silently acknowledge my own exasperation and need to be respected and listened to, and then do my best to really listen to him.

I would ask him questions, not to trick him, which he would suspect at first, but with genuine curiosity about what makes him tick. He would go on vociferously about the awfulness of a particular politician, and I might ask him: *'What qualities do you want to see in a politician? And what would that give you?'* And who knows, once he felt properly heard he might even return the question. 'Some of what I would like to see in a president, or a German chancellor,' I might say, 'is personal integrity, the courage to stand up for values, life and government experience, open-mindedness, empathy and care for the powerless. An embodiment of that would give me trust, confidence and ease.' My guess is we would probably be in agreement with quite a few of these values. I get a hint of the possibility of the heart-warming connection based on mutual respect that might follow. It opens up the possibility of also seeing Trump as a person, rather than a stereotypical tyrant, and I am less frightened.

(Except,
there may be aliens…)

The Work That Reconnects and Rebellious Mindfulness

Two years later, not a single day goes by without some media tirade related to Trump. In Noam Chomsky's view, Trump's headline-seeking antics are a distraction. 'While everything is focusing on that, the… Republicans, who are, in my view, the most dangerous and savage group in the country, are busy implementing programs that they have been talking quietly about for years. Very savage programs, which have very simple principles. One, be sure to offer to the rich and powerful gifts beyond the dreams of avarice, and [two], kick everyone else in the face. And it's going on step by step right behind the bluster.'[37] Chomsky considers that humanity has never been closer to extinction through nuclear and environmental causes than now, and he sees the Trump presidency as an unprecedented global threat to survival. But there are signs that the tide of public awareness and will to action is turning. Extinction Rebellion and other grassroot movements are gathering pace, with children taking to the streets, letting adults and governments know that they don't believe their lies any more. A large number of peaceful protesters from all walks of life are willing to get arrested during road blockades in order to draw media attention to the urgency of the situation. There is growing insight that this generation is the one that still has the potential to turn things around and avert the worst in terms of climate change; our children and grandchildren will have to bear the consequences of our inaction. At the time of writing this, May 2019, the UK Parliament has just declared a climate emergency, and the chief executive of the UK Climate Change Committee said on Radio 4 this morning that achieving net zero carbon emissions by 2025 is 'possible but brutal'.

Posters advertising mindfulness courses typically show a serenely smiling young woman sitting cross-legged on a rock by the sea, her bare skin softly lit by the rising sun. It can seem a bit of a leap from there to carrying banners in street demos, shouting 'The climate is changing, why aren't we? There is no Planet B!' Jon Kabat-Zinn, who is regarded as the founder of the secular mindfulness movement, sets an inspiring example of bridging the quiet inner and engaged outer dimensions of mindfulness practice. Having been beaten up and incarcerated for anti-war activities in the sixties, he now talks to people in power all over the world. He has no doubts about the social impact of mindfulness: 'If this is another fad, I don't want to have any part of it. If in the past 50 years I had found something more meaningful, more healing, more transformative and with more potential social impact, I would be doing that… This is our work at the moment, to see if

[37] https://nordic.businessinsider.com/chomsky

we can maintain a degree of sanity and recognition of the fears and concerns of those who do not see the world the way we do. The temptation is to fall into camps where you dehumanise the other, and no matter what they do, they are wrong, and no matter what we do, we are right.'[38]

Traditionally, the mindfulness approach to suffering prioritises looking at patterns of the mind rather than at patterns of systemic power structures. It is probably true to say that most people are drawn to a mindfulness course because they long for some reprieve from stress, rather than because they want to be encouraged to reflect on how their consumer habits within a capitalist system contribute to the demise of the biosphere. To some extent, meditators are prone to the psychological avoidance tactics human beings generally employ in order to stay happy, for example by overestimating their ability to control the environment or nurturing an unrealistically optimistic view on the future.[39] But I find that attitudes are changing.

For many years I have been running a three-day retreat with the title 'Coming to our Senses through Yoga and Meditation', and it attracts a range of participants, from seasoned mindfulness teachers to young mothers away from their children for the first time to busy professionals in search of peace of mind. Usually I emphasise the first meaning of 'coming to our senses': seeing, hearing, smelling, touching, experiencing the world through the body, 'getting out of the head' and slowing down to experience the nourishment of the moment. But more and more I introduce elements of the second meaning of the term, stopping to consider 'What am I doing?' and re-evaluating the ways we live. I make sure that people are giving their consent to this line of enquiry. 'I find it very confusing to know,' I may offer, 'that some aspects of my lifestyle are unsustainable and create suffering for others in the future, while I continue as usual, in line with most people around me. It's called "cognitive dissonance", and I find it depleting, a burden to live with. Does that sound familiar?' And I will see nods all around me.

It is not easy for anyone to know how to live with full awareness in these difficult and confusing times. It can bring up a mixture of despair and outrage, the urge to do something and the

[38] https://www.theguardian.com/lifeandstyle/2017/oct/22/mindfulness-jon-kabat-zinn-depression-trump-grenfell

[39] Oliver Bennett, *Cultural Pessimism: Narratives of Decline in the Postmodern World*

doubt that anything will be enough. I feel the temptation to bury my head in the sand, and sometimes that's what I will do. I will enjoy my bananas and mangos without a thought of the air miles they have travelled, of who gets rich and who gets exploited, and what chemicals have polluted soil, water and air. But having just written that, I question whether it is altogether true. If at all possible, I actually buy organic and fair trade. However, I can't unlearn my knowledge of environmental and social degradation associated with eating exotic fruit, the burden placed on the earth by my culinary and other cravings, my addiction to comfort. And here it is, the other feeling that is my constant companion, and I am sure that of many others: guilt about being complicit. And not wanting to feel the guilt; just wanting to enjoy life.

If there is one thing my years of mindfulness training have taught me, it is this: I have a choice where I put my mind. So does that mean I think about positive things and avoid the grimmer aspects of life? Every day I remind myself to be grateful for the many nourishing things in my life: a loving and committed husband, trees just outside the window, engaging work. And every day I search my heart for what I am trying to hide: the more difficult feelings and truths.

The environmental activist, author and Buddhist scholar Joanna Macy developed the Work That Reconnects initially during the time of the Cold War, when many people lived in fear of an imminent nuclear wipe out. She sees a 'Great Unravelling' across many sectors of life – political, environmental, social and economic – and describes the emergence of a worldwide response she calls 'The Great Turning', from an industrial growth society that is consuming the planet to a life-sustaining civilisation. 'This is a vast revolution that affects every part of our lives and our thinking, and it definitely comes from – and indeed requires – a sense of connection with future generations.'[40]

Millions of people are part of this 'Great Turning', whether they call it that or not. They make documentary films, organise awareness-raising events, chain themselves to bulldozers, demonstrate on the street, sign petitions, write to politicians, do guerrilla gardening, forego flying, boycott plastic, grow alfalfa sprouts on windowsills, meditate and name what is happening in so many ways.

[40] https://www.independent.com/news/2007/oct/25/eco-philosopher-joanna-macy-interdependence-politi/

'You can't do it alone,' Joanna said in a recent interview, still vigorous in her eighties. 'We need to sit together, grab each other and be together as we even take in what is happening, let alone how we respond. Because alone you get overwhelmed, and it becomes traumatizing. But once people have tasted that they can, with each other, speak about what they see and feel is happening to our world, a number of things happen, in addition to the fact that they fall in love with each other. There is a trust and realization of, "Oh my god, I'm not alone." There is a return to your own self-respect. I think self-respect has not been realized as such a source of strength in the individual psyche. I think people would rather see themselves facing an overwhelming foe with conviction of their purpose, than to be comfortable. People dare to be comfortable with uncertainty if they are in solidarity with each other.'

She developed a series of workshop exercises underpinned by deep ecology and systems theory that help people to work communally, creatively and mindfully with their despair about the world to empower a sustainable way of living with hope and acting with courage. In a series of four steps, which she calls the 'spiral', participants are led through a process of inner transformation. Starting with 'gratitude', we 'honour our pain for the world', 'see with new eyes' and 'go forth' into committed action.

Having received training in this work, three of us are leading a five-day Work That Reconnects retreat on Holy Isle in Scotland. Following Joanna's four-step spiral model and adding some of our own skills and methods, we introduce the participants to guided meditation, writing exercises, communication exercises and creative rituals. What she says is true; I do fall in love with my team and quite a few of the participants, and with the earth. It is disarming to witness each other's tears, open admissions of rage or feelings of impotence, as well as deep concern for the world, all within the safety of the group. Some of the interactive games and rituals take a couple of participants 'way out of their comfort zone', but they are still glad to be doing it. These are ways of reconnecting to older, almost forgotten, almost shamanic ways of sensing the interconnectedness of life, of recognising and breaking free from the species arrogance that threatens our own survival and that of other complex life forms.

Tonight, we are invited to take part in the 'Council of All Beings'; we will be dressing up to become a non-human being, an animal, plant or other element of the natural world, and will speak on its behalf, expressing its concerns. In preparation for the ritual, we are to go on a solitary writing vision quest called the thousand-step exercise. You go for a mindful walk, counting your steps, and stop after each hundredth step to write freely about what you see, hear, sense and feel. At the thousandth step you will find your being, or the being finds you.

I set out that afternoon, after our team meeting, along the stony island shore where dozens of vociferous common gulls are nesting, clearly not appreciating my presence. But as I stand still, my face bent over my notebook, they gradually quieten. I feel close to the new life in these nests, in need of protection. We have a lot in common, the birds and us humans. A little further, sandpipers patrol that part of the beach, their beaks the same orange-red as a distant buoy and a nearby empty plastic bottle, accents in the dull greys of rocks, sea, low-hanging clouds.

At step 800: *Strayed over the fence into the newly planted broadleaf forest. I recognise the signs of past farming: long, parallel furrows where former island dwellers grew their potatoes. I shake out the crumbs from my cereal bar packet, a surprise treat for some ants if they discover it before the next rain dissolves it back into the great carbon cycle.*

At step 900: *Sitting on an ancient, curved stone wall in unfurling bracken and bluebells. The signs of past cultivation strangely add to the experience of wilderness. Encroaching brambles and nettles will soon make this place impenetrable for a hundred years. Till a prince comes by – maybe… maybe not.*

At step 1,000: *I am the sky, the air. I am the atmosphere on this planet earth. My composition has changed dramatically through vast spans of time, influenced by volcanoes, vegetation and breathing beings, from mainly carbon dioxide to increasing levels of oxygen. I enable life and I destroy it. Now the temperature on earth is rising fast, huge amounts of methane from the melting Siberian tundra join with moisture from evaporating seas – it is harder and harder to protect this world. Carbon dioxide is puffed into me from countless exhaust pipes, I turn into a haze of pollutants. In large cities, defenceless lungs inhale me; I make cancers grow, cause immune-system disturbances. I enable life and I destroy it. I carry both pollen and pesticides. I nurture fledgling birds through their breathable eggshells and energise brains that invent wind turbines. I whip myself into hurricanes and flatten carefully built structures in seconds. I want to be stable for life on this planet to flourish, and it grieves me profoundly to become a force of annihilation.*

On the way home I pick up a handful of feathers and make a detour to the centre's utility room to pick up a sky-blue bedsheet, which I fasten with a yoga belt. There is gentle hilarity as we file into the peace hall attired as flowers, flamingos, cows, stones, etc. Someone has come dressed as the sea – a like spirit. We warm up for our appearance in front of the Council of All Beings by experimenting with ways of moving or staying still, as the case may be, and sharing with one or two others what we are about. When it comes to making my proclamation in front of the Council, I sense a new, more courageous, passionate voice speaking through me. Whooshing through the room in a swirl of feathers and blueness, I let go of any me-based awkwardness, trusting the truth of what wants to be spoken. And it is a great comfort and affirmation to hear the voices from the other Council members when I am finished: 'We hear you. Indeed, it is so.'

Five Vows for Protecting the World

'Vows' is a strong word to use, you could also say 'prayers' or 'intentions'. The point is to get all of ourselves behind our aspiration to act in accord with our care for the world, including ourselves. Will we break our vows occasionally? Of course - and it's not a big deal. What matters is the clarity and wholeheartedness of setting our goals.

What would be your 'five vows', or three, or ten? Would you like to close your eyes, right now, and give it some thought? Then perhaps write them down and put them somewhere safe, or secret, or where you see them regularly, as a reminder.

Or you could print out the five vows formulated by Joanna Macy, which I find deeply inspiring and beautiful:

- To commit myself daily to the healing of the world and the welfare of all beings.
- To live on earth more lightly and less violently in the food, products and energy I consume.

• To draw strength and guidance from the living earth, from our ancestors and future generations, and from our brothers and sisters of all species.

• To help others in their work for the world and to ask for help when I feel the need.

• To pursue a daily spiritual practice that clarifies my mind, strengthens my heart and supports me in observing these vows.

Virtuous Cycles

For the Woman
Picking Litter
from the Beach

Her task is vast—in fact
impossible, so why is she
humming as she snatches
plastic bits from drift wrack
all along the high-tide line?

Glum lovers pass, their world
of finite joy already waning,
while her future's filled
with a clear calling ahead
and a clean set of tracks behind.[41]

I've been thinking about the term 'virtuous'. Many Chinese analysts are worried about failing economic growth in their country, which has been hit hard by US trade tariffs. Consumer spending needs to increase, they say, to feed into what they describe as a 'virtuous cycle', in which spending generates more spending.[42]

That expression makes me laugh. I'm delighted to hear that shoppers are making different choices: that they are buying fewer new smartphones, watches, homes and designer handbags; that they travel less and have fewer children. Their motivation is probably pragmatic, neither vicious nor virtuous, but it gives me hope

[41] By Kim Stafford, from his poetry and prose anthology *Earth Verse* (Little Infinities, 2007).
[42] *The Guardian*, 19 January, 2019.

nevertheless. It is so clearly self-destructive to act as if the planet has limitless resources.

I've been wondering what would constitute a truly 'virtuous cycle'. Unlike a few centuries ago, these days we don't like to be called 'virtuous'. The term has implications of 'virtue signalling', doing something 'worthy' mainly in order to be seen as such by others. But looking at the root meaning, 'having or showing high moral standards',[43] it could be a recipe for happiness. (Of course the 'high' bit can be tricky – a hook for our inner judge, always on the lookout for opportunities to lower us.)

Research has shown that in terms of physical, emotional, mental and planetary well-being, it pays off to orient ourselves around moral principles or values, such as being ecological, altruistic and frugal. On days when I eat fewer sugary and fatty foods, I feel healthier, more content and confident. Not eating meat gives me a sense of peace. I enjoy doing an extra turn of housework, picking up the odd piece of litter or phoning a lonely person. Nobody else needs to know; it just feels wholesome, quietly joyous and connected.

And while it hurts a little, I still say 'no' to the temptation to fly to some warm, exotic holiday destination, even as many of my friends do so. Why does it hurt? Well, there is a part of me that doesn't want to miss out or be left behind. I want what others have and do. I want what is displayed in stunning images in magazines and on social media. Being left behind is a primal mammalian fear and one the advertising industry capitalises on. But as soon as I stop and mindfully enquire into my actual experience, I discover that beneath the (relative) sense of deprivation there is a quiet satisfaction from knowing that I have acted in accordance with my values. I feel good knowing that suffering in the world has been reduced through my action, or inaction, in some unspecific yet certain way. That sense of caring connection and integrity, once I allow myself to fully sense these qualities in my body/mind, provides an intrinsic reward. Feeling the satisfaction of 'leaving a clean set of tracks behind', as the poem above says, feeds the 'virtuous cycle', and I am more likely to resist the next cunningly calculated lure to spend money on things I don't need.

This doesn't mean that I don't give in to cravings. I do. I adore dark hazelnut chocolate, easy Netflix entertainment at the end of

[43] Oxford Languages

a long day, browsing eBay for particular clothing brands. I do my best to be mindful and not judge myself too harshly. Craving is a powerful desire for something that we hope will assuage the pain of a perceived lack, and the Buddha saw it as the root of suffering. Absorbing the benefits of virtuous actions alone is not enough to break the spell of deficiency. To the degree that we are in the grip of an illusory, separate, unchanging self, we will feel isolated and wanting.

Fritjof Capra, a pioneer of deep ecology and systems theory, talks about the way life on this planet has always organised itself into communities. The first bacteria that came into being three billion years ago immediately formed communities, and the same has happened at every stage of evolution or, more accurately, co-evolution since. The oceans, the atmosphere, plant and animal life: all arose interdependently.

Some say that climate change is eliciting a change in human consciousness. Twenty years ago my husband and I attempted to set up an ecovillage. It didn't work out as a housing project, but it grew a community and sowed the seeds for compassionate communication (based on Marshall Rosenberg's Nonviolent Communication (NVC)) and systems thinking. I remember interminable planning meetings in which the internal tension between the lone, heroic leader/artist/meditator in me and the patient participant in a slower, complex, emergent group process was excruciating.

Over time – and with the help of a variety of contemplative, body-based and communicative practices – transformations took hold, and I now feel tangibly different in group situations. It's hard to describe: it feels as if I am looking at people more softly, from the backs of my eyes, and speaking from the relaxed back of my body or from a sense of intertwined roots in the depths of the earth. I have come to enjoy and trust this sense of connection much more; my leadership style is more participatory, and I am quickly alerted to any internal reaction and retraction into self-protective, dualistic, right/wrong thinking. Our planet cannot survive as a life-friendly environment without more of us awakening to the truth of our interconnectedness, which leads to gladly curbing our desires and following, in Stafford's words, our 'clear calling'. Community is the key to this transformation. I see not just a solitary woman picking up rubbish from the beach but a community of happy litter-pickers, building up a rhythm aligned with the roll and rumble of the rocks and the sea.

'But is it not too late?' some may question. 'What's the point if there is only a 5 per cent chance, as some scientists say, that we manage to remain below the critical 1.5-degree global warming limit?' Joanna Macy thinks it is a distraction to think in terms of hope or to put too much weight on optimism. I need to put my mind where I want it to be and do what is right, as part of a community.

'We must make time for community,' Macy said during the 2019 summit on climate change and community organised by the Global Ecovillage Network, 'and take on this nourishing of each other. What we have got is the raw edge of consciousness together; we are 100 per cent present now and don't ask for reassurance and certainty.'

For me, one of the most powerful experiences of transforming consciousness from fearful separation into a joyful sense of interconnectedness that leads to action is to partake in the Work That Reconnects. Last year, after spending the best part of a week co-leading a WTR retreat, I felt better about myself in relation to the world than ever before, and so did the other participants. Yes, there will be cataclysmic changes for humans and other living beings, yet I am confident I can live through this time with integrity, love and courage.

The Problem of Plastic and Being Complicit

The door to the mind should only open from the heart. Joy Harjo

My fingertips are covered in hundreds of tiny circular scabs not visible to the naked eye. A magnifying glass reveals these little moon craters; you probably have some of them too, the result of accidental pricks from some rose or blackberry picking. In my case, they come from the impact of a tiny needle, shot out of a pen-sized hand-held device. I draw back the spring and press the button, with the intention of drawing blood. The red drop is absorbed by a test strip inserted into a device that measures the sweetness of my blood. If it is too sweet, I need to give myself some insulin; if not sweet enough, I need to ingest some carbohydrates. This has been happening six to eight times a day for the last seventeen years, since I was diagnosed with diabetes, and it is about to change. I have now received a device that measures blood glucose levels continuously, without the need for finger pricking. It means much better control of my condition and enhanced life expectancy. I will spare you the details of how it works; the point I want to make is about something of a perhaps more general concern than type 1 diabetes management: it is about plastics and the state of our environment.

All the devices I just mentioned are made of types of hard plastic that, unlike organic substances, don't biodegrade. My new bits of equipment involve even more robust, seemingly indestructible types of plastic. Every two weeks I unleash a bagful of beautifully designed, sophisticated medical gear, complete with tiny batteries, into the environment. I struggle with that: knowing that what keeps me alive poisons the environment. The instruction manual says, in tiny print, that the 'product should not be disposed of via municipal waste collection' and encourages me to seek out advice from the manufacturers, clearly passing the buck. Basically, there is no 'away' into which these kinds of plastics can be thrown. They don't get eaten by microbes and reintegrated into the cycles of life. They do get broken down into smaller and smaller pieces, a process that can take thousands of years in anaerobic conditions like a landfill and much faster in the ocean, under the influence of sunlight. A plastic bag can degrade in the course of a year, but into what? Into tiny, toxic microplastics, chemicals such as bisphenol and PS oligomer, that get taken up into the food chain and make whales infertile. If they do have calves, they can die of poisoned breast milk. A clear link has been shown between autoimmune diseases (such as type 1 diabetes) and plastics.[44]

The health of our beautiful planet and that of all our bodies and souls is one. Every action matters. Where do we put our single- (and multiple-use) plastics, and how do we dispose of our uneasy feelings? There is no 'away' for them either; they litter our inner landscape and block the natural flow of well-being. Human culture seems to be inherently flawed. How can it be that something as practical as a wellie, as astonishing as a parachute, as handy as a water bottle, as glamorous as a tube of lipstick, as connecting as a mobile phone turns out to destroy the basis of life on earth? We

[44] https://pubmed.ncbi.nlm.nih.gov/30590961/

can't go back to making things out of wood and animal skin – or can we? Would we not do the same things all over again, rejoice in the invention of a metal saw, praise the enduring heat of a piece of coal, revel in the lightness of a waterproof jacket, breathe a sigh of relief at the arrival of an insulin pump?

Of course, there are signs of improved, less damaging technology: compostable plastic bags, biodegradable nappies and plant-based water bottles. We hear of certain bacteria that feed on some plastics. Laws are passed, banning conventional, single-use plastic bags in supermarkets. I try to let these items of positive news in to redress the internal balance. But the uneasy feelings remain, not just with regard to plastics. The effects of our reckless over-use of the earth's resources stare us in the face: the daunting bubbles of methane rising from warming oceans, more extreme weather events that are destroying lives and homes. The novelist Annie Proulx expresses this zeitgeist well: 'I believed the rumbling climate shift caused an invisible, unspoken malaise in people the world over. Something was wrong and they felt it in their bones, even those remote in the ice, among the lianas, in thin high air, even in denying cities. Climate crisis exposed the bad wiring in the human brain.... People may have sensed that their god-given right to wrest a share of wealth from the natural world (the source of every fortune) was passing from "unlikely" to "sorry, it's over".... I was afraid then and I am afraid now.'[45]

How do we live with fear, as we witness the ravages of war and pandemics, cyclones, floods and wildfires? For some, being on some kind of spiritual path can give the sense that despite everything, we are moving towards the light; we are blessed with the potential and occasional glimpses of glorious Awakening. More than ever, this path must include a compassionate heart as the governing principle. US poet laureate Joy Harjo puts it like this:

The heart is the smaller cousin of the sun.
It sees and knows everything.
It hears the gnashing even as it hears the blessing.
The door to the mind should only open from the heart.
An enemy who gets in, risks the danger of becoming a friend.[46]

[45] https://www.theguardian.com/books/2020/oct/24/how-do-we-become-a-serious-people-again-dave-eggers-annie-proulx-and-more-on-the-2020-election
[46] From 'This morning I pray for my enemies' by Joy Harjo

Dealing with the News

'The most radical thing any of us can do at this time is to be fully present to what is happening in the world.' Joanna Macy

'Let all sorrows ripen in me.' Shantideva, Buddhist monk

If I buy a paper it tends to be on a Sunday, and I'll read it over breakfast. It's a kind of ritual that evokes childhood memories. I was brought up in in a small town in Westphalia, Germany. The *Ruhr Nachrichten* was delivered to the door every day of the week to most households in the neighbourhood. On a Sunday morning we'd buy several kinds of 'Broetchen', rolls from the local baker. The breakfast table was lavishly loaded up with boiled eggs, sliced cheeses and sausages, tomatoes and cucumber, jars of jams and honey, all looking special on the Sunday-white tablecloth. Apart from the Broetchen there would be wholesome pumpernickel, thin slices of moist, dark rye bread. A Bach motet would be playing softly on the radio. And we'd share out, more or less peacefully, the sections of the paper among the family.

I should know better by now, but I still seem to expect comfort from the weekend paper, including a vague sense of belonging to a family of other readers. There is also a sense of entitlement to a treat. Together with my Sunday breakfast, I want the paper to be a reward for a week's work. Relishing my cinnamon porridge with yoghurt and home-made rhubarb compote, I read the headlines of *The Observer* telling me that, by the year 2020[47] there won't be any Arctic ice left in the summer. This is much sooner than the worst-case scenario predictions made by the Intergovernmental Panel on Climate Change in 2007. The consequences will not just be suffered by the poor nations in the Southern hemisphere but by the rich nations too. We will be waiting for a gap in the rain while others cry for water. I lean back in my comfortable chair and turn the page.

Japan is committing to be nuclear-free by 2040, but that's not good news either, according to the analyst Mark Lynas, because they use coal instead of nuclear, which puts more dirty, climate-warming gases into the atmosphere. Green energy would only be

[47]The article in *The Observer* was written in 2017.

able to provide 1 per cent of the country's energy needs, he says. Well, I don't have the figures to refute him, but somehow that doesn't seem right.

Then there is a small paragraph under 'Financial': British wind farms now provide three million homes with light and heat, more than 10 per cent of the total of the national grid and growing. Yes, that's more like it. I only dipped into 'Financial' because of a bird's-eye photo of a traditional Indian grocery market, rows of green vegetable stalls tended by dark-haired sellers and buyers dressed in orange, yellow and white saris, forming a pleasing pattern; relaxed, natural, so unlike shopping centres. But for how much longer will it be possible for Indians to trade their own food, as the government has just opened the country's retail sector to foreign supermarkets? Tesco has had its foot in the door since 2008, in a joint cash-and-carry venture with the Indian conglomerate Tata.

Feeling slightly dazed, I carry my empty bowl to the sink and switch the kettle on for some Fairtrade coffee. I take bread out of the fridge, close it while cutting a slice and open it again to replace the loaf, thus keeping the cold in. Saving energy. The light in the kitchen is different from usual: Arctic blue, filtered through long banners of safety netting hanging from the scaffolding up the side of the house. How quiet it is, after the builders' clamour and commotion all week. I put down the margarine lid and stand still for a moment. The wind makes the soft blue plastic ripple in continuous waves, mesmerising, the sort of thing you can watch for a long time. How am I feeling? If I am honest: sad and rattled by the many difficult issues brought to the fore. Vaguely guilty. And helpless. Somehow it doesn't feel quite right to continue my cosy Sunday breakfast treat while reading about the abject poverty in other places. I remind myself that I try to save energy at home, cycle, grow some of my own food, abstain from holiday flights, support Greenpeace, even tried to set up an ecovillage. I know that there is no point in feeling guilty. And yet it is hard to live with the awareness that many aspects of my way of life actually contribute to others' suffering. As I spread marmite and tahini onto my toast, I can't help feeling the tightness in my gut – it's not good for the digestion, trying to process the news and porridge at the same time.

And still I persist, turning the pages of the paper, hoping for something more palatable to go with my piece of toast. The Duchess of Cambridge has been photographed topless by some French journalist with a long lens, and the pictures were published by a French magazine – I end up reading the whole page. The photo shown is of course not one of the offending ones; that's left to the well-behaved British nation's imagination. What we see is a close-up of Kate's face surrounded by a white veil, with the hint of a hard-done-by tightness around the mouth that doesn't spoil her loveliness: half Madonna, half bride. In the shop, I saw this photo on the front page of every newspaper. It's like being told a fairy story, all of us together, sitting comfortably. We want our chronically stressed emotional systems to be soothed; we want an escape from the tensions that come with knowing too much and doing so little.

It is getting clearer that what I need is not more facts and examples about economic decline, resource depletion, climate change, social injustice, war, the mass extinction of species, etc. The question many of us in the rich word carry around in us is: how does one cope with the inescapable knowledge that the style of life we consider normal contributes to the suffering of others, now and in the future? Or, as Joanna Macy and Chris Johnstone put it in the subtitle to their book *Active Hope*,[48] 'How to face the mess we're in without going crazy'. The 'pivotal psychological reality of our time', they say, is living with the uncertainty of whether our civilisation will survive, whether conditions on this planet will continue to support complex forms of life. Which stories do we tell ourselves within this precarious situation? Stories that will make it possible to conduct 'business as usual' or stories that may galvanise new possibilities of consciousness and action?

*

My friend Emma is a documentary film-maker and head of film and TV at Edinburgh College of Art. She tells me what weighs on her: a Syrian film-maker friend has been arrested by the Syrian police. He has been outspoken against the regime, and she is very worried about him. 'I am so sorry for his young wife,' she says in a subdued voice, pressing her hand on her heart. 'At least I can email her that we are campaigning for his release. It's heartening

[48] Joanna Macy and Chris Johnstone, *Active Hope, how to face the mess we're in without going crazy* (2012).

that so many well-known artists have signed the petition. But I hate to think what they may be doing to him.'

I've just seen a documentary called *Five Broken Cameras* about the Palestinian/Israeli conflict. Images of armed police moving in against defenceless civilians come back to me, flooding in, dry yellow earth soaked in blood, screams of anger and pain. It seems more real now, as I sense Emma's concern for her friend, somewhat less removed.

'The political situation has brought out an enormous strength in him, a passion. He is so selfless – I am really impressed by him. I have seen this in other people who live in oppressive conditions. The situation seems hopeless, and they become bigger people in response.'

'Like Chris, the guy with MND.'

'Exactly.'

Emma has almost finished a documentary called *I Am Breathing* about the dying process of a young man with motor neurone disease, who wanted to be filmed in order to raise funds for research into the currently incurable disease. His grandfather and father died of it, and he wants his son to live.

'He became more and more radiant as he grew closer to death. Everyone wanted to be near him. And he had a great sense of humour, otherwise the whole project would have just been too grim. You need that.'

The conversation turns towards what kind of meditation practices we do. Anapanasati, mindfulness of breathing and the tonglen practice have been her mainstay for many years. Breathing compassion into the suffering world. But she often feels conflict between her work and her more contemplative needs.

'Eleven-hour days to do the uni work sometimes, all that admin, and on top of that my own work. Too little time for meditation. But it's what feels right to do, right now.'

I am still getting my head and heart around the challenge of staying open, aware and undistracted in the face of the extent of deplorable happenings in the world.

'I guess it is part of your job to be faced with a lot of difficult issues, with a lot of suffering. How are your students dealing with that? I imagine they would be keen to tackle climate change and other ecological issues.'

'Well, they're not, actually. We did a module on environmental topics and the theme just didn't catch on. Not quite sure why. They say they have been brought up with climate change, it's an accepted fact. It doesn't grab them like it did our generation.'

'This reminds me of what I read in *Active Hope*,' I say. 'There are two reasons why people don't speak about the big problems. One, they dismiss it as overblown; there is nothing to worry about really. Two, they see progressive decline as inevitable and not worth talking about.'

We look at each other without words, allowing ourselves to be seen in our vulnerability and concern, staying with it all, with an open heart. Breathing with the pain, the fear and knowing we are not alone in it.

Meditation: Healing Self, Healing the World

It is my experience that the world itself has a role to play in our liberation. Its very pressures, pains, and risks can wake us up – release us from the bonds of ego and guide us home to our vast, true nature.

The biggest gift you can give is to be absolutely present, and when you're worrying about whether you're hopeful or hopeless or pessimistic or optimistic, who cares? The main thing is that you're showing up, that you're here and that you're finding ever more capacity to love this world because it will not be healed without that. Joanna Macy

The following meditation includes all the elements of the spiral of the Work That Reconnects, starting with 'gratitude', followed by a merging of 'seeing with new eyes' (we are connected to larger forces of compassion) and 'honouring our pain for the world' (breathing it into our hearts where it is transformed by compassion). It concludes with a dedication to 'go forth' and play our part in the 'Great Turning'.

Get into a comfortable position, either lying or sitting.

When you are ready, open to a sense of gratitude for the many conditions that make it possible for you to be here and meditate, starting with the earth as your physical support. Connecting with a sense of safety in the place you are in.

Developing a tactile appreciation of some of the things we usually take for granted: you are clothed in a way that gives you comfort and protection. You don't have to experience hunger and thirst. Letting that sink in.

Now bringing to mind people who have encouraged you, taught you and cared for you, including any meditation teachers. Allowing your heart to be touched by their guidance and support, letting it feed your confidence.

What else have you experienced in the last twenty-four hours that you feel grateful for? Perhaps some nourishing or fun encounters, a sense of accomplishment in work, contact with nature...

Giving yourself permission to feel the satisfaction of these experiences, helping you to become more and more settled in the body and in the present moment.

The breath itself can be a cause for gratitude, the simple pleasure of breathing in and breathing out.

Appreciating the very feeling of gratitude and other qualities that are closely related: openness, warmth, connectedness. Allowing yourself to be deeply nourished by these feelings as your breath flows through you.

If there is any resistance to dwelling in such positive states, become curious about it and do your best to befriend it, and include it in the meditation.

Now starting to develop a sense of being part of a larger field of generous and loving energy. Perhaps you visualise it embodied in the arc of a compassionate smile in the space around you, or you imagine and feel the presence of another loving and wise being, which could be a figure like the Buddha, Kuan Yin, Gandhi, Joanna

Macy or someone else you know personally. Someone ready and willing to embrace suffering, to let 'sorrow ripen' in them in order to touch the pain of others with insight and love. You don't have to do it all on your own. Let yourself be bathed in their radiant compassion.

Now, if it feels right, invite this compassionate presence into your breathing heart.

This loving presence willingly receives any pain, together with the in-breath, right into the heart, and breathes out healing towards anything that needs to be healed.

Perhaps there is a part of your body that gives you cause for concern in some way, a niggling ache or an acute pain? Let the breath reach that part, touching it with tenderness, just as it is, and receive the pain or discomfort with the inhalation into the heart. Imagining a stream of healing energy, like white light perhaps, pouring forth from the loving heart with the out-breath, bringing ease and comfort to that afflicted part. In- breath: acceptance; out-breath: healing. Settling into this intimate way of being present with discomfort. Trusting that radical, loving acceptance brings transformation and allow it to happen naturally, organically, breath by compassionate breath, not pushing for any particular outcome.

When you feel at ease in this compassionate way of breathing with difficulties, you may want to bring to mind a difficult situation in your life, something that tends to lead to an inner state of constriction. We are not trying to solve the problem right now, but simply acknowledge the difficult feelings, the way they are felt in the body: fear, sadness, confusion, a sense of separation, whatever it is. Let them be received into the compassionate heart with the inhalation, and allow yourself to feel the relief of the full acknowledgement of just how difficult this is.

The tender, wise presence in your heart knows what you most need in this difficult situation: it could be something like connection, trust, being heard and understood, a sense of self-worth, ease and relaxation, self-expression... So with the exhalation, those qualities start filling your awareness. Perhaps you could silently whisper the words that most resonate, repeating them like a mantra, letting their healing energy reach every recess of your physical, emotional and spiritual being with the outgoing air.

Staying soft and relaxed, non-attached to any particular outcome, perhaps even non-attached to a sense of self versus other, while holding the intention of healing.

Then letting some images of pain and suffering in the world arise: the plight of immigrants, exhausted after years of hardship, struggling to find a place of safety. Traumatised people in war or natural disaster zones, injured or separated from loved ones. Tortoises ensnared in fishing lines, chickens in cruel confinement. Being open to what comes to the surface. Breathing in the suffering of all those beings and breathing out what they need: safety, peace, justice, respect, whatever it is that soothes their suffering. Staying grounded and centred in your body, feeling your embeddedness in an immense field of compassionate energy. Joanna Macy says, 'The heart that breaks open can contain the whole universe.'

Allowing those images to fade and coming back to a sense of sitting in the present moment, absorbing the impact of the meditation. Just bearing witness to the suffering in the world like this is a powerful contribution to healing it. Aware that you are not on your own in this 'Great Turning' towards sustainable, life-enhancing ways of living, you may also ask yourself: is there a small and doable action that I could undertake? Take some time to visualise yourself engaged in that task, while staying in touch with the expansive heart presence developed in the meditation.

Earth in Crisis: What Is Our Calling?

Preparing food is not just about yourself and others. It is about everything! Shunryu Suzuki

A few years ago, while visiting my family in Germany, I stumbled into an interactive art installation in Düsseldorf conceived by Tomas Saraceno[49]: a giant spiderweb hung high under the ceiling of a large exhibition space. In small groups, visitors were allowed to enter this vibrating netted construction that manifested and magnified the movements of every person. It was all about the tensile connection between us; the vigorous bouncing of someone at the other end of the room threatened to throw you off your feet, and you needed to place your trust in your body to find its balance. With arms and legs spread wide, we looked like spiders. It was all quite out of control and not without some danger. Sometimes I lay down, which felt safest, and just felt the perpetual pulling through the muscles, tendons and fascia that cover the interior of my body in a similar web-like way. Collectively, we went through periods of relative stillness then stirred again into turbulence. It was a beautiful, slightly unsettling experience of surrender into interconnectedness, and I still feel its visceral echo – as if my body and brain were massaged into remembering a lost paradigm of belonging to a greater whole.

'All our relations' is the governing wisdom of indigenous tribes throughout the world. The African philosophy of *ubuntu* postulates 'I am because we are'. In this way of thinking and feeling, past and future generations, animals and trees, matter as much as present-day humans. There is some pride in being a person that future generations may think of as an ancestor worthy of veneration. You would think twice before cutting down a tree, not to mention a forest. If there is going to be a 'seventh generation' of the modern global population, how will they think of us, partakers in a mad rush towards devastating climate collapse? As they survey the landscape, will it show the barren aftermath of clear-cutting, plagues of insects and wildfires? Or might there be lush forests, teeming with diverse, mutually responsive life, all connected through immense mycorrhizal fungal networks that distribute water, beneficial microbes and nutrients, as well as

[49] https://studiotomassaraceno.org/in-orbit/

storing carbon? The science on healthy forestry has been clear for decades; isn't it heart-breaking that we still lay waste to nature in the interests of convenience and short-term profit? Forest ecologist Professor Suzanne Simard, whose courageous and inspired work led to the term 'wood wide web', writes movingly about her scientific and personal journey in her recent book *Finding the Mother Tree: Discovering the Wisdom of the Forest.*[50] I was particularly struck by the pain she felt having to poison alders and birches in a controlled trial to work out whether pines grow better with or without those neighbours.

Many contemporary analysts agree that we are the generation that may yet be able to turn things around. Globally, there has been cataclysmic upheaval, happening now, not in some future decade or century, and denial is perhaps harder to maintain. How can we utilise this opportunity, and what role can mindfulness play? It is clear that structural changes alone, although essential, will not be sufficient. We must evolve the ways we perceive ourselves within our universe, moving from being controllers to collaborators, from exploiters to nurturers, from isolated egos to partakers in wholeness. For centuries we have been shaped by capitalist, patriarchal and colonial forces. The influence is all-pervasive and affects us in ways we don't fully understand and of which we may be mostly unaware. Domination is driven by fear, and this fear is written on our frowning faces and hunched shoulders; it fuels addictive consumption and leads to a sense of isolation, meaninglessness and depression-related illnesses. We must seek change in real and deep ways; words alone are not enough.

This was also discussed recently by Dr Thomas Bruhn, research group leader of A Mindset for the Anthropocene[51] at the Institute for Advanced Sustainability Studies in Potsdam, Germany, and Laureline Simon, founder of One Resilient Earth.[52] Both are mindfulness practitioners and I found their dialogue relevant, honest and insightful, worth quoting at some length.

Thomas talked about participating in meetings with decision makers who 'would talk about these things very intelligently, but no real action emerges out of it as long as people do not find ways to connect meaningfully… In the end an approach is chosen when it resonates at both experiential and scientific levels, and when

[50] Knopf, 2021.
[51] https://www.iass-potsdam.de/en/research/mindset-anthropocene-ama
[52] https://oneresilientearth.org/how-can-we-transform-mindsets-to-address-climate-change/

it is introduced by a person whom we trust and who shares our values in terms of diversity'.

Laureline added that ' "mindset transformation" should entail: engaging in the process without knowing where it takes us, not tying ourselves to old ways of thinking, continuously grounding oneself in the moment and questioning the underpinnings of our thoughts and actions [...] and if we acknowledge that our actions are largely about controlling even when we wish to find "solutions", repair or heal, then how do we rethink agency? What would a more relational and less controlling approach to agency entail?'

Similarly, Thomas feels that 'science is helping me through the crumbling of my old mindset and emergence of a new one. Complex systems science addresses emergence, self-organisation and more fluid relational dynamics that differ from mechanical systems. That's exactly what I observe in my own becoming. But I also feel I "understand" less and less, and feel how scary it is to let go of belief systems and assumptions that I have lived with for decades.'

Laureline offers reflections on collective trauma and safety: 'Part of my spiritual practice is to ask myself in any situation, what am I afraid of and how do I feel safe? [...] The question of safety is both about the inner feeling and the outer conditions. How do we maintain safe conditions for humans to develop within planetary boundaries? And can the development of our inner safety help us deal better with volatility, ambiguity and uncertainty so that we may not have to rely on existing structures to feel safe?'

What is the pattern of the changes that are starting to happen? Thomas thinks that 'the earth is reflecting back to us that it is reaching certain limits and that the path we have been taking has no future. But I don't see a kind of breaking, more of new relationship patterns emerging here and there, connecting and forming new resonance fields. At some point it will have become a totally different system, just the way natural systems transform [...] And this gives me far more hope than a revolutionary shift from an old system to a new one, according to some binary logic. It means that if we stay present in this relationship and grow a full acceptance of that relationality, different relationship patterns emerge in us and around us. [...] I feel confident that life will find responses that are different from anything that we can imagine in our human form.'

Laureline replies: 'I can totally relate. At the same time, when I get in that mind space, it becomes almost futile to work for the preservation or the restoration of life on earth. Do you feel the same? What drives you in your work if your mindset is transformed to the point that you no longer feel a need to preserve, heal, or restore human or non-human life?'

Thomas: 'That's a very good question that I run into regularly. What comes to mind is that I love the world that I experience right now. I love the people that I know. I love forests. I love the oceans. And I am here to learn how to act out of that sense of love and care for the world. Which doesn't say that I could ever save anything, probably not, but I feel that process is meaningful, regardless of how much I personally achieve or whether this particular form is meant to persist. I see beauty in this existence.'

I recognise my own development in much of what is expressed in this dialogue, particularly in:

• Cultivating humility as a teacher and communicator: letting knowledge emerge from collective, ground-up, experiential processes, rather than presuming myself to be the expert who tries to control the situation through top-down presentation.

• In mindfulness enquiry situations, or any other communication, being alert to and letting go of the desire to fix, to impose my solutions, out of some discomfort with tension.

• Engaging in trauma work: recognising elements of it in personal, intergenerational and collective spheres, and bringing healing by befriending the protectors and exiles. I find Internal Family Systems[53] a most effective tool for that. There are no 'bad parts'.

• Taking time for daily mindfulness, compassion and insight practice, with confidence that it is essential for the prospering of the whole.

• Enjoying the beauty of nature and the arts, immersing myself in them as much as possible.

• Trusting that every little effort counts. Relaxing and enjoying the process of the re-emergence of 'we consciousness'.

But it's not an easy task to change our ways, even if we have

[53] https://ifs-institute.com/

some clarity on the level of rational and emotional understanding. Creatures of habit and seekers of comfort that we are, it is only too easy to acquiesce to the non-creative ways of living prescribed by modern market forces. 'Consume doom doom doom' goes the refrain of an activist song,[54] but it's no good being too gloomy about our complacent and destructive ways either. Ursula Le Guin says, 'To use the world well, to be able to stop wasting it and our time in it, we need to relearn our being in it.' So what will help us to joyfully 'relearn our being' in the world, hopefully leading to more planet-friendly behaviour? In his poem 'For all', Gary Snyder pledges 'allegiance' to:

one ecosystem
in diversity
under the sun
With joyful interpenetration for all.

Snyder's call is fuelled by being out in wild nature, in the 'rustle and shimmer of icy creek waters'. Since access to such wilderness is limited for most of us, perhaps a meditation will have to do as a means of stimulating our felt sense of belonging to all life, through deep time.

I invite you to slowly read through this reflective meditation on 'Touching Deep Time'.[55] I suggest you take time to close your eyes between the paragraphs and let the words and images resonate through your being.

Meditation: Touching Deep Time

Sit comfortably and begin by giving your hands a brief massage. Then let one of your hands rest nestled in the other, perhaps supported on a cushion, for ease in your shoulders and neck. Sense the aliveness of that hand, the warmth and weight of it, how it tingles with energy.

Remember some of the things the hand has done today: it helped you get clean, dressed and fed. Perhaps it has done things for others too, like written a text or an email, caressed a child or pet, or waved

[54] https://soundcloud.com/campaign-chorus/xr-songs-consume-doom-doom
[55] Loosely based on the 'Cradling' exercise in the Work That Reconnects, where the hand and other limbs are held by another person.

to someone. But now, nothing needs to be done. It can simply rest, cradled by the other hand and held in kind awareness. Feel your breathing in this quiet spaciousness, and let your breath be a thread throughout this exploration: breath, hand, heart.

Now we start to reflect on the relatedness of our hand to the extremities of other living beings; how in the course of evolution, this hand has been a fin, a wing, a paw or a hoof. It's an ever-changing story of theme and variation. This hand is our link with sister dolphin and brother horse.

In this lifetime, in our mother's womb, this hand grew together with our heart, from the same stem cells. At some point the hand resembled the paddle of a turtle. At birth, this tiny hand, with its perfect little fingernails, was able to firmly grasp and hold on to its mother's hair.

Soon this hand began to explore the world, playing with food, with toys, learning which things are dangerous, too hot or too sharp. Held by other hands, you learned to walk. Encouraged by others and drawn by natural curiosity, you learned to draw and write, to shuffle cards. This hand worked out how to tie a shoelace, hold handlebars, use a hammer, deal with money, perhaps how to play an instrument.

This hand has changed its appearance over time. Once it was incredibly soft and smooth, and gradually has become drier and more wrinkled. It has been shaped by immersion in the great elements, earth, water, fire and air. Its form, scars and callouses tell stories of its encounters with the world. So much life experience of giving, of creating, are evident in this hand.

Now we use our imagination to reach out with our hands to other beings, starting with a person dear to us. Holding their hands, we allow our care to flow from the heart through to them and receive their love in turn. Perhaps your breathing supports this exchange of loving energy, of giving and receiving with your exhalations and inhalations. Hand – heart – breath.

Now we bring to mind a relative stranger, the postman perhaps, or a checkout assistant. In our imagination we are allowed to hold their hands, and we connect with their humanity. How their hands have gone through the same journey of evolution as ours, have learned skills for living in similar ways, have sought connection with others just as we do. Not so many generations ago we shared an ancestor. Like us, they need love, friendship and self-expression in order to thrive.

If it feels right, we now allow our hands to reach out and hold the hands of someone with whom we have some difficulties. Is it possible to connect with their humanity too? Can we sense their vulnerability, just like ours? The longing to be seen, to be respected, to be in harmony? Staying in touch with the give and take of our breathing and a felt sense of deep-time relatedness, we can perhaps allow some of our small-self fears and resistances to melt away.

In this way, in your own time, let yourself hold the hands of human beings of any age, colour or gender and perhaps particularly those who experience fear and pain. People in hospitals, prisons, refugee camps, wherever your imagination takes you, letting love communicate itself directly into their being. You may want to include other mammals, birds, fish, trees and the life in the soil, including the vast fungal networks connecting all plants.

Let your hands touch beings that are no longer alive, some of the extinct species, that 99.9 per cent of all that have ever lived on earth: grandmother mammoth, grandfather saddle-backed giant tortoise. Rest in your breath and open to that awe-inspiring sense of connection with life through deep time.

And finally, reach out into the future, making contact with our children's children's children, to the seventh generation maybe. Let them know you care.

Now let yourself rest and breathe, simply letting life flow through you.

For me, such explorations lead to an experience of awe and a re-evaluation of my place on the earth, feeling myself to be both more and less precious. An image arises of my skeleton ossified in stone, like an ammonite, discovered by some future being.

Anchored in Strength and Compassion: Stories that Transform

I've learned to trust my actions. I offer the beginning of a suggestion, or a recognition of what's happening, or maybe some kindness. Most of the time someone else will then offer something, and the group will start to shift as we respond to each other. In the middle of everything, a 'knowing' comes, not a solution, but a way of navigating the territory.
Liu Yingzhao

Liu Yingzhao is an executive in Silicon Valley, California, who lives in a Buddhist community an hour's commute away. It was on Buddhist Door Global,[56] as part of the 2018 special issue on 'Women of Buddhism' that I read about the influence of her spiritual practice on her work (as Director of User Experience Design at LinkedIn). The quotation above appeals to me; her words mirror my experience of working things out effectively and harmoniously in a group by relaxing the 'me' that wants control and instead trusting in a process of collective emergence. It's heartening to hear stories of others who consciously pursue this respectful, improvisatory and kindly way of going about finding solutions. It's a radically different kind of story from the culturally prevailing one, which paints 'power over' as the best way to achieve an individual's goal.

We are all shaped by the stories that we regularly imbibe, and I want to pay more attention to what I expose myself to. That's part of my New Year's intentions: being more discerning about what and how much I read and watch. Recently I took part in a couple of five-day online retreats in which the leader encouraged everyone to carefully choose the input that we expose ourselves to. A retreat at home highlights the habits we have fallen into, and I noticed a little pang of withdrawal at the thought of not watching

[56] Liu Yingzhao and Buddhist Alchemy: A Silicon Valley Executive Talks Spirituality and Integration (Buddhistdoor Global)

the next episode of the TV series *His Dark Materials* in the evening. The results of even a few days of screen fast (not counting the Zoom screen, out of necessity) were less distraction in meditation, a sense of being more in charge of my life, greater clarity about my priorities and more sensitivity to beauty and enjoyment.

To be honest, I will probably still sometimes consume some of the films and series available on mainstream outlets, simply because it's comforting to fall back on the kinds of stories we have all been used to since childhood: stories of good and evil, envy, revenge and power, misguided ambitions, etc. The settings and costumes can be a feast for the senses, and after a few episodes the actors almost become family. But more and more often I find myself skipping over scenes depicting violence, or I abandon a programme altogether, because it feels like an assault to a mind that is ethically sensitised through meditation.

Finding Liu's story required a little active research, an effort I am glad to have made. It took me to other inspiring women writers who meditate, such as Ruth Ozeki and Elizabeth Lesser. Lesser has written a book called *Cassandra Speaks* that looks at how 'the human story changes when women are the storytellers'. She describes how she came across a box of books left by her son, who had just graduated from St John's College (USA), which is also known as the 'Great Books School' because over the course of four years, every student reads the same hundred books, the 'canon of Western thought'. They were almost exclusively by 'dead white men' and 'shockingly misogynistic,' says Lesser. Then she pulled out a book that had been on the bestseller list a few years back: *The 48 Laws of Power* by Robert Greene. He had synthesised centuries of thought from 'masters of power', such as Machiavelli, Mao Tse-tung and Socrates. Law no 2: Never put too much trust in friends, learn how to use enemies. Law no 4: Always say less than necessary. Law no 7: Get others to do the work for you, but always take the credit. Law no 8: Keep others in suspended terror: cultivate an air of unpredictability.

I wanted to know what the other laws were – maybe the author was unduly selective? I found an animated version of the forty-eight laws on YouTube, listed with almost nine million viewings. Law no 3: Conceal your intentions. Law no 6: Court attention at all costs. Law no 11: Learn to keep people dependent on you. Law no 12: Use selective honesty to disarm your victim. And so on… I don't want to put too much of this content into your mind, even if it is likely to be there anyway, embedded into the deep strata of our conditioning. So this is what individuals in positions of power feed on! I feel sorry for these feared and lonely kings and queens of doomed empires, and sorry for the enormous suffering that follows in the wake of their actions...

What would the culturally imparted stories of power have been if the female principle was also represented? If, in Lesser's words, we would not 'only revere the strong and silent type; it would also be cool to be talkative, brave to cry, noble to feel and relate'. I was deeply touched by a story she tells about a woman called Antoinette Tuff, and I hope that passing it on to you will help to root it into my memory, and maybe into yours too, as an example of courage we can draw on when confronted by violence.

Antoinette Tuff was the bookkeeper at an Atlanta elementary school who prevented another massive school shooting in 2013. For an hour, she stayed with the deranged twenty-year-old gunman in a small room and talked to him, dissuading him from using his loaded rifle on the hundreds of children right outside. Although Tuff had several opportunities to escape, she kept up the connection with the would-be shooter, 'anchored to my own strength and letting empathy and connection lead the way,' as she described later. 'I just let him know he wasn't alone. I kept saying, baby, we don't want you to die today. You belong to us. Just put your gun down. I won't let anyone hurt you.' And that's what happened: the gunman put down his weapon and the SWAT team came in to gently take him away.

Anchored in strength and compassion. That sounds like a good motto for the difficult times we live in. I have my own close-escape story. About twenty years ago, on a wet and windy spring day on the River Kelvin Walkway in Glasgow, I was confronted by a young man with a cleaver who demanded my bag. As it happened, I was on the way to the bank to deposit several hundred pounds, the hard-earned income from months of teaching yoga (this was in the days before direct banking). I didn't want to hand that money over to him if I could avoid it. Interestingly, I had actually approached the man just minutes before, asking whether he needed help, as he seemed lost. Maybe it was this basically kind orientation that gave me the confidence to do just what Tuff had done – root into my strength, stand my ground, and reach across to him by talking gently. 'You don't have to do this.' He ran away as others approached.

Positive stories are around if we know how to look. I have a subscription to the magazine *Positive News* and regularly read about individuals and small organisations contributing to a fairer and more sustainable world. It's by no means only women who are doing their best to help shift the patriarchal and capitalist paradigm through both inner work and activism.We don't have to be special or original in order to play our part. We don't have to be high earners in Silicon Valley, or decorated authors or ordained Buddhists. What we do need is a clear sense of our moral compass and inspiring stories that bed us into a community of like-minded people. We need to find and treasure, tell and retell the stories that truly move us, as well as resist the lure of stories that only propagate greed and violence.

An important element of the stories I keep close to my heart is the wisdom to hold those stories and the views expressed in them lightly. It is not worth falling out with our fellow human beings over different views on politics, religion or COVID-19 vaccination. Important and inevitable as stories are, they are just that, stories. How things really are is ultimately beyond the grasp of words and reason and can only be understood by the heart. So let's keep the heart open.

What are the stories that gladden you and embolden you to be all you can be?

Small Losses and Great Grief

He picks up what he thinks is
a road map, and it is
his death; he holds it easily, and
nothing can take it from this firm hand.

William Stafford[57]

I am writing in the rickety rain shelter on the leafy border of our allotment's flower and vegetable patch. A loud thunderstorm is rolling in, and I watch the big pink cosmos petals getting pleated by the downpour. A raindrop falls heavily onto my writing hand

[57] From 'My Father: October 1942', quoted by Kim Stafford in *Living our Dying*.

– there's a leak in the roofing felt. The weather matches how I feel: salty water behind my eyes, close to seeping through at the slightest escalation.

What's happened? Larry, my life companion of thirty years, left this morning to go on a retreat in the Spanish Pyrenees; no physical contact, no phone or letters, for over four months. During the retreat he will be ordained as a Buddhist, the opportunity of a lifetime, much looked-forward to and prepared for, and we have sent him off with plentiful appreciation and celebration. And while the nobleman is off on his quest for the Holy Grail, travelling through pestilence-ridden lands, I am left behind, much less heroically, to guard the castle.

No doubt here too, through necessity, inner riches are to be discovered. To start with, the challenge of dealing with loss. Returning to the empty flat after giving Larry a lift to the railway station, intense feelings were coursing through my body and mind. But what were they exactly? Convention says 'sadness' and 'grief' and 'loneliness', words that felt like disconnected stories keeping me in my head. That's not the most useful place to be in a situation like this, my mindfulness training advises.

I was impelled to stay intimately connected with the actual sensations: a tearing in my chest, an overall sense of weakness, of smallness, of vulnerability. Being attentive in this way felt in itself comforting and caring, close. I wanted to feel close. I walked through the flat tentatively, uncertain how to be with myself, what to do, in this new and yet familiar space.

The phone buzzed: a message from a good friend. At our last meeting there had been some tension, and her gentle words released something. I curled up on the couch and started whimpering, like a dog left tied up outside a shop. The same fundamental, mammalian separation pain. That felt good, healing, allowing the feelings to wash through me, not expending energy trying to be stoic. (Even if a small, critical part of me thought that stoicism is a better strategy and I shouldn't be so self-indulgent, and I certainly shouldn't let other people know about it.) I allowed the sobbing to go on for a while.

The deluge at the allotment has run its course, the cosmos and daisies are shining brightly back at the sun again. I pick the last of the raspberries and some dripping, floppy lettuce for dinner. Back at the flat, I almost see my beloved through the half-open door to his study, facing his computer: the familiar shape of his back, his over-grown hair needing a trim. I almost see his posture, which speaks of alertness, commitment, open-heartedness – spreading his nets wide, as a poet, publisher, tai chi teacher and activist. His presence, mysteriously, is more palpable and clearer than when he was here 'in person' a few hours ago. Maybe the right word for my feelings is the Finnish 'haikeus', which captures both sadness and gratitude, apparently. Or maybe there is no right word, just this searching for some way to give the feelings a home.

Ah, grief, I should not treat you
like a homeless dog
who comes to the back door
for a crust, for a meatless bone
I should trust you.
I should coax you
into the house and give you your corner,
a worn mat to lie on,
you own water dish.

Denise Levertov[58]

The last project Larry completed before his departure was the publication of a book which he co-edited called *Living our Dying*.[59] Richard Holloway's endorsement summarised it: 'It will not only help you to die a good death, it will strengthen you to live a good life.' I dip into it for some guidance in this transitional moment. It covers many variations of the basic human experience of loss and grief. My husband isn't dead, he's only gone for a long time, but who knows? Any parting with anyone could be the last moment of seeing them alive. The upheaval of losing something or somebody we thought was essential to our lives and dreams is universal. Perhaps you too have had a recent separation or bereavement, and your grieving is still vivid and raw. I hope something in this text will speak to you, soothe you and give you strength.

You may also experience and recognise 'Great Grief' – a feeling that rises in us as if from the earth itself – about the state of

[58] From 'Talking to Grief', quoted by Jane Wilding in *Living our Dying*.
[59] https://playspacepublications.com/living-our-dying/

the world. The decline of life-supporting conditions on our planet is becoming more and more apparent, and the spread of wildfires and destructive floods figure constantly in the daily news. The world is 'sick, lost, harrowed, broken, toxic, violent, and full of shame' in Em Strang's words.[60] Grief educator Ted Bowman finds that people experiencing loss or heavy anticipatory grief 'yearn for words and acknowledgement'[61] – perhaps from poetry such as this, by Maya Angelou:

Now if you listen closely
I'll tell you what I know
Storm clouds are gathering
The wind is gonna blow…

Alone, all alone
Nobody, but nobody
Can make it out here alone.[62]

Certainly the presence of others, on the page or otherwise, helps. When writing, I am imagining you reading this; I am not alone, we are sharing the burden of grief, and I can feel uplifted by that. But even if not for the eyes of others, expressing how we feel helps to process difficult states of mind. There is a well-known saying in therapeutic-writing circles: if it is not mentionable, it is not manageable. After the suicide of her brother and her father, Jayne Wilding found that the 'grief was difficult to speak of and I felt very alone. Like Anne Frank, my diary or journal became my friend and confidante'. What also helped was 'to connect with nature and the natural cycle of the year, where death has its place.'[63]

In his deceased father, Kim Stafford recognised 'the predicament of being human. He was denied certainty, but blessed with a sense of engagement with what comes.'[64] I take heart from that and celebrate the opportunities that lie ahead for me, over the next four months in particular. They are wise words for dealing with our 'Great Grief' too. Let's keep engaging and sharing!

[60] From 'If I die sooner rather than later….' by Em Strang, in *Living our Dying*.
[61] https://playspacepublications.com/living-our-dying/
[62] From 'Alone' by Maya Angelou.
[63] 'After Suicide', by Jayne Wilding, in *Living our Dying*.
[64] In *Living our Dying*.

PART III

~ Are Rituals Necessary? ~

Mindful Christmas!

Even the most secular-minded practitioner of mindfulness will be affected by this ritualised time of the year that is Christmas. It evokes childhood memories and family customs, and there are choices to be made: you could spend it in a fog of general over-consumption or you could find ways to stay clear, conscious and connected and actually enjoy it more.

I wrote my PhD thesis on ritual, many years ago, and my curiosity in this area has persisted. The title of my thesis was 'Gestures towards emptiness: an exploration of ritual with reference to Buddhist tradition and innovation'. Shortly after starting this arts-based research, I discovered I had type 1 diabetes, the start of a lifetime of injecting insulin. I became interested in the ritualised elements of diabetes management, particularly pricking my finger up to ten times a day to take readings of my blood sugar levels. I made artwork using handmade paper as blotting paper for the remaining blood on my fingertips. The phenomenon of repetition, one of the hallmarks of ritual, grew into one of my enduring fascinations.

Repetition reassures us on a visceral level of our place in an ordered universe. Doing the same thing at the same time, like the first cup of tea in the morning, puts the world to rights. This could either be a largely unconscious act, keeping us in automatic mode, or it could be the cue for waking up into a more sensory and alive presence. How does the tea actually taste this morning? Mindfulness fights the dulling aspects of repetition while using it as the structural bedrock for regular practice that liberates insight and creativity. 'Mindfulness isn't difficult; we just need to remember to do it,' Sharon Salzberg famously said. We forget, again and again, but slowly our brains rewire, and we are able to stay present more of the time. Life appears in brighter colours and sharper outlines, and we feel more intimately connected with it. So we do our best to remember. More recently I resolved again to take the pricking of my finger as an opportunity to drop into more heart-based awareness, thus using to my advantage a daily and often wearisome reoccurrence.

During my training as a mindfulness teacher, the question of ritual was raised; the trainer was quite adamant that there was no place for ritual in secular mindfulness. What she may have meant was that there is no collective recitation of articles of faith, no chanting of hymns or mantras, no wearing of special garments signifying ecclesiastical hierarchies. But for a sharing at the end of the course we were asked to bring an object that symbolised our inspiration for living mindfully. We sat in a circle around a central arrangement of flowers, rocks and lit candles. One by one, we talked about our aspirations and then placed our own little stones, photos, alarm clocks, etc. into the mandala. A poem was read. In the ensuing silence there was a palpable sense of significance and connection.

Rituals are a brilliant vehicle for discovering and celebrating our values, thus keeping them alive and consciously operational in everyday living. They are also a direct and powerful way to strengthen a sense of belonging and community. It would be very hard to maintain connection with one's values without at least occasionally being mirrored by like-minded people. I think that rituals are therefore going to play a significant part in the flourishing of the mindfulness movement, and it will be interesting to see what forms they will take. I am part of a small group of people, mainly former students of mine, who meet weekly for meditation and take it in turns to offer some light facilitation. The meditation usually leads into some verbal sharing, with a lovely sense of spaciousness and deep listening. Not a meeting passes where there isn't some expression of appreciation and gratitude for what we are doing. Is this just a habit or edging towards ritual? The traditional chanting of the 'Refuges', which is part of Buddhist meetings, has the same purpose; it is essentially a way of acknowledging the value of the meeting and ensuring its continuity.

The festive period may or may not provide suitable conditions to clarify and celebrate our values as mindfulness practitioners. Christmas has many functions: it is a holiday, an opportunity to strengthen bonds with family and friends, a religious festival or a retail opportunity. On a mythical level it is similar to ancient solstice rituals, celebrating light and new life. The birth of a child connects us with hope during the darkest period of the year; it reminds us that there are beginnings inherent in endings. Human beings have arrived at such understandings about life and death with or without religion. One of the central tenets (if that is the right word) of the mindfulness movement is that by embracing our inevitable pain and fears, we create the conditions for the arising of well-being. Dark inner states of mind can shift: when we live mindfully, we will eventually enjoy new-born, shining, infectious inner gladness and joy.

Reflections: Celebrating Mindfully at Christmas

How does Christmas fit in with your religious (including atheist and agnostic) background?

Which values spring to mind as important during this time (such as celebration, enjoyment of the moment, kindness, generosity, stillness, letting go, acceptance, etc.)?

How could your mindfulness practice help to strengthen and express such values during the festive period (particularly perhaps with regard to care for the environment and communication which truly connects)?

What rituals of your own making could move your heart and those dear to you in the direction of more peace and contentment? (We have tied ribbons with celebrations and wishes onto fir branches, for example, saying them aloud for everyone to witness.)

How can the giving of presents become a practice of mindfulness? (I am aware, for example, of how I can fret about getting a present right in order to feel good about myself and look good, rather than taking it as an opportunity to simply feel my love for the person and put myself in their shoes. Holding such inner processes in kindly awareness is a gift of kindness to myself.)

There is a well-researched link between happiness and meaning. The merriness of your Christmas depends on how close to your deeper values you steer. Rich food, alcohol and extravagant presents probably don't quite hit the spot for most people, if they are honest.

The season can throw meaninglessness, old psychological wounds or family conflicts into stark relief, and it can all feel like hard work. And being alone at this time can be equally, if not more, challenging. It is emotionally draining to try to be merry when, underneath the jokes, we sense unhappy voices from the past, aching to be heard.

Perhaps the festive season has some elements of retreat for you, with a deliberate withdrawal from some of its more distracting elements. My husband and I tend to be at home between Christmas and New Year; we switch off the phones, refrain from digital communication, don't watch movies and meditate more. Doesn't sound like fun to you? Try it – even for a day or two.

Meditation: Adoration of the Inner Baby

Here is a little gift to yourself and your inner baby to soothe any old pain. You just need to make ten minutes of quiet time for yourself.

Sit in a comfortable and alert posture. Let your body and mind relax by tuning into some present-moment awareness of physical sensations, including the breath, or sounds.

Now remembering what it is like to hold a baby or a small infant. It could be a baby you know or a general sense of a small human being. It could also be a pet. Feeling the sensations of holding it close to you, the warmth, the weight of it, perhaps noticing a scent.

Becoming aware of the emotional response in you. Caring for new life is a natural, innate part of being human, so most likely you will feel some warmth and tenderness. Where do you feel it in your body? Your heart, eyes, lips, hands?

If you find it hard to contact such feelings right now, you may want to bring to mind another kind and compassionate adult you know, smiling at both you and the being you hold. Or you could visualise an image of a loving, smiling face, perhaps even a traditional painting of a Madonna and child, if that works for you.

Being aware of yourself as a caring and compassionate adult, you can now sense the being you cradle to be yourself as a baby. Sense where the baby wants to be and how it wants to be held – close to your heart maybe, or in your lap? Letting yourself breathe in its sweet baby scent and feel its beating heart. Maybe it wants its head to be supported and its cheeks gently stroked? Maybe it wants to hear some soothing sounds?

Sensing the mood of this little you – is it quite happy and content, or feeling hungry, lonely or scared? Communicate to this little being, through your tender smile and touch, that all its feelings are welcome, that you love it unconditionally. And that you do your best to satisfy its needs, for nourishment, comfort, safety, love. What else does this little you want? Play, perhaps?

Letting yourself be enchanted by the loveliness of the baby you: its innocence and beauty, its vulnerability. Is the baby really getting it - revelling in this adoration? Are there perhaps others around too, welcoming this little one into the tribe?

A baby cannot be expected to have to do anything to be loved; just being there is enough. In the same way, you can now let go of any further doing or striving and simply continue to sit, in natural, easy, open-hearted awareness.

Reminders of Meaning

In the repetition and order, ritual imitates the rhythmic imperatives of the biological and physical universe, thus suggesting a link with the perpetual processes of the cosmos. Barbara Myerhoff

A few years ago, I attended a conference at Samye Ling Buddhist Centre on 'Mindfulness in Society' which was broadly concerned with how mindfulness can retain its 'heart' as it becomes more and more accessible to people. The setting of a secular conference in a monastery run along traditional Tibetan Buddhist lines was a contribution to the theme in its own right. The temple and surrounding architecture felt like an enshrinement of spiritual values.

I was moved by a film shown one evening about Akong Rinpoche, the former abbot of the monastery, who made headlines a few years ago when he was brutally murdered. Escaping the Chinese invasion of Tibet, then working as an orderly in an Oxford hospital, he then founded Samye Ling in the early sixties, together with his close friend, Choegyam Trungpa Rinpoche. I was impressed to see how many lives he touched through the many charitable humanitarian aid projects he set up, from soup kitchens in Glasgow to education for orphans in Tibet, Nepal, India and Africa. He literally touched the heads of thousands of devotees with blessings as he regularly travelled through these countries. I was curious: what gave him the strength to bounce back from his traumatic experiences? He had seen many of his friends and family perish under appalling conditions: after crossing the Himalayas through uncharted mountain passes, they had lost all their possessions, run out of water and food, and many of the few who made it to India died of diseases their bodies could not cope with. Somehow he managed to continue the spiritual journey he was destined and groomed for as an officially recognised, incarnated, high-ranking lama. What made it possible for him to stay on track, to fulfil his life's purpose in circumstances that must have been so utterly foreign and disorientating?

Spending just three days in this Tibetan monastery in Dumfries and Galloway, the very fabric of the colourfully painted buildings and the dignified presence of the monks and nuns in their maroon robes suggested an answer to me: he continuously and ritually affirmed his life's purpose. In Mahayana and Vajrayana Buddhism, the basic motivation of a practitioner is called the 'bodhicitta'. At its core it is the dedication to work for the benefit of all beings, based on recognition of the mysterious interconnectedness of all life. Filling one's heart with that connection to larger life allows an unburdening from the fears and traumas of the small, deluded self that believes in its separateness. This orientation is kept alive by regular study, meditation, art and devotional practice. For hours every day, the monastics chant verses that celebrate the spiritual achievements of enlightened masters and reiterate the pathways towards liberation. For most visiting Westerners, the bone-shaking sounds of large drums and trumpets and the hundreds of images of Buddhas and Bodhisattvas may be strange, remote and exotic. For Akong Rinpoche, it may have been what healed the trauma of emigration and kept his altruistic orientation alive over the course of his remarkable life.

I study the paintings that cover every available space in the temple; they evoke a pantheon of spiritual teachers and archetypal Buddha figures, painted in a style that follows very clear rules and leaves little room for individual expression. The figures are seated in blue skies, and something about the clear lines and empty spaces opens my mind, a recognition of being held in something bigger – kind and wise. But they also look foreign, and I am sure that despite my own studies of Tibetan Buddhism over the years and the presence of similar images in my home, much of their original meaning and subtlety is not accessible to me.

In the afternoon we have a workshop on engaged Buddhism, and the voices of the teachers are almost drowned out by the mighty drum sounds from the temple next door, where the monks and nuns are chanting ancient verses to Chenrezig.[65] It's as if each beat is saying 'Let go! Let go! Stop identifying with yourself. Surrender to this bigger reality we are all part of and partake in this wave of compassionate activity.' Without strong reminders of our true vocation, we get distracted and lost in our mundane routines and rituals, operating largely on autopilot.

Meditating is sometimes compared to making art. If I bring to mind the faces of some famous artists, like Joseph Beuys or Louise Bourgeois, what strikes me is the expression of unremitting alertness and curiosity in their eyes. Most artists are committed to their daily stint in the studio, whatever else may be going on in their inner or outer lives. Their work is ruled by repetition and ritual, as it is for most of us. But inherent in making art is a conscious enquiry into the dynamics between routine and fresh presence. 'Where is this work going? What is it that matters here?' The artist asks these questions within a framework of experience, history and formal constraints. From time to time she steps back,

[65] The Bodhisattva of Compassion in Tibetan Buddhism, also known as Avalokitesvara.

asking existential questions that risk bewilderment, uncertainty, being lost. She gets into the habit of questioning her habits, while valuing them.

Routines and rituals help us make meditation part of the fabric of our lives. Just as the artist puts on her special apron, primes the canvas and lays out the brushes, we get out our mat and light a candle or a stick of incense. It's not helpful to ask ourselves every single day whether we really want to sit down and meditate or do our mindful movement practice. We just do it, slotting it in after our morning cup of tea, or whatever other, already established regular activity we can piggy-back onto. Sometimes we are just not so keyed in to our deeper motivation; we may be simply glad that, in the midst of a busy life, we somehow got ourselves onto our cushion or mat at all. Our mind and body might be a bit fidgety or not quite woken up yet. Then it is useful to be able to fall back onto the familiar rituals established at times of greater clarity and vision. Rituals help to keep the momentum going.

Stepping into the ritualised environment for our practice, taking in the images, objects and scents that remind us of previous meditative experiences, helps get us in the mood. Then we go through the stages of mentally entering the meditative space which we are accustomed to. Our routine of setting up our posture and initially settling the mind around the breath helps us get closer to ourselves and how we are feeling. From that intimate self-connection, we may set an intention for this period of practice based on what we sense we need: this could be developing certain qualities, such as calm or kindness or spaciousness. Then we commit ourselves to a practice that provides the conditions for the arising of such states: focussing on the breath, developing kindness or 'just sitting'. Many regular meditators I know are drawn towards more formless ways of meditating. Perhaps this creates a much-needed counterbalance to the target-driven culture of modern living. Giving ourselves permission to 'do nothing' also creates a gentle, open space for the healing of emotional wounds that very many Westerners carry within them from their childhood. With a more open approach to sitting, we are more likely to allow these healing processes as part of an overall journey towards integration, rather than viewing them as obstacles to practice. We become skilful creators of our own selves.

Part of this intention-setting can be reconnecting with the greater picture of why we are doing this, which for many could include an altruistic dimension. One of my recurring intentions is to relax the sense of self and let go into a flow of connected energy through space and time. For me, the image or statue of a Buddha or Bodhisattva or a mantra provides a beautiful and direct link to such aspirations. At times these symbols resonate deeply within the mystery of my mind, at other times they are a bit flat, without that inspiring dimension of depth. I consider cultivating symbolic links to the ineffable as essential to my progress and am very curious about how this dimension of mindfulness training can be made accessible to a wider public who are not explicitly aligned to a system of religious beliefs.

When I offer retreats for a non-Buddhist population, I am often in a quandary about placing Buddhist images on a small central table (which I keep calling a 'shrine', despite my best intentions, just as I occasionally lapse into referring to the practice room as the 'shrine room'). On a recent retreat I put a postcard of the serene face of a wooden Buddha on the mantelpiece and just a vase of flowers, candles and incense in the centre. I noticed one of the participants, whom I knew as a stout atheist and allergic to rituals, take an interest in the postcard. 'What do you make of that?' I enquired. 'He looks happy,' he replied. 'Calm and confident.' There is nothing quite like a human face to convey emotional states. We are primed that way – as babies, the first thing we respond to is a smiling human face.

Later that day, we performed a collective ritual, where everyone offered something to the shrine table: an object they had brought or found that stood for their intention for the retreat. People presented semi-precious stones, shells, lockets, a sculpture of a spiral. My contribution was the image of the Buddha, and I like to think we were all grateful to have his beauty and serenity to gaze at before and after our meditations, providing an anchor in the ups and downs of our inner experience and seeing in him the qualities we aspire towards.

One of the reservations about rituals that people often voice is that they can become stale and empty of meaning and don't meet their need for authenticity. Two of the hallmarks of ritual in all cultures through the ages are repetition and invariability – they should feel ancient and connected with universal laws. There can be warnings not to tamper with them or they may lose their power. 'Change the unchanging ritual, and there is no point of rest,' Michael Tippett wrote in his opera 'The Midsummer Marriage'. But when one looks closely at how rituals evolve, particularly in societies where they are not written down, one sees that they are constantly changing. That's how they stay alive.

These days, many people make up their own rituals to mark important occasions like weddings and funerals. Likewise, we may want to create ways to support our mindful and compassionate way of life.

Ritual Support for Meditation at Home

Keep your meditation mat, stool, cushions, etc. in a dedicated space.

Set up a little shrine or altar (or whatever you are comfortable calling it) on a little table, box or part of your bookcase. Assemble some images, sculptures and other objects that you associate with your values. These could include embroidered cloth, semi-precious stones, crystals, flowers, candles and incense, as well as less traditional items. (Favourites on my shrine are a tiny blackbird and a shiny red plastic heart. They are my granddaughter's favourites too, and we engage in ongoing trade negotiations. She will bring a little flower as a gift for Tara,[66] who might give her something else in return, like a little jewellery box full of tiny shards of amber.) As you sit down to meditate, gaze at the lovely things on your shrine and let them smile back at you. Different meanings will arise at different times. The face of a loved teacher warms your heart and reminds you of their confidence in your practice. A bird's skull reminds you of impermanence and using this precious moment well. From time to time, shift objects around or exchange them.

Get into the habit of reflecting on your intention at the start of each meditation.

Collect poems or sayings, and keep them in a special book near your place of practice, ready to dip into for inspiration.

Light a candle, at the very least. Like incense and a bell, they stimulate your senses, reconnecting with previous meditations and getting you in the mood.

---

[66] The female Bodhisattva of Compassion.

~ Mindful Communication ~

The Art of Listening

When you talk, you are only repeating what you already know. But if you listen, you may learn something new. The Dalai Lama

To listen is to lean in softly with a willingness to be changed by what we hear. Mark Nepo

When we feel truly understood, something deep inside relaxes: we breathe more calmly and smoothly. We stop **trying** to be heard and understood – such a relief! At times of great emotional intensity we may even cry, so good does it feel to be heard at last. So often, our need to be heard is frustrated by people giving advice, telling their own story, belittling our experience or pitying us.

During the last couple of decades, through my studies of NVC and my work as a coach, I have dedicated myself to cultivating the art of listening. One of the most powerful changes that has made communication satisfying for me has been learning to listen to the deeper needs that are being expressed, often hidden behind judgements. When someone says, 'they are only interested in their own advantage', what I hear is a need for care, to matter and for mutuality. When such underlying universal needs are recognised and their qualities given some space to be felt, then the space between people starts to sing, and hard edges soften.

At the heart of skilful communication are openness and receptivity: a quality of curious presence, the preparedness of body, heart and mind to be affected and to respond. This expresses itself in attention to detail, being non-judgemental, willing to accept uncertainty, not knowing where the encounter is going to go and trusting intuition. Sounds like a description of mindfulness meditation, doesn't it? It could also be an introduction to improvisation, something I studied at music college many years ago and still love to do. Every communication is an opportunity to play together in this spirit of adventure, whether with one other person or in a group.

The first step is observation (or lack of it): how we are so tempted to create a bite-size and biting (i.e. judgemental) story around our experience that then defines our reality. 'My boss deliberately ignores me' went round and round in Jane's head, together with possible explanations as to why this was so. (She was a participant in a course on mindful communication.) We tried to tease out what kind of behaviour would be observed by a camera in the office, the bare facts. We got to: 'My boss's face is neutral, and she mostly interacts with the whole group, rather than with any individuals.' By asking the question 'What did you actually see and hear?' we brought mindfulness into play. A large part of mindfulness practice consists in noticing, through the senses and free of judgement, what is happening in the moment. It activates a calmer way of being, a process that occurs even when being mindful in hindsight, remembering what we saw, felt or heard in past moments. By tapping into that mode of being, Jane created a wider perspective and started to have more of a sense of choice.

But she was still pretty worked up about the situation, still rehearsing her story about what she thought her boss was thinking. She is not alone in getting almost addicted to mental calibrations of this kind. Our big human brains have evolved to do that very thing: assuming the worst about things and thereby keeping us safe (even if not happy). We had another look at her judgement that her boss deliberately ignores her. Though not based on observational facts, it is actually a valuable part of her experience, giving her clues to what she is longing for. If we were to tell ourselves we were 'wrong' for having judgements, we would just heap more suffering onto an already painful experience.

So next we looked at needs: related to her charged interpretation of the situation, which of the many universal human needs that underlie our feelings and behaviour were not met for Jane? Recognition? Wanting to matter? Care? As we were making these empathetic guesses, Jane was nodding, breathing a little more deeply, starting to smile. Care and warmth – those qualities resonated most deeply with her. The sense of relief about having these needs acknowledged was palpable.

Later on in the session, when we had all had a chance to identify our unmet needs in our own scenarios, we spent ten minutes in meditation, getting in touch with those qualities that touched us most deeply. Peace, warmth, being seen, respect: what does it feel like, in our flesh and bones, when they are present? Can we allow those qualities to suffuse our body/mind, letting them deeply nourish us? Afterwards, Jane said it had felt 'like a treat'.

Later in the course, we rehearsed, in role play, how we might interact with a person we have a conflict with, learning to switch between empathy for the other person's feelings and needs and for our own. Often solutions will arise that nobody had thought of before. This kind of 'work' can be great fun, in the midst of real-life challenges.

In the Spirit of Improvisation

Little improvisation games can also instil that spirit of openness to new possibilities. Some time ago I went to a meeting of mindfulness practitioners interested in academic research. I was invited to say something on the subject of mindfulness and creativity. I decided to start my short contribution experientially, asking people to engage in some movement improvisation. It was a confined space, filled with tables and chairs, with little room for moving about. So we played with two simple forms of physical expression: standing and sitting. You had a choice of how long to sit or stand, changing as many times as you wanted. 'It's about being aware of yourself and at the same time maintaining a broad awareness of the whole group,' I explained. 'Be aware of the whole happening you are a part of, the particular sculptural configuration of shapes in this room at any moment and how it changes. Be curious about what makes you alter your position. Enjoy the quality of listening, including to any possible feelings of apprehension or shyness.' Soon the atmosphere in the room became charged with heightened awareness.

In the reflection afterwards, some people said that they found it easier to be mindful in movement than in sitting meditation, and particularly within a playful context. Others said that they felt not only alert and calm (as in sitting meditation) but also connected to others. We talked about the potential transformation of an element of self-consciousness (in the meaning of shyness or awkwardness) into losing a sense of separate self, experiencing the release of being part of something bigger.

Play and experiencing belonging and interconnectedness are among the universal needs we all share. Being aware is another of these core needs which lead to a sense of fulfilment. When 'needs awareness' becomes part of the training, life opens out in unexpected ways. 'Oughts' and 'shoulds' shrink and lose some of their stifling control, and we meet life's challenges from a feeling of abundance.

Doing Conflict Better

Myres Castle, near Auchtermuchty in Scotland, was built in 1530 on even older foundations and is now used as a luxury wedding venue. Because we know the owners, a group of us are here, at an out-of-season price, for a week of writing. As well as revelling in a luxurious Victorian bathtub, strolling through the Venetian-style gardens and getting deliciously lost in the maze, I sit in a romantic turret inside one of the towers composing this chapter. The name Myres is related to the swamp that surrounded the castle in medieval times, a natural defence that probably played a role in choosing its location. The expression 'mired' means to be 'bogged down' in a difficult situation, so Myres Castle seems to be an apt place for writing about conflict.

As far as I know the castle has never played a significant military role, but one of its towers features a signature 'battlement', a defensive wall incised with square gaps along the top. Ask anyone to draw a castle or build a sandcastle and they will come up with this regular, rectangular design, called crenellation. When under attack, defenders would hide behind the parapet, dart out into the crenel to shoot an arrow and hastily duck back to safety. This basic structure must have been very useful, because one finds it all over the world, going back to ancient Egyptian and Syrian settlements. 'Shoot and duck' is the adrenalin-soaked principle behind trench warfare and any cops-and-villains movie, where the black-clad protagonist inches towards the edge of the wall with a cocked gun in her extended hand. Watching such scenes makes me draw my head in between my shoulders, like a tortoise, shielding my brain and my soft vital organs.

Tortoises and crabs protect themselves with exoskeletons, grazing mammals with horns, cats with sharp teeth and claws, bees with stings, and jellyfish, those strange, translucent beings which will probably survive us all, with the aid of poisonous chemicals. Coral fish withdraw into rock crevices for safety, herrings into shoals, badgers into burrows, and we, having by and large given up on wearing metal suits of armour, cover the earth with concrete walls and barbed wire fences, and bolt ourselves and our property down with security locks. Just as in the animal kingdom, sometimes these defence structures are fake, as with pretend eyes on butterfly wings or faux battlements and burglar alarms. They have become signifiers of power, and at the same time indicate vulnerability.

Sometimes castle entrances were attacked by battering rams, a drama we are familiar with through many movies. But more often, castles succumbed to sieges or 'saps', where the attackers would dig a tunnel leading to the wall. Once the target was reached, the wooden support structure holding up its walls was set alight, and the resulting collapse would bring down the rampart above. Eventually people stopped building 'true' castles, as the ever-expanding defence features made them too uncomfortable to live in. But we all live in residences with varying degrees of fortification, protecting and separating us from the elements and each other. Castle mentality is embedded in our way of life and language, when we talk about feeling 'undermined', for example, or our confidence being 'sapped', receiving a 'battering' or being 'besieged' by unwelcome callers. Conversely, we 'attack' a project or 'conquer' cancer. These are all indications that we are experiencing ourselves essentially as either victims or attackers, trapped in polarisation.

Whether as a result of our evolved genetic predisposition, social and political power structures or personal trauma, most of us operate in this dualistic framework, and our go-to attitude in conflict is that of win/lose. We want to feel and be seen as superior to our opponent, a short-term gain that comes at the cost of continued tensions, which really makes it a lose/lose situation. No wonder many of us are afraid of conflict and avoid it if we can. In group settings we try to stay behind the parapet, safe – but incarcerated in ossified and destructive power structures; safe – but limited in our scope for true connection; safe – but frustrated in our collective, creative flourishing.

The most insidiously penetrating and powerful weapons yet developed by living beings are probably language and thought, and much of those ways of operating are aligned with an older, reptilian survival apparatus in ways that render them just as automatic and instinctive. When we are in a conflict situation with someone, the compulsion to hear blame directed towards us and tell ourselves stories of who is at fault is almost irresistible. Without a strong dose of self-awareness, the tactics of blaming and the compulsion to be right can backfire and create misery for ourselves behind our heroically upheld barricades. On a personal level, we ruminate, lose sleep and become depressed, and on a global level we wage wars without winners. The costs of continuous quarrelling are denuded and barren inner and outer landscapes and joyless relationships.

Over lunch in the Victorian kitchen, formerly used by the servants, under the shadow of the row of bells connected to the upstairs rooms, I discuss this theme with one of the writers on this retreat, John, a former family therapist. How can we loosen the entrenched (another warfare term) defensive patterns of positioning ourselves in close relationships? His work brought him to the insight that the most important way to create trust is to let go of expectations about what people are thinking and wanting, and accept uncertainty. He describes an inner movement towards radical openness, doing our best to let go of the habit of telling ourselves stories about what others' intentions are, and relaxing into not knowing, trusting that new solutions will emerge out of even little shifts in relational patterns.

The NVC trainer and writer Miki Kashtan investigates what makes some of her relationships largely conflict-free. 'So far, I've identified two main ingredients for this magic. One I call the assumption of innocence, which is about a fundamental, implicit trust of each other. In these unique relationships, when one of us does something the other doesn't like, we nonetheless trust each other's basic care; we assume the best about each other's intentions. The second ingredient is that when conflicts do arise, we attend to them. The two aspects reinforce each other.' [67]

NVC has developed some excellent tools for attending to

[67] https://thefearlessheart.org/flow-decision-making-and-conflict/

conflicts.[68] One of the principles its founder, Marshall Rosenberg, articulated is this: 'Conflicts don't exist on the level of needs, but on the level of strategies.' When we enquire with spaciousness, care and courage into the needs and values behind our own and other people's adversarial stance, we will always find common ground, a new playing field from which unforeseen solutions can emerge. Unfortunately, we are often too scared to take the time to empathise with others, fearing that we will lose out, that we will be taken advantage of. Mindfully and compassionately being aware of and managing the arousal of our threat system is an important part of creating peace.

The film *War Horse* (which is based on a novel by Michael Morpurgo and is also a popular musical) offers a heart-rending example of literally touching the common ground between the Germans and the British in the First World War. A horse gets itself entangled in barbed wire on the devastated no- man's-land between the two armies, and soldiers from both camps work together to free it and guide it back to safety.

Some peace-making, and hopefully not just temporarily, is also needed in our neighbourhood. My husband and I have recently bought an elevated ground-floor tenement flat in Glasgow. The flat includes a strip of front garden to the left of the entry stairs. It is almost barren at the moment, and we are very much looking forward to developing it by planting a holly and hawthorn hedge and thereby creating a shielded, bird-friendly seating area for enjoying the late-afternoon sun. We made sure that the garden was in our title deeds, but the wall and railings are communally owned. We think it would make sense to take down the railings, in keeping with several other hedge-framed gardens in the street, including the one adjacent to our new garden. The railings are nothing special: standard replacements of the original ornate nineteenth-century iron fences that were melted down for war machinery.

So I wrote to the seven other flat owners in the building to explain our plans and ask for permission. It turns out that people didn't actually know that the railings are shared property, and although at first the people we talked to agreed with our plans, in the end three people objected. There were two reasons given: first, symmetry. The right-hand garden has railings, with several

[68] See https://www.cnvc.org/for more information on the principles of NVC.

large hydrangea and heather bushes growing through them, and no seating. The second reason is safety: people want to use the railings at the side of the stairs as handrails.

Even as I write this, a part of me is instantly arguing that the railings are too far from the door and too low to be useful for that purpose. That there are other houses on the street that have asymmetric front gardens. And that they can't really stop us having a hedge anyway, so why are they so unreasonable? What's the point of having a railing slowly rusting away underneath it? And it's not as if we intend to shape it into a tall crenellated battlement, shooting arrows at passers-by… As I say, that's a part of me speaking, the 'shoot and duck' part.

Another part is interested in transcending this knee-jerk reactivity in the interest of achieving understanding, peace and harmony. Using NVC tools, first I give myself a little empathy – acknowledging the feelings of frustration and annoyance and also the needs for privacy, autonomy, creative expression and harmony. I invite those qualities to suffuse my organism, allowing them to calm down the threat system. Then I remind myself to 'assume innocence' and put myself into the neighbours' shoes, guessing their feelings and needs. When they say 'symmetry', what need is met by that? Perhaps they are a little worried about the overall appearance of harmony and order? I can relate to that. Maybe they also feel a little envious and would like to be part of the garden creation in some way? Is it about creative expression and inclusion? And being heard and taken into consideration? My heart softens towards them a little more. And then safety. Sure, we are all getting older, and a proper handrail seems a really good idea. I am also wondering whether there is something territorial going on; people may be a bit wary of us, the newcomers, and need some reassurance that we fit in.

I wish I had sent the email after I had written this piece, which helped me to become a lot clearer and calmer about the issue, less in the grip of 'othering', more ready to surrender the internal image of the enemy. The email I sent is probably okay but misses out on some of the finer points of empathetic understanding. I thanked people for expressing their views, said we'd keep the railings, referring to symmetry and safety, and didn't mention the hedge. I imagine future, relaxed, neighbourly conversations taking place over a beautifully maintained border, but who knows what else may emerge.

On the last day of the retreat I climb up into the tower to have another look at the mock battlement. Time has softened the edges, and I take a picture of puddles of soft rainwater left in indentations – maybe birds come here to bathe. Looking out over the well-maintained fields and gardens, I reflect on some of the wonderful aspects of culture that have developed in the protection of the crenellated crowns and battlements of castles: protection of natural forests, research, libraries and compositions of timeless music. And yes, a lot of the wealth accumulation of Scottish landowners, for example, was dependent on the ruthless exploitation of human resources, in particular through slavery.

For better or worse, conflicts are embedded in the DNA of all organisms, shaping the way they look, how they take in their environment through the senses, how they feel, think and try to control an environment of limited resources. The issues at stake are self-preservation, propagation of the species and general flourishing.

Wisdom traditions suggest that softening the sense of a separate self helps us to be less dominated by these preoccupations and achieve true happiness and peace. True, but it's probably wise to expect conflicts nevertheless and aim to get better at them, perhaps even enjoying this dance between withdrawing into safety and softening again into an open-ended relational field, where everyone's needs are celebrated and where life feels a little less like a struggle.

Reflection: From Judgement to Connection

This process follows a classic NVC model of working with difficult situations. There are four steps: Observation, Feelings, Needs and Requests.

Bring to mind a situation that bothers you in some way and where you hold some judgement or blame, either of yourself or others, with some 'oughts' and 'shoulds' and 'shouldn't haves'.

Consider the objective situation – what happened and what you saw and heard – as much as possible free from interpretations.

Connect with your feelings; allow them and hold them in compassionate awareness. This is a difficult situation, and it is normal to feel angry, sad, fearful, etc.

Ask yourself what needs of yours are not being met: to matter, to have respect, safety, etc.

Give some time to feeling those qualities, letting them bring you some ease.

Ask yourself whether there is something you may want to request of yourself or others that is precise and doable, and a genuine request rather than a demand. For example, a request to yourself may be to go through a similar process for the other person in a conflict, in order to develop deeper understanding of what is going on for them. You would then guess their feelings and needs. A request to the other person may be quite concrete, such as: 'Would you be prepared to call me in future when you know you will be late for a meeting?'

~ Silence in the Digital Age ~

Meditation is not so concerned with how much thinking is going on as it is with how much room you are making for it to take place within the field of your awareness from one moment to the next. Jon Kabat-Zinn

For almost everyone these days, engaging with social media is as common a way of communicating as phoning once was. When I was a kid, we didn't even have a landline. Now babies grow up with smartphones: alluring, forbidden toys and their caregivers' constant distraction. I remember when the people with headphones appeared: on walkways, buses, at traffic lights, lost in their own worlds, hunched over their personal device, ears and eyes closed to the world around them. Surely this craze wouldn't last, I hoped, surely it was too obvious what was being lost: the sensory richness and vividness of fully lived experience, the opportunities to connect with fellow beings in the real world. I resisted owning a mobile phone, not to mention a smartphone, as long as I could and was happily ignorant of social media. As a mindfulness practitioner and teacher, there were principles to uphold! Needless to say, I eventually had to cave in. Although written just a few years before the publication of this book, the piece that follows, tracing that transition into the fast-moving digital age, already feels as if it dates from a bygone age.

From Letraset to Facebook

Twenty years ago, I made my own posters with glue and Letraset letter stencils and papered the city with my adverts for yoga classes. Certainly a time-consuming way of doing it; my computer word processor now does a neater job in a fraction of the time, but without the smell of glue and the rustling of paper, the satisfying sense of having made something, holding it up and admiring it. Putting up posters in wholefood shops got me talking to shopkeepers; on the way I'd bump into people I knew and I got some exercise. Now I spend more time in front of this square, bright, humming computer screen than anywhere else on this earth, except my bed. I have not lost the nagging sense that this is a strange, disembodied way of living. But I need to make a living as a self-employed mindfulness teacher, and people need to know I am here.

A few years ago, I had a Skype call with Raymond Lam (senior reader on the website Buddhistdoor Global)[69] to discuss the possibility of offering a regular blog on mindfulness. At some point I mentioned that I had trouble attracting interest for some of my courses. He said that Facebook is now what the telephone and email were in previous decades: if you don't use it, you are off the radar. He wasn't the first person to stress the importance of social media for self-employed teachers looking to promote their work, but something about his calm, youthful, confident presence, sitting there with his headphones in his sun-filled office in Hong Kong, spurred me into action.

Someone had actually already set up a Facebook page for me some time back, but I lacked confidence and conviction to use it. I mentioned the issue to my peer-coaching partner Kanya in Bangkok, and she, bless her, taught me how to use Facebook via screen sharing on Zoom. 'And you need more friends!' she said.

So I put a little effort into getting more friends (being quite unceremonious about it, as seems to be the custom), and this morning, when I log on – oh my god – this influx of interesting photos, tips and films comes rolling in on my 'timeline' and leaves me reeling. This is all so terribly alluring, and I could spend all my time just sitting at my computer absorbing all this info and still feel I haven't done justice to it, or to these people, my newly confirmed friends. I see how addictive and stress-inducing this could easily become. I could be tempted to spend even more of this precious life sitting in front of a screen than I already do. People come to my mindfulness courses to regain sane, sense-based, present-moment perspectives on life, and here I am, engaging in the very activities I tell my students to resist the lure of!

I have become all eyes and brain, with hardly any awareness of body or breath. So I put the computer to sleep and go for a walk along the River Kelvin, just a few steps from our door in Glasgow. It's a bright autumnal Saturday morning with lots of people out and about, many of them with mobile phones in their hands or pockets. There is also the sniffing presence of lots of dogs. Everywhere, photos are being taken: a baby carried in a sling on

[69] https://www.buddhistdoor.net/features/bringing-mindfulness-to-life

mum's belly in front of a red-leaved maple tree. A group of mum and dad with toddler, kneeling in fallen leaves, trying to get the child to smile. Now I understand: these photos are ending up on Facebook, or Instagram, or whatever else is out there! My mind is faltering, witnessing this parade of communities, digital and analogue. Disorientation is taking place: what is real? (Not a bad question to ask.) I am reminded of a cartoon I saw in the paper of a woman with two kids picking blackberries, their outfits and baskets matching the berries. The bubble text says, 'Isn't it fun, kids? It's like being on someone's lifestyle blog.'

A couple of weeks later, I have my own smartphone! Walking along the muddy Kelvin Walkway on a chilly Sunday morning, I am holding it close to my lips. Surreptitiously I am murmuring these words into it, while at the same time trying to enunciate clearly. The phone translates the words, more or less accurately (I've no idea what 'fun and Mel vapour Currys pollution' was supposed to have meant), into text, which I can then access on my computer. Is this the beginning of a new era of effectiveness for me or the beginning of the end of spacious, innocent, direct, technology-free immersion in the 'real world'? I am still not too sure. When I finally signed on the dotted line of the contract, I had the sneaking feeling I was making a deal with the devil. 'I'm sure you made a good one,' my friend Cate wrote back after I texted my new phone number to all my contacts, which the sales assistant had successfully transferred from my ancient, barely used Nokia. Despite having stated my intention not to use my new phone for phoning or texting any more often than before, I already had to deal with lots of replies to my message.

'I predict you will love the camera,' another friend had texted. As I walk along the river, I see the landscape bobbing up and down to the rhythm of my steps, as if my eyes were a hand-held camera. They capture: the pale pink, orchid-like blossoms of Himalayan balsam against the solid red sandstone pillars of Queen Margaret Bridge; exhilarating blue-white sky reflected in quiet black puddles; a skinny little boy hanging on to his week-end daddy's arm while trying to skip. Actually, that's not exactly what I'm seeing; my mind is adding meaning to the raw data, interpretations and stories. In any case, carrying the new phone in standby mode in my coat pocket takes me out of automatic pilot. Any moment carries potential and is also enough in itself. I stroll into a huddle of joggers with a fascinating variety of running styles; take in a dog owner with long, glossy, dark curls, who jerks the lead attached to his curious terrier while mumbling 'sorry' to nobody in particular; catch sight of a toddler in a flashy buggy complete with a built-in holding contraption for his bottle, which for some reason makes me think of the luxury car he will drive in some not-too-distant time in the future.

Ambling along reflectively, with my smartphone at the ready, I feel part of this morning river-walk scene. People are still noticing and acknowledging each other, according to the unspoken rules governing contact between strangers in this part of the world. In Glasgow, people will often smile at each other, but not too brightly and not for too long. I wonder how the quasi-intimacy with widening circles of digital connections will affect these conventions over time. I acknowledge both excitement and concern.

Repeatedly I am drawn to watching the dogs bouncing along the path, gazing up attentively at their owners, racing after balls. There is something reassuringly straightforward about these wagging tails, these noses close to the ground. My spine comes alive in old-brain resonance, wagging a phantom tail. There is a simple joy in being alive – and also to know this. With or without taking a digital snapshot.

Silence

After the final hugs and goodbyes, I walk through the house, closing windows and checking whether anything has been left behind by any of the retreatants. I notice a pale blue, small, squarish book on the lounge table, with the title written in large silver letters: *Silence: In the Age of Noise*. What have my students been reading during this five-day, largely silent retreat, I wonder, and discover that the book was written by a Norwegian explorer, writer and publisher called Erling Kagge. He once spent fifty days walking solo across Antarctica, looking for silence. The opening sentence reads: 'Whenever I am unable to walk, climb or sail away from the world, I have learned to shut it out.' My first thought is: 'It doesn't work like that. Anyone who meditates knows that.'

But I am intrigued nevertheless – this little bestseller has been published in fifty languages, and maybe there is something here for me to discover.

I have the good fortune to stay on in the studio we used as a meditation hall for another couple of days on my own. It's an exceptionally warm early-September day, and the Argyll coast, with its many small islands and promontories, looks spectacular. But after these days of intensified meditation practice, even a common chaffinch at the bird feeder is enchanting to me, and it is utterly satisfying to just sit and do nothing. My heart is content and mellow, feeling the continued presence of the beings I have shared this space with and gratitude for the people looking after this place. I am alone, yet connected; everything I see has a quiet *suchness* about it. I know it will change, but right now, I get what the eighteenth-century Japanese Buddhist hermit monk Ryokan expressed in this poem, one of the few I know by heart:

My hut lies in the middle of a dense forest;
Every year the green ivy grows longer.
No news of the affairs of men,
Only the occasional song of a woodcutter.
The sun shines and I mend my robe;
When the moon comes out I read Buddhist poems.
I have nothing to report, my friends.
If you want to find the meaning, stop chasing after so many things.

The extremity of Erling Kagge's search for meaning is undoubtedly part of the appeal of his book. Living vicariously through the author's chosen deprivations, we shiver with him in below-zero temperatures and enduring frostbite, and smell the stench of the New York underground sewage system he chooses as his three-day route through the city. We intuit what kind of experiences he was accessing: 'One universe stretches outwards, the other inwards.' But does our fascination help us reach that elusive silence in ourselves? Since we can't reasonably be expected to follow him in such dangerous explorations, where does that leave us? He recommends stopping for some conscious breaths from time to time, curbing social media and other input, getting absorbed in small sensory experiences and spending a few days away from the city. Advice you'd find in a mindfulness manual, but he doesn't go as far as recommending the systematic practice of meditation, even if he mentions his own meditation and yoga practice at one point. Would that have lessened the book's popularity, I wonder?

Whether it is a question of exposing ourselves to the rawness of the elements or taking those quests more metaphorically and charting scary, unknown territories in ourselves, most of us don't cherish being too far outside our comfort zones. Kagge mentions some research conducted by the universities of Virginia and Harvard, where people are left in a room for up to fifteen minutes without music, reading material, the chance to write or their smartphones. Most felt discomfort and, in a variation of the study, even chose to do something unpleasant, like giving themselves electric shocks they knew to be painful, in order to reduce the length of their period of seclusion.

Why are we so afraid of stillness? When we turn silent, on a meditation retreat for example, first we may encounter a degree of sadness, related to having been out of touch with ourselves for so long. Perhaps a vague, disquieting sense of having lost connection with our life's purpose, with our deeper values. And we often meet worried and critical inner parts of ourselves: 'You're no good at this! You should try harder!' Underneath those tense, harsh admonitions, we sometimes sense sad and desperate, vulnerable child parts of ourselves, which are longing to be fully seen and accepted, to be loved. Without experience and confidence in our inner communication, as well as awareness and compassion skills, we are afraid to get embroiled in this inner quagmire of unpleasant emotions and will do anything to avoid the experience. Much of the 'work' we do on a retreat is to befriend these internal patterns, understand how they are trying to serve us and feel more at ease with them. Likewise, we do our best to accept the inevitable intrusions of outside noise, coughing, a neighbour's hedge cutting, into the quiet space we have so carefully created.

I would like to think that it would be in most people's reach to learn to be happy and comfortable in their own company and even to relish that fifteen-minute spell of silence in a room by themselves, if it came to it. It just needs regular, committed practice. At the end of the retreat, everyone, even those who were initially apprehensive of the silence, spoke in the most glowing terms of the effects of it (in combination with the other practices we engaged in). How it deepened their sense of intimacy with themselves and enhanced their sense of belonging to the community. How it heightened their sensory enjoyment of the food we shared. How they treasured going off on their quiet, solitary walks. At the end, they were reluctant to switch on their mobile phones again.

I regularly attend retreats led by Vessantara[70] who often speaks of the 'depth dimension of the present moment'. I like the sound of that; it invites me to relax and let go into the mystery of my experience right now. There is nowhere else to go. From here, the future will take care of itself. It can happen anywhere, as I am typing this and you are reading it. Stop for a moment and listen to the silence that surrounds your experience. There is so much more silence than sound, just as there is so much more space than matter in the universe.

Shutting anything out (as Kagge repeatedly advises) is a noisy thing to do; it keeps us on a level of vociferous reactivity. It's often an impulse born of aversion, wanting things to be other than they are, and activates our threat system: fight, flight, freeze. For inner silence to have a chance to show itself and sweeten our lives, a shift has to occur: into an expanded, open and inviting way of perceiving. We listen with tenderness to what is happening, both outside and inside ourselves, and the listening opens into spacious awareness. Whether or not there is thinking ceases to matter. All experience is welcome. End of rant.

Ranting, of course, also interferes with inner silence. Anything that tries to bolster up our own sense of a separate self, in opposition to the 'other', has that noise-aggravating effect. On the retreat I mentioned the concept of 'selfing', the fear-driven process of asserting an independent sense of 'me and mine'. It is interesting to observe it coming and going during the day. At times we are happily absorbed in an activity or resting, without much of a sense of self, and then suddenly something is perceived as a threat and we start contracting around some imagined kernel of selfhood. I gave an example of how it kicked in for me on the retreat, related to decaffeinated coffee. I don't drink 'real' coffee, and when I observed more and more people who normally drink

[70] www.vessantara.net

the 'real', heartrate-raising stuff also going for the decaf, I got a little anxious, because there was only one packet left to last the retreat. A bit embarrassing, but there you are.

The next day, at the beginning of our mid-morning practice session, I found three sachets of decaffeinated coffee on my meditation cushion. I enquired (since I am allowed to speak) who had made that delightful offering. Everyone shook their heads, denying responsibility. 'It must be Robert then,' I said, as he hadn't arrived in the room yet. But it wasn't him either, as he made perfectly clear, non-verbally. During our final evening meal, the silence formally over, someone asked whether the decaf case had been resolved. 'I bet it was Mary,' she suggested. 'What makes you think that?' I asked. 'Because she is so kind and generous,' she replied. 'I think it was Thom,' someone else suggested. 'Why?' 'Because he is so modest, he would never tell.' 'No, it was Helen, I'm sure. She always has such good ideas.' Then Chris piped up: 'I wonder why nobody thinks it was me.' The table erupted into hilarity.

Erling Kagge does, of course, have a point: if we are lovers of silence, it is wise to minimise our exposure to distractions. Mary Oliver, in her poem 'The Old Poets of China', puts it like this:

Wherever I am, the world comes after me.
It offers me its busyness. It does not believe
that I do not want it. Now I understand
why the old poets of China went so far and high
into the mountains, then crept into the pale mist.

Meditate or Facebook: Meeting all of our Needs

One of the recurring themes in my mindfulness classes is to look, with curiosity and kindness, at what keeps people from doing their daily practice of sitting or other kinds of formal meditation. We make a list: not enough time, doing chores, watching movies, going on Facebook. If there is time (!) in the class, I introduce the 'two chairs' exercise. It is a quick and effective way of working with two seemingly mutually exclusive courses of action. You find out which needs you are trying to meet through each activity (meditating or Facebook is a common pair of seemingly conflicting interests) and seek to integrate all those energies, rather than feeling judgemental and dispirited about 'letting yourself down'. In the exercise you sit down on each chair in turn, expressing the needs met by that choice. You go back and forth between the chairs, making sure that the two parts really hear each other.

In last night's class I asked for a volunteer to demonstrate how it is done, and Marlene placed an interesting part on the second chair (the first chair being 'the meditator'). She had had a 'bad week'; a work-related conversation had caught her unawares, and she had sunk into depression. The thing she did instead of meditating was sitting and staring at the floor, ruminating. She put 'the ruminator' on the other chair, which was a new experience for me. In mindfulness circles rumination is often treated as something to avoid at all costs, so I was interested to see how this would go.

As she was sitting on the chair as the ruminator, I asked her what ruminating was giving her. At first she couldn't come up with anything – she said she had let herself down, after having done so well in the first part of the course. Together we teased out that the needs behind going over the same work conversation again and again were **clarity, resolve and a sense of ease.** She sat on the chair and let herself feel the validity of these needs. When she sat on the other, 'mindfulness' chair, she found that, actually, clarity, calm and ease were the main states of mind she hoped to get out of it too, and often did. Finally, she stood between the chairs, with her hands open to both. What came up for her was an insight that the ruminating part had the best of intentions for her, but that her needs were better met by mindfulness practice, and in particular mindful movement and body scan, because they got her out of her head into a more whole and resourceful way of being.

I thought that this was an interesting way to approach rumination. Rather than battling it as the sure route to the hell of depression, we took a friendly interest in it and discovered its true intention for her. In this scenario both parts wanted the same thing, which makes the resolution quite straightforward. This is not unusual, and it can be quite an eye opener to find that supposedly conflicting activities have similar desires at their core.

So what did the Facebook-craving people come with? The needs most often named were not, as one may expect, **community,**

belonging and friendship (although they were mentioned), but **relaxation, stimulation and ease**. And they all said that those digital ways of trying to meet those needs actually didn't work very well, that they often felt flat and empty afterwards. The learning here was to bring more qualities of ease and relaxation into meditation, so it doesn't become too much like hard work. One person, a psychologist who wanted a sense of community from Facebook, said that the kind of communication going on there was mostly superficial and not really meeting his need. He came up with the idea of making loving-kindness meditation a regular part of his day, to let himself feel a more ongoing depth of connection. Others mentioned meditation apps that connect you with other meditators in real time.

Parts work: Between two Chairs

This exercise is a coaching tool and based on NVC. It can be used for any kind of conflict and decision-making process, with a guide or alone, moving from one chair to the other. The physical aspect of it seems to be an important part of the integrative effect, but it could also be done as a written dialogue. This is how it goes:

> Stand between the chairs and become aware of the conflict you want to explore; one part of you wants to do one thing, the other part wants to do something else. It needs to be binary: either/or. Get a sense of which part wants to sit on which chair.
>
> You decide which part wants to talk first; let's call it Part A. Let it express what's important about the activity, which needs and values are being met.
>
> Part B listens and then feeds back what it has heard, in particular the needs that are important to Part A.
>
> Part A takes in what it feels like to be fully acknowledged in that way.

Part B asks whether there are more things wanting to be said, and the process can be repeated.

Then Part B has its turn and gets fully listened to and reflected back, taking in what it feels like to be fully understood in its main intentions and needs.

When both parts have fully heard each other, you stand between the chairs with both hands open and recall all the important needs.

Consider that both sets of needs can be met. Slowly bring your hands together in a bowl shape, containing the essence of those qualities, and savour them.

Reflect: what could that look like in practical terms?

Make something

When I joined Facebook, I was slightly concerned that it might turn into another addiction, like binge-watching television series on Netflix (something I have to be careful of!). I was aware of the effects of dopamine, which is released when someone responds to you on social media. You want more of that, and you could get it for the relatively small effort of just 'liking' something. So why not go for it, again and again: it seems so harmless and connection-promoting. But so far, it hasn't turned out that way, I am glad to say. The holiday adventures of a friend of a friend just aren't that much of a page-turner, as it were. But every so often I come across a little Facebook gem, a link to an interesting article or a witty exchange that stays in my mind. Like this one, about a week before Christmas:

> G: Don't buy anything.
> Me: Make something.
> A: Like, what???

Until very recently, people constantly made things. They sewed, knitted, wove, embroidered and darned their clothes. They carved, hammered and incised tools, toys and weapons. They shaped stone into houses, clay into pots, grass into baskets, flour into bread, fruit and vegetables into conserves and mammoth ivory into talismans. Their bodies, in turn, were shaped by the repetitious actions, as were their minds and communities.

I am sure some of this shaving, whittling and pounding was a bit of a grind at times. People must have got repetitive strain injury. (In an experiment, a stonemason using Stone-Age tools took four hundred hours to make a replica of the thirty-centimetre-high figure of the 'Lion Man', estimated to be forty thousand years old.) Maybe it was a bit mind-numbing as well, even if it was done in community, with plenty of chatting, chanting and storytelling going on. But it was also an enviably healthy way to spend one's time: rooted in sensory experience, with a sense of purpose and belonging. The writers Richard Mabey and Kathleen Jamie visited an exhibition of 'Ice Age Art' in London in 2013, and, looking at small sculptures bearing the imprint of their Palaeolithic makers, agreed that they 'felt something strangely akin to homesickness'.

The prevailing production sound affecting my ear these modern days is the plasticky clicking of the keyboard, accompanied by the background hum of the hard drive. You could say I am kind of making something: a Word document that transports ideas into the brains of other people who have the matching equipment to decode them. But something is lacking. I am out of direct touch with my body and with other people, an experience that registers subconsciously as an emptiness. But relief is only a mouse click away: buying something or watching a movie will fill that gap nicely, won't it?

Not surprisingly, there is a rising movement opposing this materialistic, digital obsession (and maybe you are already part of it?): a renewal of craft activities. Vintage sewing patterns are being reissued, knitting and sewing courses are thriving and millions of people watch YouTube tutorials about all manner of manual skills. Programmes about competitive baking, gardening and pottery attract large numbers of viewers, and the Transition Town movement talks about 'The Great Reskilling', preparing for post-industrial survival.

I was fortunate in that my mum taught me to knit, sew and alter clothes, and I often have a little project on the go. Much of my wardrobe consists of slightly adjusted second-hand clothes, and I also 'repurpose' objects, like turning a couple of old dresses or jeans into a shopping bag, with nice long handles to carry over the shoulder (not all shopping is frivolous, after all). By the way, I just read in *Positive News* magazine that it takes approximately fourteen years to drink the amount of water used to make just one pair of jeans. (I wonder: is that drinking continuously or a couple of litres a day?) That's a lot of water in countries where water is scarce. And research shows that the average person wears their outfits only six or seven times before binning them.

What motivation could swing you into action, away from the lure of the screen? Saving the planet; enjoying the simple pleasure of handling materials; getting hooked on the magical transformation of a ball of clay into serviceable mugs; the sense of accomplishment; the soul-nourishing effect of a personal touch in your environment; activating the soothing system of the brain to counteract stress; or becoming part of a community of makers that reaches back to the Stone Age?

Many of us enjoy the privilege of choice: we could either make or buy that dress (and buying it would possibly even be cheaper than making it). We decide to make it because it is not about the product so much as the enjoyment inherent in seeing something you imagined take shape in your hands. It doesn't matter how long it takes – four hundred hours, four hours or four minutes. In any case, whether it is a luxury or a necessity, whenever we get our hands into something, we can allow ourselves to really enjoy every moment of the process. In that way we heighten the beneficial effects of the activity through mindfulness: the art of being present, curious, free of judgement if not of discernment. We hear the sound of roasted hazelnuts being crushed for a chocolate cake; revel in the shape, scent and colour of the flowers we arrange into a bouquet; satisfyingly sense through the whole body the sawing of a piece of wood. We might take in how relaxed we are while knitting and how much we enjoy learning something new, like turning the heel of a sock.

And then, I guess, we could take a selfie alongside our proud achievement and post it on Facebook.

~ Befriending All the Parts ~

Internal Family Systems

Wholeness does not mean perfection. It means no part left out.
Frank Ostaseski[71]

Mindfulness is a way of being in wise and purposeful relationship to one's experience, both inwardly and outwardly. Jon Kabat-Zinn[72]

For several years, my journey in mindfulness has been enhanced by the integration of 'parts work' in the tradition of Internal Family Systems or IFS. It is a form of therapy developed by Richard Schwartz and complements mindfulness approaches beautifully, bringing awareness to aspects of the psyche that are often hidden and create tension. It works on the premise that the way to overcome a difficulty is by facing it. This is a truth known to spiritual seekers, modern mindfulness practitioners and therapists of various schools alike. By using IFS methods of inner dialogue, you not only turn towards the difficulty, willing to experience the discomfort, you also give it a voice and hear what it has to say. You get a sense of it as a persona inside you, with its own history, agenda, likes and dislikes. Often these protecting parts come in pairs – a conformer and a rebel, for example. They all have a positive intent for you, even if they often couch it in ways that make that hard to see.

When you let these parts know that you understand their intention to serve you, to keep you safe and well regarded in the eyes of others, for example, they often relax. The more specifically you can name the need they are trying to meet, the better. They enjoy being thanked for the hard work they have been doing for a long time, often without any acknowledgement.

When they are fully heard, other, more vulnerable inner-child parts can be accessed and healed. The protectors, like the inner critics (and there are seven different types of critics, according to Jay Earley: the perfectionist, the inner controller, the taskmaster, the underminer, the destroyer, the guilt-tripper, and the

[71] In: 'The Five Invitations: What Death can teach us about Living'.
[72] In his foreword to the 2015 Mindful Nation Report.

conformist) came onto the scene early in your life in order to protect the child that was receiving harsh parental criticism. By internalising those critical voices, the child tries to make sure it doesn't have to experience the pain and fear of disconnection again. When we re-parent those hurt parts of ourselves, the whole inner system recalibrates itself, and we experience some freedom from those old patterns of self-blame.

There is another important part of the system: the aware, witnessing self. Schwartz calls it the '8 C Self', as it is characterised by qualities such as curiosity, connectedness, courage, confidence, clarity, compassion, calm and creativity. A large part of the effectiveness of this approach to finding ease from disempowering inner voices is simply knowing that they are there and that they are not all of you.

Learning how to apply this system is not hard for someone familiar with meditation. Jay Earley's books and online courses are valuable resources.[73] I learned IFS initially as part of my coaching training with Martha Lasley and Guthrie Sawyer[74] and continue to develop it in my work with peer coaches and clients. I have got to know many parts of my inner system intimately and recognise their voices when they try to take over the seat of awareness.

Exercise: Befriending a Protector

What inner voice is preventing you from being your most resourceful and flowing self right now? Some inner critic maybe, a doubter, rebel or underminer? It may be related to something happening in your life at the moment, such as a difficult task that lies ahead of you, a recurring difficulty in your meditation practice, a fallout with a friend or perhaps a reaction you have while reading this book. Notice the thoughts, feelings and mood connected with that reaction. Most likely it will feel very familiar.

Turn towards that inner part now with the intention of getting to know it – not to change it.

[73] Such as *Self Therapy*.

[74] *Coaching for Transformation*.

If there is some objection to doing this work (like 'I don't have time right now' or 'Is this safe?' or 'Can I be bothered?'), acknowledge that concerned part first and ask it to step back. If it doesn't want to do that, ask whether it would be open to having a conversation in order to be heard more fully. (In which case, you'd ask it the questions below.) If it isn't open to that either, it's probably not a good idea to pursue this inner dialogue at this time, at least not on your own. When we are very blended with our protectors, we may need someone experienced in this kind of approach to guide us.

When you have a sense of which part wants to be heard first, ask it some of the following questions:

What is it like to be you? What does it feel like to be in your skin?
What would you like to be called?
How are you serving me?
What are you afraid would happen if you didn't do your job?

Then thank the part for the work it is doing. Name the needs it is trying to meet. (For example: 'I can see that you are trying to make sure I use my time most efficiently. Thank you for your vigilance.') How is it receiving that acknowledgement? If there is a sense of relief, allow that to be experienced as full body sensations. Ask it some more questions:

If you knew that your concerns were being taken care of, what would you rather be doing?

Sometimes the part will transform, in its own time, from a critic into more of a mentoring figure. Or it may find a wise ally within the inner system. But it cannot be pushed into it. It fulfils an important function in the inner family of parts, and usually it will only fully release its grip when the exiled, hurt little-child parts it protects have received some healing and 'released their burdens'.

Teddies, Babies and Buddhas

'Do you have a teddy or a similar cuddly toy?' my supervisor asked.

No, I didn't. I looked around and grabbed a small cushion from the nearby heap of meditation gear.

'Will this do?' I could see myself in the small window on the Skype screen, clutching the square, cream-coloured substitute to my chest. Hugging something soft seemed to viscerally inspire confidence that this difficult stuff I was dealing with was manageable. Like any human being consoling another in distress, I might cocoon that tight spot in my solar plexus in warmth and acceptance. A couple of minutes passed. Gradually, breath by breath, a sense of ease and relief was starting to spread through my body. With the gentle encouragement of my guide, and feeling just a little sheepish, I slowly stroked the cushion a few times, and the effect deepened. I was now more aware of my heart area, where I felt both an ache and a softness, a warmth with a tinge of sadness. Call it compassion. I remembered Chris Germer's kindly voice from a self-compassion retreat: 'It is not easy to be a human being.'

Following that therapeutic supervision session, I investigated teddies on the internet and bought a pre-loved one I liked the look of on eBay. He arrives in a haze of apple-scented perfume. I take to him straightaway. (Why am I so sure about the gender of my teddy bear? Because in German it is masculine, 'der Teddybär'? It would be interesting to ask my three-year-old granddaughter what she thinks its gender is.) His big head has quite an emotional impact; it takes up more than a third of his body volume, and is broader than, and almost continuous with, his shoulders. I'd like my teddy to have a bit of a neck, though, so I take up needle and thread (pleased to have some of the right golden-beige tone in my collection) and tuck in his cheeks a fraction. Yes, the resulting heart shape has definitely nudged up the level of cuteness. I try him for cuddliness, his furry belly reassuring and warm against my solar plexus, his little black nose pressing on my chest bone. Wanting to feel more contact against my lower belly, I pull on his stubby legs. They are a bit too short. Just then my husband enters, looking somewhat incredulous. 'Meet Teddy,' I say. 'Isn't he cute? I just hope he'll grow a little.'

Maybe I am too old for a teddy? But did I ever have one as a kid? I can't get a visual recall of any soft toys I may have played with as a toddler. On our next phone call, I ask my mum. She doesn't remember. She says there was no money for many toys and repeats what she has said many times: that I was happy to be left on my own in a playpen, or, as a baby, in a pram out on the balcony, with dappled light coming through the trees, playing with my hands. She had been following the educational theories of those times: feed them every four hours, don't respond to their crying or you'll spoil them, give them lots of fresh air. I hope I did have a teddy; I think I would have needed one. And something makes me think I did have one… When I hold my new teddy, my thumbs keep stroking the inner ears and the paws, expecting to feel something smooth and velvety, something different from the general rough-and-tumble hairiness of the pelt. As if I had performed this tiny, comfort-giving action many times in the past, going with and pushing against the grain of exquisitely fine, silky material. Next time I'm in town I go to the fabric shop and buy a strip of teddy-coloured velvet. I cut out little half-moon shapes for the ears and little oblongs for the paws and patiently, with small, neat stitches, sew them on. I am a little surprised at how much I am enjoying this, how much pleasure I receive from holding the little body against me, the sense of bonding.

It reminds me of holding our granddaughter Fiadh when she was a baby and of holding my friend Liz's three-month-old baby. Willow has almost constant skin contact with someone, mostly her mother, and generally doesn't wear a nappy. 'Attachment parenting', it's called, and 'Natural Infant Hygiene'. Taking inspiration from mothers in the less-developed world, Liz tries to tune into the elimination needs of her baby. When they are outside in the garden, the perennial borders frequently get fertilised. Indoors a potty is ready at all times. When the pee starts flowing, Liz makes a soft 'ssssssss' sound. According to the theory,[75] Willow will soon start to respond to the sound by emptying her bladder on cue and will effectively communicate her need to go. After a few months she may be nappy-free and may use the potty on her own as soon as she starts walking. Most importantly, she will grow up with the happiness-boosting experience that her primal needs are met. Studies have shown that carrying babies

[75] Ingrid Bauer, *Diaper Free*, 2001.

with skin-to-skin contact improves the baby's growth, regulates the heartbeat, maintains body temperature, stimulates digestion, reduces crying and fussiness, supports deeper sleep, reduces stress hormones and enhances the ability to recover from stress. 'Plus,' as Ingrid Bauer writes, 'it just plain feels good. Really good. The bond between baby and mother, as well as the well-being of both, is strengthened immeasurably through touch.'

Last week I carried nappyless Willow in a sling right up close to the front of my body for a couple of hours. It did indeed give me that good feeling and provided an opportunity for her mum to have an afternoon nap. As I was not so tuned into her 'elimination needs' and was somewhat slow to disentangle the complicated sling mechanism, my clothing was gradually suffused with warm moisture. I reminded myself that urine is sterile when it leaves the body. And till a few hundred years ago people used urine to clean their clothes. Still, to be honest, I did notice a mild reaction. But overall, the mostly sleeping, contented baby and I were peacefully at one, enjoying the simultaneous and mutual giving and receiving of comfort. Perhaps I was the more conscious partaker in the exchange, but did that really matter? I could feel those happiness hormones, oxytocin and opiates dispersing ease and relaxation through my body. Yes, very similar to holding Teddy and feeling at the same time held by him. But with the baby, it was more direct, more intense, more responsible and more challenging. Predictably enough, the baby started to get restless, began crying, and Liz thankfully reappeared.

While nursing Willow, Liz told me a childhood story of how she accidentally dropped her teddy bear on a steam-train line. The train stopped for her to retrieve him. When, years later, she introduced the same teddy to her young son, he felt that he was in need of repair. He put a bandage around his head and sewed up the holes to prevent more of the stuffing falling out. This was probably as therapeutic for him as it was for the teddy.

Caring stimulates the soothing system as much as being cared for does, and sometimes even more successfully. The soothing system is one of at least three emotion-regulating systems that have evolved to keep us safe and thriving. According to Professor Paul Gilbert,[76] an expert on the subject of depression and compassion, these systems are, first, the threat and self-protection system;

[76] Paul Gilbert, *The Compassionate Mind*, 2009.

second, the incentive and resource-seeking system; and third, the soothing and contentment system. In our fast and competitive modern world, many people are overwhelmed by the stress that can inadvertently result from the almost automatic operations of the first two systems. We react to our relatively harmless daily problems as if they were life-threatening tigers on the savannah. And we can easily get caught up in a rat race for rewards that are rarely examined with reference to our deeper values. This is just 'normal' living, and on top of this our resilience inevitably gets tested by more traumatic life events: an unexpected death, a cancer diagnosis, bullying, losing one's job or a partner, etc. The soothing system is there to restore healthy, calm and balanced states of being, but we are often at a loss as to how to activate it successfully. Some of the socially accepted and commercially promoted ways of relaxing, such as watching TV, drinking alcohol, consuming sugary and fatty foods or shopping online, often don't really work. Rather than recuperating, we end up feeling distracted and numb instead. The widespread interest in mindfulness and compassion-focussed methodologies speaks to the burgeoning need for more effective ways to let go of stress, heal trauma and relax into a sense of wholeness, meaning and wellbeing. Whether it's because of the pressure of stress, disillusion with a materialistic lifestyle or faith in the scientific evidence, people are now regularly practising sitting meditation, and they do so in their millions.[77]

I am full of amazement that all these people are actually managing to do it. Because, let's face it, meditating is not always easy. In particular, how do we deal with that uncomfortable initial stage when we sit down and, rather than dipping straight into that deep pool of bliss and tranquillity, find ourselves assailed by the unprocessed material from our busy days? By the restless thoughts about tasks left unfinished? Or the nagging suspicion that we may have, yet again, somehow failed to come up to scratch? Or some intense feelings of hurt, sadness or anger we have worked hard all day to keep at bay?

Maybe this is where the teddy could come in handy. Perhaps not literally, though it may be worth trying to have him or her (I did ask my granddaughter, who helpfully said, *'he is a girl teddy'*) sitting in your lap while you meditate. But there are other ways

[77] Two to five hundred million, according to a 2021 report. https://disturbmenot.co/meditation-statistics/

to incline our body/mind towards a state of safety and ease, right from the start. Here are a few ideas:

Think of the earth as your friend; let there be a sense of mutuality in the contact of your body with the ground.

Bring to mind a past episode of caring for another being: when you made that encouraging remark to a colleague, gave your child an encouraging pat or stroked the cat. Dwell in the good feelings that engenders.

Conjure up the presence of a compassionate being who accepts you as you are right now, either someone you know personally, a famous teacher like the Dalai Lama or a more archetypal figure like the Buddha. It could even be your pet.

In these ways you deliberately create a friendly inner milieu within which a readiness to embrace your experience as it is can grow, and that is ultimately the most effective way to find release from suffering.

Knowing this has made a big difference to my practice and teaching of compassion and metta (loving kindness). In Buddhist traditions, these meditations often start with developing loving kindness for oneself, before directing it towards other beings. Sometimes one imagines the presence of a compassionate teacher first. For people brought up in modern societies, self-love can present a big hurdle right at the start. Many of us struggle with feelings of unworthiness and guilt that have been quite puzzling to Eastern teachers, such as the Dalai Lama. Whether as a result of insecure early attachment, the influence of the Christian religion or living in a climate of competitive materialism, it is quite common for people to have a sense of never being good enough, however hard they might try. We live in a 'trance of unworthiness', as Tara Brach calls it. Tragically, sometimes 'trying' to feel loving kindness for oneself just becomes another task that is beset with the fear of failure, another nail in the coffin of self-blame. We may faithfully repeat phrases such as 'May I be well, may I be happy', trying our best to mean it, but in our heart of hearts we doubt that we are worthy of happiness. Chris Germer talks about the common experience in loving-kindness meditation of a 'backdraught', a term used by firefighters: when they open a door to a place where a fire has been deprived of oxygen, it will explode in their faces. Likewise, 'if our hearts are hot with suffering – self-hatred, self-doubt – when we begin to practise, sympathetic words can open the door of our hearts, causing an explosion of difficult feelings'.[78] Germer says that this experience is part of the healing process.

One pathway towards healing is to connect with our innate predisposition towards caring. As mammals we are hard-wired to respond to other beings in distress. We may feel a lack, current or past, of being cared for, but we can empower ourselves by remembering our own caring abilities. Even without 'trying' very hard, most people will be able to recall a kindly action they recently performed: stroking a pet, making someone a cup of tea, texting a reassuring message or, indeed, putting a bandage on a teddy.

The primary function of a soft toy is to help a child in the difficult period of separation from their mother. Teddies fall into the category of 'transitional objects', a term coined in 1953 by Dr Donald Woods Winnicott, a prominent paediatrician and psychoanalyst. One of his students, Dr Steve Tuber, wrote: 'The baby knows the teddy bear is not Mom, but the baby can get a certain satisfaction. It is neither Mom nor totally just a stuffed animal.' And does the child at some age outgrow the need for this kind of substitution? The *New York Times* published an article that suggested that as many as 25 per cent of young women going to university take along something identifiable as a childhood transitional object: soft toys or scraps of a favourite old blanket.

And it's certainly not just women who continue using such comforters, although men will not so readily admit to it. Research done in 2012 by the hotel chain Travelodge revealed that 35 per cent of adults in Britain still sleep with a teddy bear to help them de-stress and sleep at night. Apparently, seventy-five thousand forgotten bears were left behind in its 452 hotels in England in the previous 12 months and had to be reunited with their distressed owners, many of whom were not children. A quarter of the men who took part in the survey (which included six thousand adults) admitted to taking their teddy bear away on business. At home, they hide the stuffed toy so visitors won't see it.

Something told me that the shuffling, hunched-over, unkempt old man, a former engineer who came to me for help in dealing with depression, wouldn't respond favourably to a suggestion that he might cuddle a teddy. But he had read about the beneficial

[78] In: '*The Mindful Path to Self-Compassion*', 2009.

effects of yoga and was willing to give it a go. We went through a few gentle lying-down yoga poses and finished with a body-scan meditation. 'Remember what it feels like to hold a baby: the mutual receptivity, the giving and receiving of warmth. Imagine you have a similar relationship with the ground; imagine a reciprocal connection with the earth. A sense of receiving and being received.' I was delighted and somewhat surprised to hear from him afterwards that my suggestion had made sense to him. His eyes had a hopeful glow when he glanced up at me through his scruffy white eyebrows.

Clearly the imagination plays an important role in self-soothing. A transitional object can turn into an imaginary friend, like Winnie the Pooh. The telling of stories about the object can become as effective as physical contact with it. And the time will come when we are able to leave the house without clutching a bear (if need be!), confident in our inner resources for dealing with stress. You may, for example, call on the presence of a 'compassionate other'. The neuroscientist Paul Gilbert has explored the power of creating compassionate imagery to activate the soothing system. You can tailor the qualities of such an ideal figure to suit your needs, but he finds that certain key qualities work well: a wise mind, strength and fortitude, great warmth and kindness, and an attitude of non-judgement. 'If you are struggling, try this exploration,' he writes. 'If you could design the ideal *compassionate other* for a child, what qualities would they have? How would they change as the child grows and what would they be like when the child is an adult?'[79]

For some people, the 'compassionate other' takes the shape of a traditional spiritual figure, like the Buddha, God or Holy Mary. Depending on the type of religious background, there can be a sense of a divine presence as a constant companion and the relationship can be cultivated through regular prayer and devotional ritual. For many people in the modern world this kind of direct and innocent faith connection is no longer available, or even desirable. We have become quite sophisticated in our psychological understanding of processes of projection and my see such figures as an outward manifestation of our longing for love and wholeness. But whether we 'believe' in the existence of such spiritual entities or not, the fact is that imagining ourselves to be in

[79] Paul Gilbert, *The Compassionate Mind*, 2009.

their presence can have a powerful effect anyway. Tara Brach gets around the complexities around belief and deities by suggesting we visualise the arc of a compassionate smile in the space around us, as well as in our own bodies. This seems to work well for many people.

The Buddha didn't want images of himself made, but it's not surprising that it turned out otherwise. This is the way the mind works, from when we were babies – it responds instinctively to images of faces, particularly a smiling one. As meditators, we have the option to use the faculty of the imagination to enrich and deepen our experience. Holding the image of a compassionate figure steadily in our minds deepens concentration and the qualities we sense emanating from them can lead to the direct experience of states that can be difficult to put into words, touching on the very nature of existence, its ungraspable and luminous nature. I enjoy visualising a being that knows more than 'me' and is more compassionate than 'me' and open myself to that influence. It's a relief not to have to do it all myself.

The relaxing and expanding experience of surrender to something bigger than ourselves can also come about when we tune into the company of people we meditate with, either in the same room, on a digital platform, or simply in our imagination. It becomes 'our', rather than 'my' meditation and we can allow ourselves to be carried by the collective effort.

Meditation: Opening to Loving Presence

Bring your awareness to your contact with the ground, through your feet and sitting bones. Experiencing the relationship to the ground as a mutually receptive and nourishing one: you are aware of the earth and the earth is aware of you.

Notice your breath and how it may change, allowing it to deepen naturally. Letting the breath spread any feelings of warmth, pleasure, peace and safety through your whole body. If it feels right stay in touch with the breath throughout the meditation.

If it feels right, bring your hands to the centre of the chest, feeling the breath and being present with the giving and receiving of care and love. If it is helpful, bring to mind an image of caressing a baby, or stroking a pet, accessing that natural capacity for caring we mammals all share.

Exploring the nuances of that tenderness.

Perhaps your lips are slightly curling up into a smile? Where else may that smile live in your body? Your heart? Your belly? The palms of your hands?

Maybe you can imagine and feel the arc of a smile in the space around you, and you allow yourself to bathe in the presence of compassion.

If any resistance or difficult feelings arise, see if you can find a way to include those in the meditation. Let them be bathed in kindness. Listen to the sound of your inner voice; let it be reassuring, kind. Perhaps gently naming the qualities you experience or want to invite: acceptance, calm, joy, etc.

Follow your intuition: what works for you? What allows you to continue dwelling in a state of love and wellbeing, relaxed and effortlessly? Imagining others around you? Or a particular landscape?

Before finishing, imagine yourself in the next few hours or days, still in touch with this loving presence.

PART IV

~ Being Present ~

Getting the Most out of Summer

Nothing Gold Can Stay

Nature's first green is gold,
Her hardest hue to hold.
Her early leaf's a flower;
But only so an hour.
Then leaf subsides to leaf.
So Eden sank to grief,
So dawn goes down to day.
Nothing gold can stay.

Robert Frost

Once you realise this floating life as the perfect mirage of change, it's breathtaking – this wild joy at wandering boundless and free. Han Shan

When I was a child in Germany, summer was a never-ending outdoor adventure story. It was easy to leave behind the tight rhythms of the school term and float free. There was boredom at times, but somehow that was part of the seasonal languor. The weather helped – usually there were weeks of sunshine, interrupted only by the occasional thunderstorm.

Uncharacteristically, it hasn't rained in Scotland for weeks. Letting go into that summer feeling, however, doesn't come quite so easily any more. I remember being able, even as a young adult, to lie down on a stretch of grass in the sun somewhere, inhale the scent of ripe seeds and dry soil and surrender to the earth. I felt like some kind of beautiful, long-limbed animal. An antelope, maybe.

Today the part of me that knows how to be on holiday has turned into a pale, insignificant presence, squashed aside by the feisty, tireless 'inner worker'. I blame the phone, tethering me to the ever-present possibility of work or social opportunities. I did go to the allotment today, but all I could see were the weeds that need pulling and the bare patch that needs resowing. Eventually I sat down and had a conversation with these two parts of myself and found out what their good intentions for me are. The inner worker wants me to feel a sense of purpose and meaning. She is afraid that if she were to relax, I may flounder and drift. The inner holidaymaker wants me to 'melt into life'. That sounded quite spiritual and meaningful to the inner worker, and she relented a little, allowing me to have a blissful afternoon nap, curled up on a sheepskin in the dappled shade of the plum tree.

I was pleasantly surprised by the shift I experienced on waking, extending my limbs into the warm summer air, luxuriating in innocent, bone-deep deliciousness, without a hint of censure. Yes, that's the wish in many emails: 'enjoy the summer!' come true.

Then I remembered a recent coaching session with a client, who was so intent on enjoying the summer that she got out of the habit of meditating. She arrived at an interesting insight: she was afraid of the summer ending. She dreaded how the darkness might affect her mood. So she tried to get the most out of summer, with lots of travel, physical activity, good food and family time, trying to enjoy it all mindfully. But there was an uncomfortable, driven edge to her pleasure-seeking, and she was reluctant to sit for any length of time and experience herself more fully. She recognised that her fear of facing impermanence actually limited her enjoyment of the moment. Part of the homework we designed together for her consisted in looking up poems on impermanence and using them to inspire her meditation. It helps to see that facing change is not easy for any human being and that it is also the doorway to 'this wild joy at wandering boundless and free', as Han Shan puts it.

October Walk in the Botanic Garden

Walking through the gates of the Botanic Garden, head down and halfway home already, I have passed the sycamore before I am stopped by its compact presence. I look back at its solid shape, still in possession of most of its dark green leaves, and appreciate the contrast with the surrounding trees that are well on their way into their skeletal phase. Some remaining yellow ash leaves look much brighter than one would expect on this dark rainy day. They seem magically self-illuminated, like a smartphone screen. I continue walking more slowly, listening to the rain on the umbrella, feeling sheltered and comfortable, like waking in the middle of a wet night in a good tent.

This is Just to Say

This is just to say

I have eaten
the plums
that were in
the icebox

and which
you were probably
saving
for breakfast

Forgive me
they were delicious
so sweet
and so cold

William Carlos Williams

I was reminded of this poem recently when it was recited in the film *Paterson* by Jim Jarmusch. The movie is as countercultural as it gets: nothing (or almost nothing) more dramatic happens than a bus breaking down. It has no sex in it, but breathes tenderness right from the starting scene, where you see a couple waking up, entwined in each other's arms, streaks of golden-white morning light playing on their skins. You see this scene repeated throughout the film, with variations in posture and light, as the days of the week unfold. He is a bus driver in Paterson, the town William Carlos Williams lived and wrote in, and also writes poetry, jotted down in spare moments around his shifts. She is a designer/artist in waiting, developing her style at home by painting every surface large enough: crockery, curtains, clothes and even home-made cupcakes in black-and-white patterns.

This slow-paced, meditative film has been surprisingly well received. Paterson, the film's as-yet-unpublished, quiet hero, doesn't own a mobile phone or other screen device. He still writes everything by hand, in a notebook with unruled pages. As the camera bouncily follows his daily bus route, you are impelled to view the scene through a poet's eye. Everything is given significance as potential material for poetry. Ordinary house walls in juxtaposition with other ordinary house walls, in a particular slant of light. The rambling conversation between passengers or with his colleagues: all worth taking note of.

The film is an unpretentious lesson on how to lead a meaningful life: no need to try to be famous. Just be as present as you can to the detail and beauty in everyday occurrences. The half-guilty taking of plums from the icebox or a box of matches with large blue lettering on it become an opportunity to write a love poem. An artist keeps the senses well tuned; they are the indispensable tools of her trade. She uses the variations within the regularity and predictability of an established timetable to keep a creative edge, thus avoiding dullness. The same skills are necessary for sustained mindfulness practice.

The day after watching the movie I taught one of my 'yoga for mindful living' classes. In yoga you have a relatively limited repertoire of poses and movement sequences, and in order to keep the practice fruitful over the years, you have to know how to bring it sensuously and imaginatively alive. I read the poem 'This is Just to Say' and encouraged people to give themselves permission to enjoy the sweet juiciness of their bodies in movement. One simple means to contact this inner aliveness is to notice the effect of performing a movement only on one side, pausing before repeating on the other side. For example, you may bring your torso into a lying-down twist, where your bent knees point to the left and your outstretched left arm and face turn to the opposite side. After a few breaths you return to a neutral position, before turning the knees to the right. In that pause, when comparing the sensations in the two sides of the body, you inevitably notice certain differences. Maybe the side you have just stretched feels bigger, different in shape, in closer contact with the ground, more tingly and alive. There is some scientific underpinning to this change. During a prolonged stretch, cells in the fascia (the soft tissue that connects bones, organs and muscles) elongate. When they return to neutral, these cells get filled with fluid, and their size increases up to a third. You literally become more plump and juicy.

It could be said that the main character in the film *Paterson* is the town itself, brought to life through the eyes of Paterson the bus driver, and, before him, William Carlos Williams, who wrote an epic poem called *Paterson*. Likewise, in mindful and insightful living, it is this whole marvellous, interconnected world that we pay attention to. We aim to be a little less ruled by the demands of our restless, craving, small selves. There can be a gradual maturing of our understanding of what it means to really enjoy ourselves.

Before the Soup gets Cold

'Vanities!' shouts the first assistant director, and the vanities – hair, makeup and costume – hurry over to descend upon him as if he is carrion, plucking at his hair and straightening his shirt and tickling his eyelids with their soft brushes. It takes only thirty seconds or so but in those thirty seconds… he has the strange sensation that he is gone, that he is suspended, and that his very life is an imagining. In those seconds a whirl of images whips through his mind, too quickly and jumblingly to effectively identify each as it occurs to him: there is the scene he's about to shoot, of course, and the scene he's shot earlier, but also all the things he sees and hears and remembers before he falls asleep at night…. But by the time he's finished shooting the scene, he won't remember.
From *A Little Life* by Hanya Yanagihara

Ignoring the good Buddhist in me that advises being fully present and doing one thing at a time, I often indulge in the habit of reading during mealtimes, particularly when I am on my own at home. I may take a few moments to appreciate the sights, tastes and smells of the food, and then I lose myself in the story. Coming across the scene quoted above, however, I am stopped in my tracks. I read it over a couple of times, spoon suspended over the freshly made beetroot soup. 'By the time he's finished shooting the scene, he won't remember…'. A sense of urgency arises from some deep place within. 'Wake up!' I say to myself, 'life is short. Honour these whirling thoughts and images that are hoping for an airing; catch them while they are whirling a little closer to the surface right now!' A small window of choice has opened: will I stay submerged in this familiar pattern of pacifying half-admitted feelings (is it loneliness?); have the next spoonful, and the next, while turning the pages and then move onto the next thing on the agenda; or will I take heed of the stirring in my soul and do something different? Will I tend to this little spark of creativity? I put the bookmark between the pages and stand up. I stretch and speak a few sentences about this moment into the notepad on my phone. When I go back to the soup, it is still warm.

Being or Doing? Or Both? Or Neither?

On arrival at the allotment plot, I immediately see what needs doing: weeding, above all, throughout the year. And sowing, planting, watering, mulching, dividing, deadheading and composting. Rigging up protective netting for the kale (birds love it); placing collars, made from cut plastic bottles with a ring of copper tape, over young courgettes and sunflowers as slug barriers; replanting tiny, self-seeded poppies to more convenient and picturesque places. I do 'stand and stare'[80] a fair amount too, but often with an eye for improvement. 'If I were to thin out that rampant euphorbia, maybe I could grow a whitecurrant bush there. Would it get enough light throughout the season?'

There is nothing wrong with doing. Without my (and my husband's) vigilance and commitment, there wouldn't be a garden. We wouldn't be eating our own lettuce and radishes; we wouldn't enjoy so many home-grown leek and potato soups or rhubarb crumbles. We wouldn't have vases full of free flowers most months of the year. When our even more industrious allotment neighbour of many years gave up his plot after a bad dose of Covid-19, a young couple took over. After an initial burst of enthusiastic digging, weeding and marking out new beds, all went quiet. The weeds took over, and you could get a glimpse of what would

[80] 'What is this life if, full of care / We have no time to stand and stare?' From: 'Leisure', W. H. Davies

happen if human activity ceased altogether: the site would be a nitrogen-rich heaven for nettles, dandelions, dock leaves, brambles, buttercups, ground elder and forget-me-nots. The apple trees would do well, for a while, and so would the Jerusalem artichokes, mint and lovage. I don't blame the young people; they have their lives, their careers to grow. For a garden to flourish, you have to be present in it, often.

I love tending our Plot 60. It does all the good things for my body and mind that research mentions;[81] it often tangibly improves my mood, steadies and balances me. There is something straightforwardly useful and wholesome about gardening, when many aspects of modern life are so complicated and removed from sensory reality. I love the smell and feel of rich earth on my hands; I feel enticed to enrich and collaborate with the natural environment, and I enjoy giving away split-off plants and surplus products to neighbours. It also gives me the opportunity to explore that koan[82] of 'being' and 'doing'. Digging up potatoes can be an unhurried, mindful, purposeful pleasure, or it can almost recede into the background while the mind unhappily and busily churns over some apparent or threatening calamity. We are so compelled to sort things out by ruminating over them. In order to use to the full the beneficial opportunities presented by gardening, some training of the mind through sitting practice will be of great benefit. It will open up more choice and agency with regard to our mental states in any situation, whether physically active or not.

Our plot is only five minutes' walk from our home, and when it is dry and reasonably mild (not something to take for granted in Scotland) I will go there in the morning to do some physical warm-ups and meditate outside. In the same way as I avoid looking at my phone before meditating at home, I hold myself back (not always successfully) from starting to pull out some of that stealthy ground elder, couch grass and bindweed before getting ready to sit. The lines from a poem by Rumi come to mind:

Don't open the door to the study and begin reading.
Take down a musical instrument.

---

[81] https://www.sciencedirect.com/science/article/pii/S2211335516301401

[82] According to the *Oxford Dictionary*, a koan is 'a paradoxical anecdote or riddle without a solution, used in Zen Buddhism to demonstrate the inadequacy of logical reasoning and provoke enlightenment.'

Let the beauty we love be what we do.
There are hundreds of ways to
Kneel and kiss the ground.

Today the sky is clear, and I choose a shady corner of the allotment between the apple trees to set up my blocks for sitting meditation. Afterwards, when I open my eyes again, the sun has reached the crown of the trees, and dappled light amazes the skin on my face. Early-morning city sounds are starting to clank and whirr. A rustling of leaves nearby. Sitting peacefully, thoughts arise in tandem with everything else, coming and going, no big deal.

Meditation: Just Sitting

Getting a general sense of arriving in the body, in this place. A few deeper breaths help us to be grounded and settled. Feeling a sense of the earth, vast and ancient, holding us.

Becoming aware of the hands, where they are resting, what they are in touch with: air, skin, clothes. What is the energy in the hands like – are they still expecting to do something? Letting the hands realise that now, nothing needs to be done.

Letting the feet know that now, there is nowhere to go.

Letting the face know that now, there is nothing to communicate and nothing to hide from the world.

Letting the belly be soft and get on with its business of digesting. It knows what to do.

In this atmosphere of quietness, the heart might open naturally, like a flower when the conditions are right.

Allowing a sense of belonging, without having to do anything to prove your worthiness.

When the urge to do, to ponder, to fix something arises, sense the vitality of that energy. This is how life expresses itself; let it brighten the moment. Perhaps your breath can ride that energy, tame it with ease, channel it into contentment.

If it feels right, you may drop in the question of 'being' versus 'doing'. How is it playing itself out for you right now? Is it about both? Or neither?

Sitting with ease, for as long as feels right.

Draw it as it is

At last it's warm enough for morning meditation outside at the allotment again. The grass paths haven't been cut for a while, and my canvas flats immediately get drenched in dew as I make my way to our far-end corner plot. It's like walking through a meadow, far away from the city. Our plot is a little hidden paradise, bordered by the River Kelvin and a small stretch of no-man's-land. After some warm-up chi kung, I put down a sheet of blue plastic, an old sheepskin and two blocks of polystyrene meditation blocks (salvaged packaging material) and settle down in cross-legged position facing the morning sun. I arrange some paper and drawing utensils in front of me: I am planning on some drawing meditation.

Opening into awareness brings the sound environment to the fore, which is dense this morning: blackbirds, police sirens, the rush of the river, a song thrush, some hammering from a building site. My body feels good here. Next to the cultivated crops there are nettles, ground elder, buttercups, foxgloves, the smell of foxes: enough wilderness for a sense of homecoming.

At first my mind gets caught up with some gardening jobs, as this is the time for splitting and re-siting perennials. It engages the mind just like an art project: weighing up and playing with variables such as the height, shape, flowering time and colour of various plants. An element of intuition is involved: will this rose thrive next to that apple tree? As in any emergent art project, trial and error play a crucial role – in this case it will be weeks and months before the implications of decisions made now will become visible. Some plants have been here for a long time, and I know their names, rhythms and habits, recognise their leaves and roots; others I have recently bought from a garden centre, and it remains to be seen whether they like it here and whether I will be able to distinguish them from weeds early next spring. My own ignorance, foxes, human thieves, frost and snails are among the challenges they have to survive in order to become part of this ever-changing art installation.

Having let the mind run with this for a while, I am now ready to focus on the present moment. I want to use drawing to become more intimate with life. I dip my water-soluble pencil into a patch of wet moss and start drawing a foxglove just coming into bloom. At first I follow the outlines, attracted by the repeating rhythm of the curved flower petals. A gentle wind keeps everything moving. I stop – what do I really see? Shifting and vibrating shapes and spaces, in shades of green, purple and brown, dark and light. The word 'foxglove' seems an artificial separation, a provisional approximation of interpenetrating processes. I begin drawing the spaces between interweaving lines and shapes, not concerned about which parts of which separate species they may belong to. The labelling part of the brain relaxes, together with notions of 'right' or 'wrong', and my pleasure in the process increases tangibly. The ease deepens when I switch to making marks without looking at the paper for a while, getting drawn into what presents itself to the sense of seeing without aiming for accurate representation. Then I do the opposite, letting go of what it looks like 'out there', focussing only on what is emerging on the paper and being open to what that stimulates. I like the imprecision and variability of the half-dissolved pencil line and keep moistening the pencil tip on the dew-covered grass. Becoming interested in the feel of the pencil on the finely textured paper, as Paul Klee said, I 'take the line for a walk'. There is an increasing tenderness here, in the quality of my gaze, the contact with the paper, the sense of being held in the environment.

Then I put down the pen, lift into my posture a little more and close my eyes, letting my attention follow the curves and edges of my breath in the same innocent, open way. The border between my body and the breath seems tenuous; there is a just a swell with variations. What would it be like to draw the breath or the experience of breathing? At first I produce regular curves, like a schoolchild's picture of waves, but as I get close to the sensations, new questions pose themselves: how sharp is the peak of the in-breath? How even is the gradient of the out-breath? With great absorption and interest, I follow the breath's accelerando and ritardando. Finally, I let go of the pen, the breath, everything, and just sit.

Drawing Meditation

To stimulate and refresh your meditation practice, throughout a whole week you may want to precede each day's sit with a period of drawing. Keep note of any insights. Here are a few ideas you may want to try out.

If possible, find a spot outside in nature – otherwise sit in front of a vase of flowers or other natural objects.

Choose paper and some mark-making implement, like a pen, pencil, crayon or charcoal. Make sure you are sitting comfortably and have easy access to the art materials.

Be aware of your posture, your breath, the feel of the pen in your hand. Sense the connection between your heart, eyes and hand.

Connect with your intention for this session.

When you feel settled, start drawing what you see in a continuous line, without looking at the paper. It is obvious that no one can expect you to come up with a good likeness, so relax any goal orientation and perfectionism. Just 'take the line for a walk'.

Then only look at the paper, and let yourself be guided by what is already there – you may want to play with repetition and contrast, varying the tempo and pressure of the line-making.

Be aware of the qualities of connection: of eyes on object, pen on paper. Does it feel tender, passionate, curious – or more neutral? Be open to experiencing some mutuality, of being touched by the object in return (whatever that means to you). Be as interested in inward as in outward seeing. 'One eye sees, the other eye feels,' Paul Klee said.

After ten minutes, put down your pen, close your eyes and watch your breath, following it with the same relaxed, continuous attention, delineating its peaks and troughs with care and precision. What happens when you open your eyes? Would you like to draw the experience of breathing?

Picking Blackberries

As I walk along the fence of the allotment site, a window opens into deep foraging time. I am walking carefully, steadily, gaze turned towards the edible potential to my left, with senses open to the wider environment. Calm, content, alert, I could keep going like this all afternoon. It makes me think of an ancestor a hundred thousand years ago, gathering berries in a container woven from grass. A warm, gentle wind, intense brightness when clouds give way – a gift this late in the summer.

There is a mild burning on the inside of my third finger where it was touched by nettles, and rubbing with a dock leaf hasn't completely taken it away. A 'be careful' message enlivening the skin. Thorns are ready to rip into my scarf, which I hold close to my body. There is barbed wire, too, and you have to reach a little further at this time of the year to get to the last crop of blackberries. I'm aware of the whole body, the reach, balance, in-breath, contact with the fruit, careful release, out-breath. Some of the berries are too soft to come off the branch whole, and dark, sticky red juice runs down my fingers into my palm. Others are too firm and don't yield to a probing tug. They are for later, or for others, whose anonymous presence replaces the 'wanting for oneself'.

A sense of plenitude, gratitude. There is still this, despite the acidification of the oceans, the diminishing of species. There is, in fact, always only this moment. I think of my mother who is getting near the end of her life. What is it that will matter at the end of our span, give a sense of satisfaction, of a life well lived that will let us go from this world gracefully? For me just now, there is little doubt about the value of taking this time out from the computer, working on my autumn programme, to fill a small plastic tub with the last of the blackberries, my scratched skin absorbing that strong, clear September sun.

Found

I've lost:

Three hours of work on the last chapter
Friends I thought I had for life
The golden cross pendant my godmother gave me
Faith in God
Frequently, my equanimity

I almost lost:

The way out of the woods
My passport and smartphone at the Dutch tulip show
My virginity before I was ready
Three months' earnings when I was mugged
Consciousness

I could easily lose:

The ability to walk down hills
More of my teeth
The man I will marry next month
The German names of birds
My sanity

No doubt I will lose:

My life and identity
My possessions
My achievements
My family and friends
Anything 'me' and 'mine'

What cannot be lost:

a black-and-white cat
stalking the edge of the field
ready to pounce

Appendix

A Needs Inventory[1]

The following list of needs is neither exhaustive nor definitive. It is meant as a starting place to support anyone who wishes to engage in a process of deepening self-discovery and to facilitate greater understanding and connection between people.

SUBSISTENCE & SECURITY

Physical Sustenance
Air
Food
Health
Movement
Physical Safety
Rest/sleep
Shelter
Touch
Water

Security
Consistency
Order/ Structure
Peace (external)
Peace of mind
Protection
Safety (emotional)
Stability
Trusting

FREEDOM

Autonomy
Agency
Choice
Independence
Power
Self-responsibility
Space Spontaneity

Relaxation
Humour
Ease
Joy
Play
Pleasure
Rejuvenation

CONNECTION

Affection
Appreciation
Attention
Closeness
Companionship
Harmony
Intimacy
Love
Nurturing
Sexual Expression
Support
Tenderness
Warmth

To Matter
Acceptance
Care
Compassion
Consideration
Empathy

[1] Based on the Needs Inventory on nvc@baynvc.org

Kindness
Mutual Recognition
Respect
To be heard/seen
To be understood
To be trusted
Understanding others

Community
Belonging
Communication
Cooperation
Equality
Inclusion
Mutuality
Participation
Partnership
Self-expression
Sharing

MEANING

Sense of Self
Authenticity
Competence
Creativity
Dignity
Growth
Healing
Honesty
Integrity
Self-acceptance
Self-appreciation
Self-care
Self-confidence
Self-connection
Self-realisation

Understanding
Awareness
Clarity
Learning
Discovery
Stimulation
Making Sense of Life

Meaning
Aliveness
Challenge
Consciousness
Contribution
Creativity
Effectiveness
Integration
Purpose

Transcendence
Beauty
Celebration of Life
Communion
Faith
Flow
Hope
Inspiration
Mourning
Peace (internal)
Presence

big fire. Windhorse Publications suggested an excellent editor and I have received editorial input from a number of other people as well - thanks to all of them. Luke Winter coached me in the pre-sale fundraising process and Lou Fox McLoughlan made the beautiful little video to go with it. It was a pleasure to work with Gerry Cambridge on the book design. Joy Charnley did a great job proof-reading.

'Who do you imagine as your readers?' I was often asked. The people who I pictured in a crowd behind the computer screen, nudging and cheering me towards the finishing line are also those who I feel much gratitude for and without whom the book would probably not exist: the students in my mindfulness and teacher training courses, retreats and CPD workshops, the wonderful human beings I supervise in their mindfulness work and those that have become friends and collaborators and form part of my Sangha of fellow practitioners. Many of you have read the book, or parts of it at various stages, offered suggestions and endorsements and wanted to see more. In no particular order: Vidyamala, Rick Hanson, Choden, Vajragupta, Charlotte Procter, Kristine Jansen, Chloe Homewood, Anna Stallard, Dan Marcus, Joy Charnley, Fiona Comfort, Adam Burnel, Ann-Marie Wall, Kay Young, Louise McAllan, Aly Findlay, Judy Jamieson, Liz Henderson, Anna Edgar, Anna Zubrzycka, Lizzie O'Brian, Cat McCaw, Jane Negrych, Moira Munro and many more. Heartfelt thanks also to everyone who expressed their support through the pre-sale book fund-raising appeal. And my family rooted for me all the way through.

I am so lucky there was a person who held me and the project all the way along, with unwavering love, literary advice and practical help: my husband Sukhema (Larry Butler), collaborator on many projects mentioned in the book. He carefully read and commented on every page of it, and his creative ideas have shaped much of the content.